Praise for *"Mom, sex is NO b...*

"I love talking to audiences of any size about G... when I talked with my son and two daughters a... cold terrified. Sharon Hersh has written the definitive book on how to engage our children on issues we know are so fundamental to their well-being and yet unnerve us to discuss with candor and clarity. Sharon is real, profoundly wise, and doesn't swerve from the heart of Jesus as she invites us to consider our own sexual redemption as the better doorway to inviting our children to more than mere morality—to the glories of our God, who longs for relationship with us."

> —Dan B. Allender PhD, president of Mars Hill Graduate School and author of *The Wounded Heart, To Be Told,* and *How Children Raise Parents*

"In a world where our children and teens are encouraged to believe in boundary-less sexual practice and expression, we must develop strategies for leading them to the fulfilling knowledge of a biblical sexual ethic. Sharon Hersh's *"Mom, sex is NO big deal!"* is a practical tool that equips both moms and dads to understand present cultural realities and apply God's Word to those realities in ways that will help our daughters see, live, and experience God's wonderful gift of sexuality to its fullest. Thanks, Sharon, for another wonderful resource!"

> —Dr. Walt Mueller, president of Center for Parent/Youth Understanding and author of *Understanding Today's Youth Culture* and *Engaging the Soul of Youth Culture*

"Sex is a BIG deal in today's culture. Yet as parents, most of us feel woefully inadequate in talking *with*—not *at*—our daughters. This book will show you how to listen while providing you with exactly what to say in a variety of situations."

> —Susan Alexander Yates, speaker and author of several books, including *And Then I Had Teenagers: Encouragement for Parents of Teens and Preteens*

"Sharon Hersh is true to fabulous form in this book for moms. Thorough, honest, and realistic, *"Mom, sex is NO big deal!"* is a must-read for anyone raising a daughter. Right after giving birth isn't too early to pick it up!"

—NANCY RUE, best-selling author of the Lily, Sophie, and 'Nama Beach High series for girls

"Mom, *sex is NO big deal!*"

a hand-in-hand book

"Mom, *sex is NO big deal!*"

Becoming your daughter's ally
in developing a healthy sexual identity

sharon a. hersh

SHAW BOOKS

an imprint of WATERBROOK PRESS

"MOM, SEX IS NO BIG DEAL!"
A SHAW BOOK
PUBLISHED BY WATERBROOK PRESS
12265 Oracle Boulevard, Suite 200
Colorado Springs, Colorado 80921
A division of Random House Inc.

All Scripture quotations, unless otherwise indicated, are taken from The Message. Copyright
© 1993, 1994, 1995, 1996, 2000, 2001, 2002. Used by permission of NavPress Publishing
Group. All rights reserved. Scripture quotations marked (NIV) are taken from the Holy Bible,
New International Version®. NIV®. Copyright © 1973, 1978, 1984 by International Bible
Society. Used by permission of Zondervan Publishing House. All rights reserved. Scripture
quotations marked (KJV) are taken from the King James Version.

Names and details in some anecdotes and stories have been changed to protect the identities
of the persons involved.

ISBN 0-87788-202-9

Library of Congress Cataloging-in-Publication Data
Hersh, Sharon A.
"Mom, sex is no big deal!" : becoming your daughter's ally in developing a healthy sexual
identity / Sharon A. Hersh.—1st ed.
     p. cm.
   Includes bibliographical references.
   ISBN 0-87788-202-9
   1. Mothers and daughters—Religious aspects—Christianity. 2. Sex instruction—Religious
aspects—Christianity. 3. Parenting—Religious aspects—Christianity. I. Title.
BV4529.18.H48 2006
248.8'431—dc22

                                                                    2005035103

Printed in the United States of America
2006—First Edition

10 9 8 7 6 5 4 3 2 1

To all girls and moms who wish someday their prince will come.
May they know that He already has.

CONTENTS

FOREWORD

How different my life would have been if a book like this had been available to my mother when I was a teen. Chances are good that if you're reading this, you know that sex is indeed a big deal, such a big deal that it affects much of who we are and how we live.

I can still recall the exact thoughts going through my mind the night before I had sex for the first time. *Are you really ready to do this, Shannon? What if it hurts? What if he tells?* All of these concerns seemed to be risks I was willing to take. I was only fourteen, and the guy who was rocking my world at the time was a handsome eighteen-year-old football player I'd just met the week before.

There had been no talk of us dating. He made no promises. He'd never even said, "I love you." There had just been a lot of flirting and sexual innuendos as we swam together at an apartment pool. I was blown away when he asked if we could spend some time alone together the next day. *Wow,* I thought, *he's a senior and I'm a freshman, and* he's *interested in* me!

I allowed that boy to visit me the next day, but I decided at the last minute that I *wasn't* ready for sex. However, he *was,* and he was much bigger and stronger than I was. I froze out of fear, and I silently and passively allowed the most precious gift I could ever give to a man to be stolen from me by a boy who probably didn't even know my last name. I told myself that it was no big deal that my virginity was stolen. I never shed a tear, and I never told anyone.

For the following five years, I blindly drifted from one sexual relationship to another, feeling as if sex was the price I had to pay to get the attention and affection I so desperately craved. I tried to keep my double life a secret from most everyone, especially my parents.

Maybe you are thinking that I wasn't very smart or that I came from a broken home or that I wasn't a Christian at the time. The opposite is true. I was an honor student growing up in a two-parent home and serving as the president of my youth group. My parents would testify that no matter how hard you try to raise responsible children, not even good Christian girls are exempt from these kinds of sexual temptations and experiences—not even *your* daughter.

More than two decades later, if anything has changed for teenage girls, it's that the battle they must fight for sexual purity has grown even more intense, especially with the invention of the Internet. When we were growing up, pornography was in brown paper wrappers behind the convenience store clerk's counter. Today millions of pornographic images can be ushered into your daughter's mind simply with the click of her mouse. Gone are the days when we could assume that pornography and sexual temptation were "men's issues."

As the author of *Every Young Woman's Battle* and a teacher on the Teen Mania Ministries' campus, I hear from thousands of girls each year who have bought into the lie the world tries to feed us: that sex isn't a big deal at all. There is a terrible gnawing in their spirits that sex is perhaps a much bigger deal than they ever imagined, or else their regrets, guilt, fears, and emotional pain wouldn't feel so crippling. I can see it in the face of every young woman who dares to look me in the eye when she confesses her sexual misdeeds. It's as if she's crying out, "Why didn't anyone tell me that my heart would ache so badly?"

Looking back to my teen years, I never confided in my mother about my sexual and emotional struggles because I simply didn't feel I could. She seemed to live in her world and I lived in mine, and the gap between those two worlds seemed too wide to be bridged. I wouldn't wish that feeling of isolation on any teenager, or on any parent. That's why I'm so excited about this book. Sharon helps you understand your daughter's world, how your world appears to her, and how you can build a bridge to connect the two of you so that you can help her make the healthiest sexual choices possible.

It's *never* too late to begin living as a woman of sexual and emotional integrity. Even if your daughter has crossed many sexual boundaries already, there is hope that with the guidance and unconditional love of a true ally, she can experience the healing and wholeness that only one Lover—Jesus Christ—can offer us.

And who is the best person to teach her how a woman can look for love in all the *right* places instead of settling for a cheap, destructive imitation? Yep. It's *you*, Mom! You *are* the woman!

—SHANNON ETHRIDGE

ACKNOWLEDGMENTS

With deepest gratitude and respect to:

John and Kathleen Baker, my dad and mom, who have given me the gift of modeling a lifelong marriage.

Kristin, my dear daughter, who proves on a daily basis that you can be a real girl in this real world and yet long for more in a more real world.

Graham, my amazing son, for putting up with me while writing yet another book for girls.

All the girls who have whispered to me their stories and urged me to write this book for their mothers.

Dan Allender, my friend and teacher. This book is a small repayment of a debt of gratitude I owe you for teaching me about pain, problems, and the gospel.

Judy Bruce, my brilliant friend, who kept telling me that this is the subject matter that most needs Jesus.

Peter Hiett, my pastor, for teaching me to be a bride who dances.

Dr. Jeffrey Satinover, for telling the story of "The Feathers of the Skylark," and Michael Cusick, of *www.restoringthesoul.com,* for first bringing this story to my attention.

Steve Siler, of *www.musicforthesoul.org,* for compiling the amazing project Somebody's Daughter to help families with sexual addiction.

Traci Mullins, my braveheart editor, thank you. You know all that those two words mean.

Jennifer Lonas, Amy Partain, and Jessica Barnes, for going above and beyond to help research and verify the statistics in this book. Thank you for your hard work.

Don Pape, my agent extraordinaire, for encouraging (no, forcing) me to write this book.

All the people at WaterBrook/Shaw for publishing books about parenting—the most important task in the kingdom.

You're on Holy Ground

Teenagers are less likely to start having sex when their mothers are involved in their lives [and] have a close relationship with them.

—2002 National Longitudinal Survey on Adolescent Health

"R emind me, Mom," my seventeen-year-old daughter pleaded. "Remind me why I want to wait to have sex."

Kristin sounded tired. We were on our way to a local church to participate in a mother-daughter forum for middle-school girls and their moms. We were brainstorming together about some of the possible questions the girls and their moms might ask. When I suggested that they might want to talk about boys, dating, and sex, Kristin sighed and asked me to remind her of her reasons for waiting to have sex.

I knew that her request was really a code—a question that reminded both of us of hundreds of conversations we'd had about sex; a question that revealed all we have come to believe about the symbolism and sacredness of sex; a question that flies in the face of a cultural mandate about girls and sex; and a question that opens the door to answers about so much more than just sex.

I also knew why Kristin sounded so tired. She was just a few months from graduating from high school, and the pressure was on to have sex with her boyfriend of six months. The pressure didn't come only in the relationship with her boyfriend. It came from her close girlfriends—all of whom had already had sex. Now before you make judgments about Kristin's friends, you should know that they are nice girls—cheerleaders, athletes, honor students, Christians. And her boyfriend is a wonderful young man—from a strong religious home. My daughter's peers are not so different from the teenagers who crowd the hallways in most high schools.

Consider the following statistics on teenage sexual activity:[1]

- The 2002 National Survey of Family Growth reported that of girls and boys between the ages of fifteen and seventeen, 39 percent of girls and 36 percent of boys engaged in sexual intercourse. That percentage increased to 45 percent for both boys and girls between the ages of fifteen and nineteen.[2]

- In 2002, 58 percent of teenage girls reported having sex by age eighteen and 70 percent reported having sex by age nineteen.[3]

- Between 1988 and 1995, the number of girls having sex before age fourteen *doubled* from 4 percent to 8 percent of the survey population. Although the percentage dropped slightly between 1995 and 2002—from 8 percent to just under 6 percent—this remains a matter of significant concern.[4]

- In 2002, the biggest percentage jump in sexual activity among teenage girls occurred between the ages of sixteen and seventeen. By age sixteen, almost 27 percent of girls reported having lost their virginity compared with 43 percent by age seventeen.[5]

- Eighty-eight percent of teens who take an abstinence pledge break it. Of teenage girls who took an abstinence pledge, 25 percent had sex by age sixteen and 50 percent had sex by age eighteen.[6]

These are just a few of the statistics about teenage girls and sex. These statistics are overwhelming—detailing for us teen sexual practices, teen sexual diseases, teen pregnancies, and the often-resulting teen depression and teen suicide. All of these subjects make us want to throw our hands up in despair because they should not describe our teenagers.

Some researchers suggest that these statistics are not reflected among Christian teens. Abstinence-only advocates are quick to point out that there is a downward trend in sexual intercourse, at least for teenage boys. According to the 2002 National Survey of Family Growth, more than one-third (37 percent) of the older teenage girls who said they were virgins cited faith and high moral standards as the reasons they abstained from sex.[7] I'm grateful for any good news that we can find in this arena. However, hundreds of conversations with teenage girls in my office suggest that teens from religious homes don't always tell the truth on sex surveys, and that even when they do tell the truth, parents don't always hear what they are saying. In my experience, most adolescent girls I see disclose to me that they have engaged in sexual activity. But when I ask parents what they know about their daughter's sexual experience, they most often respond, "We're sure she's never done more than kiss a boy, if that." And then, with a flicker of panic in their eyes, they say, "Why are you asking?"

Even if our daughters do make firm and faith-based decisions about sex, we cannot discount the world's influence on them and the toll it takes on their resolve. Their friends have compelling reasons for engaging in sexual activity—they believe that they are in love; it's fun and it feels goods; it makes them feel grown up and independent; it provides them with a sense of emotional and relational connection; and it really does seem like the "normal" thing to do. The culture of teen sex underscores what our daughters are up against.

- A 2005 Kaiser Family Foundation report states that 70 percent of the top twenty TV programs that teens watch contain at least some sexual content, with 45 percent of them showing sexual behavior of some kind. Of those programs with sexual behavior, 8 percent showed intercourse behaviors.[8]
- In 1999, "42% of songs on the top 10 CDs…contained sexual content; 19% included direct descriptions of sexual intercourse."[9]
- There are an average of ninety-three sexually explicit scenes per hour in music videos.[10]
- According to a 1988 report, each year American teens view approximately *fourteen thousand* sexual references in the media.[11] Although this statistic is more than fifteen years old, it is staggering to imagine how many sexual references today's teenagers view in their completely media-saturated world.
- Thirteen- to fifteen-year-olds say that television, movies, magazines, and music are their primary sources of information about sex.[12]
- A national NBC/*People* magazine survey conducted in conjunction with the Katie Couric special "The 411: Teens and Sex," reported that half of the teens surveyed said they received "a lot" or "some" information about sex from friends and media sources, such as movies and television.[13]

If you walk through the hallways of your daughter's school, you will see firsthand how all these statistics intersect with real teenagers in their real lives. Take clothing, for example. Teenage girls wear tight shirts that reveal their belly-button rings and low-riding jeans that reveal their thong underwear. Boys wear T-shirts with sexually suggestive tag lines, such as "Knotty by Nature." Then there's the language. Both boys and girls call out sexually graphic teasers about "hooking up with" and "getting on" each other. And now you know the statistical reality: approximately 50 percent of these teenagers will engage in sexual activity this year.[14] Parents who watch their daughter drive off to a social event or get into a car with a boy to go to a party have to wonder whether this predicted sexual activity will take place *this* weekend. And even if a teenager doesn't engage in sexual activity, she is still subject to a profane culture that makes sex casual at best and meaningless at worst.

When you walk through the hallways where your daughter spends time and makes powerful connections with her peers, you may want to take out your disinfectant, wear a blindfold, or put in earplugs. May I suggest instead that you take off your shoes, because you are on holy ground. It is in the midst of this simultaneously sexually advanced and sexually ignorant culture that you have an unparalleled opportunity to connect with your daughter not only about sex but also about her body, her self-esteem, her relationships, and the deepest longings of her heart.

I was challenged yet again to address the beauty and complexity of God's design in my daughter and myself when Kristin asked me to remind her of why she's choosing not to engage in sexual activity, even though many of her peers are not making the same choice and her culture bombards her daily with evidence that suggests she is a "freak." I didn't always view the subject of teen sex and questions about oral sex, masturbation, contraceptives, and french kissing so positively or passionately.

A few years earlier I had come face to face with my own cowardice and ignorance when my daughter and I were sitting in our pajamas flipping through magazines. In my book *"Mom, I feel fat!"* I wrote about using the culture to connect with our daughters about body image and self-esteem. My daughter and I often used teen magazines to talk about teen issues. Kristin was looking at an issue of *Seventeen* magazine. One article caught my attention: "The Sex Questions You Can't Ask Anyone Else…Answered." I started reading over Kristin's shoulder and discovered that nameless, faceless editors were educating my daughter about eight ways to tell if a boy is your soul mate, how to hide a hickey, and techniques for becoming a good kisser. I wanted to grab that magazine and tear every page to tiny pieces. How dare *Seventeen* magazine teach my daughter about love, kissing, and sex in such sophisticated, conspiratorial tones?

Yet I knew that even if I banned Kristin from reading *Seventeen* magazine and cut the cord on the television, she would still be in a world of peers who were being influenced by these shiny, glamorous, seductive messages about sex. And what had I done? We had had "the talk" when Kristin was twelve years old. Oh, there had been small conversations leading up to the big talk about the wonders and mysteries of the human body. We talked about menstruation, but I never mentioned masturbation. We talked about ovaries, but not oral sex. We talked about procreation, but never french kissing.

Seventeen magazine brought me face to face with my own ignorance about my daughter's world and with my own meager offerings about the subjects that she and her friends thought about and talked about all the time. It struck me that the culture gives one message about sex: it's a big deal to think and talk about, but engaging in it is no big deal. I had given my daughter quite a different message: it's not a big deal to think and talk about, but engaging in it *is* a big deal.

Everything was completely mixed up!

I know that I am not unlike many well-meaning parents. We hold up sexual *purity* to our daughters as if it is the biggest goal of the adolescent years—the pinnacle of achievement. But we are really limited in talking about why and how it is important and how to reach this goal. As a result, our daughters don't talk to us about their questions and doubts. How can they question this ideal without feeling as if they are bad? And they certainly don't talk to us about their experiences—whether it's a heart that beats faster at the sight of a certain boy, a first kiss, or further sexual activity—because that would mean that they are really bad. Often we cripple our children if we only give them rules but neglect to equip them to handle their feelings, to think for themselves, or to be filled with awe and wonder at their amazing design. Most of us don't have a vision for how the subject of sex can become a means to romance our daughters' hearts to a more intimate relationship with us and with God.

As my daughter and I sat sipping hot cocoa and looking through magazines, I became acutely aware that I had not offered her much of a choice. Her culture was holding up sexual *activity* as the pinnacle of real living, and television, music, and movies are brilliant in portraying why and how. "Just say no and wait for sex, and one day you'll understand it all" was not a powerful enough incentive for Kristin to hold on to her values when she wasn't entirely sure why she held them or whether the "sacrifices" she was making were worthwhile. Why not just give in, be like everyone else who is hip and cool and having fun, and experience life and love! Which would you choose?

This book is a crash course in how to talk with our daughters about sex. We moms don't need to become disgusted, judgmental, hysterical, or afraid to protect our daughters from the sexual traps of the day. Rather, we need to become informed (more informed than our daughters!) about the realities of today's adolescent world, compassionate toward teens who are looking for love in all the wrong places, and passionate about sex as a means of understanding far more than hormonal realities (although those are important). Once we understand the true purpose of sex, we will gain a better understanding of our sacred selves and the Sacred One who designed us as sexual beings.

In no other arena of life has the Enemy of our souls been more powerful. Sexual abuse, assault, disease, and confusion reign. Why did the one who prowls about seeking to devour[15] choose sex as the ground on which to wage all-out war? Why not academics, physical health, or even religious life? The apostle Paul provides an answer that today's culture has missed entirely: "There's more to sex than mere skin on skin.... There is a sense in which sexual sins are different from all others. In sexual sin we violate the sacredness of our own bodies, these bodies that were made for God-given and God-modeled love."[16]

Part 1 of this book will give you tools for understanding your daughter's world and using her questions about her body and her experiences with her peers to lead her to understand her awesome design (body, soul, and spirit) and the symbolism and sacredness of sex. You will also have an opportunity to courageously look at your own sexual history and understand how it has formed what you believe about yourself and sex. As you combine your own story with an understanding of the body, soul, and spirit connection to sex, you will become a powerful ally for your daughter, offering far more than a superficial skin-on-skin understanding of sex.

In Part 2, "Building a Bridge Between Your Worlds," we will tackle tough topics like masturbation, oral sex, and the morning-after pill. We will also talk about palm-sweating, heart-racing, and skin-tingling romance, kissing, and flirting. Throughout the book you will find interactive Just for You and Just for the Two of You sections that include questions and exercises to help you fully formulate your own convictions about sex so that you can become your daughter's ally as she forms her own convictions. You will discover that the conversations you and your daughter have as you work through these exercises will help you form a relationship with your daughter that even the most heartbreaking struggles or glitzy media cannot shake.

The questions some of you have about your daughter and sex come from heartache and confusion. Perhaps your daughter has already engaged in sexual intercourse, has a sexually transmitted disease, has been through the agony of date rape, or is questioning her sexual orientation. Part 3, "Conquering Roadblocks to Relationships," will help you discover or rediscover the promise of the gospel—that God can redeem anything and that sexual sin or hurt cannot diminish or destroy the hope He offers. You will discover that unthinkable struggles become the most profound context in which to invite your daughter into an unshakable relationship with you and with God.

Since that moment when *Seventeen* magazine brought me face to face with the truth about my mothering, I have spent countless hours with my own daughter as well as hundreds of other teenage girls talking about the amazing design of the female body, God's delight in creating us for pleasure, the fun of flirting, the promise of romance, and the heart's deep longing for connection. We have talked about the symbolism of sex—an outward act representing an inward reality—that makes it sacred. We've watched movies, listened to music, and scanned advertisements, looking for both the truth and lies about sex. I've confronted my own past and dreamed with girls about their futures. I now know—heart and soul—that I have far more help to offer my daughter about sex than all the editors of all the teen magazines combined. And so do you.

Of course, I also know some heartbreaking stories and staggering statistics about teens and sex. When a girl shows up in my office after being date raped or after performing oral sex on a boy and then discovering that it was demeaning and meaningless, I am sometimes tempted to conclude that the Enemy has won. But then I remember that night in the car when my tired teenage daughter asked me, "Remind me, Mom. Remind me why I want to wait to have sex."

Hand-in-hand mothering is a way of parenting that uses the sometimes overwhelming daily struggles that our daughters face to connect with them in powerful, life-changing ways. We become our daughters' allies. An ally is one who knows the enemy, understands the battle, and is always ready to lend a hand. This book will help you be the most effective and powerful ally your daughter can have as she grapples with her questions about sex.

As mothers we probably won't overthrow today's deceptive and destructive sexual culture. In fact, we may not make the slightest impact on the culture. But we can have a profound impact on our daughters. One on one—in powerful mother-daughter alliances—we can remind girls that sex is a big deal because *they* are a big deal. They were created—body, soul, and spirit—to experience relationships that honor the way they were designed, enliven their passions, and strengthen their connections to others and to God.

"Remind me, Mom. Remind me why I want to wait to have sex," my daughter asked.

I responded with fierce purpose and passion, praying like crazy that my answer would revive Kristin's heart: "Because, my dear daughter, you want *more*."

Part I

Understanding Your Worlds

A woman's heroic journey always begins in partnership with her mother, the woman from whom she takes the imprint of what it means to be a woman.

—Chrstiane Northrup, *Mother-Daughter Wisdom*

Chapter 1

Sex and Your Daughter

Afterward, they stood on the balcony as the sun broke through the mist that had shrouded the castle for so long. The sun shone on the beautiful Belle and her handsome prince, whose love had finally broken the spell.

—From the Walt Disney book *Beauty and the Beast*

I thought I loved him and he loved me." A flicker of pain flitted across my fifteen-year-old client's face. "We met at the mall," Morgan began her story of teenage romance. I suspected how this story was going to end but focused on Morgan's retelling of her experience.

"I was hanging out with my friends, and we ran into these guys at the mall. I thought one of them was really hot, so when he asked for my number, I gave it to him. I couldn't believe it when he called me. He was sixteen, and I was only thirteen."

Already my heart was racing. I felt like I do when I'm watching a frustrating horror movie, and I want to shout to the main character, "Don't you see what's happening? He's going to trap you, murder you, cut you up into pieces, and hide you in the freezer!" I wanted to shake Morgan and warn her, "Don't you see what's happening? You're thirteen. He's sixteen. He's going to trap you, use you, and break your heart. Run!"

Morgan continued. "We started talking on the phone every day. We'd text-message each other all day long. I told him everything—about my parents' divorce, my dad leaving, my annoying brother. I even told him about my dream of playing college basketball and maybe being in the pros. We were like best friends. He told me about his life too…" Morgan's voice faded, and I knew that she was remembering this seemingly magical first romance, and then I saw that flicker of pain again.

Morgan looked like the typical teenage girl. She was wearing jeans, a tank top, and flip-flops. Her toenails were painted pink with little while daisies on each big toe. Her parents had sent her to see me because they feared she was depressed. She'd stopped eating, didn't seem interested in her friends or her usual activities, and spent a lot of time in her room listening to sad or angry-sounding music. They suspected that she might be struggling with their divorce. In a way they were right. But as soon as Morgan started talking about her summer romance, I knew that this was about more than a broken family. It was about a broken heart.

Morgan began the summer before her eighth-grade year wanting to hang out with friends, practice her basketball skills at summer camp, sleep in late, and find a boyfriend—hopes that most middle-school-age girls have. In 2004 *Young and Modern* magazine asked teenage girls to rank what they wanted most from high school. More than 80 percent listed dating or a boyfriend as their top desire.[1] More than good grades, extracurricular achievement, or girl-friends, teenage girls want romance. We'll talk more about this a little later in the chapter, but I share this statistic now for two reasons: to highlight that boy-crazy girls are the norm in the teenage years and to help you imagine Morgan's (and, later, your daughter's) story.

I imagined Morgan giggling at slumber parties with her girlfriends about the boy she'd met at the mall. I suspected that she and her friends had plotted together how she could be with him, what she should say to him, and whether she would kiss him. I knew that Morgan had stars in her eyes and that, at this point, everything she hoped for was mostly innocent.

"He started coming to my house when my mom was at work," Morgan continued. "We started kissing…and stuff," she said, looking at the floor.

"Had you ever kissed anyone before?" My question surprised Morgan. I think she was ready for admonishment, not curiosity.

"Not really. I kissed a boy at camp when I was in the fifth grade. But it was really a dare from my friends, and I missed his lips."

I smiled until I saw that flicker of pain again. "What did you feel when it became more than just kissing?" I asked.

"I was scared—" She stopped in midsentence.

"Was there anything about kissing him and his touching you that you liked?" Morgan looked embarrassed. I knew that she was looking to me for cues as to what was okay to talk about.

Teenage girls often hold back in talking openly about sex because moms send verbal and nonverbal cues that *they* don't want to talk openly about sex. *Seventeen* magazine surveyed its teenage readership to find out how often they talked to their moms about kissing, making out, and other sexual contact. Ninety-five percent of those surveyed said they never discussed these subjects with their mothers.[2]

I have learned that girls often do not talk to their moms about physical contact with their boyfriends during the early stages of a dating relationship because they fear judgment or restrictions. Sadly, when guidance from mom is not invited or accepted early in a dating relationship, her input will be absent later when the stakes are much higher. So girls look to *Seventeen* for answers to "The Sex Questions You Can't Ask Anyone Else." I knew it would be important for Morgan to understand her responses to this boy's advances, but we would have to talk about that later. I sensed that Morgan wanted to get her story over with.

"Anyway,"—she started talking faster—"by the end of the summer, we were so close. I thought I loved him and he loved me. So we had sex." Morgan stopped abruptly.

This time Morgan didn't look at the floor. She looked me straight in the eyes. She almost seemed to be daring me, "Go ahead. Tell me I'm bad."

Of course I wanted to talk with her about having sex, and I knew we would eventually, but I also knew that she hadn't told the hardest part of the story yet. And she needed to tell it.

"What happened to your relationship?" I asked.

I could see Morgan clench her teeth. She answered, her voice completely flat, "I never heard from him again. He's such a jerk. It doesn't matter."

Tears welled in my eyes. "Oh, Morgan, I'm so sorry."

"You are?" she asked. "It's my own fault. I was so stupid."

"You deserve so much more than you experienced. He *was* a jerk. And you're not stupid. You thought you were in love. You wanted to be in love. What's stupid about that?" I asked.

And then Morgan started to cry. I knew we would have many more conversations about her experiences, but I hoped they would be conversations remembering our shared tears. Morgan already knew that I, like most of the adults in her life, thought sex was a big deal. I prayed that she was beginning to believe that I thought *she* was a big deal.

EVERY GIRL HAS A STORY

Studies show that in the year 2000 approximately 19 million new STD infections were reported. Forty-eight percent of these new cases (9.1 million) were among young people between the ages of fifteen and twenty-four.[3] In addition, approximately 900,000 teenage girls between the ages of fifteen and nineteen became pregnant in the United States that same year.[4] Although the teenage pregnancy rate dropped 22 percent between 1986 and 2000,[5] the statistics are still staggering.

When we read the statistics about teens and sex, we have to remember that they represent more than just numbers; they reflect teenagers' lives and stories.

Each of us attempts to make sense out of life through stories. If we can't tell a story about ourselves, then we are nothing more than detached bundles of facts, dates, and faces signifying nothing.

—WILLIAM H. WILLIMON, *Reading with Deeper Eyes*

If statistics are all you think about when you look at your adolescent daughter, you will be tempted to lock her in her room and throw away the key. Or maybe you'll give her a good book on abstinence or send her to an abstinence-only conference. Both of these are good ideas. But they can also make your daughter's story irrelevant. When you preach "Just say no" without showing any interest in who your daughter is, what she daydreams about, and how she interacts with her peers, your words become law without any heart. When some boy at the mall asks your daughter for her number, tells her she's "hot," and listens to her stories, who do you think she finds more appealing?

The statistics are sobering. The real-life stories take place on a continuum from engaging in a romantic chat with someone in an Internet chat room to pursuing boys or men for sexual intercourse. In this chapter we will look at the sexual temptations that teenage girls from middle school on up face today. This will not be a chapter for the faint of heart, but it will arm you with essential information about the sexual lives of teenagers. Today's girls think they know a lot about sex, probably more than their mothers know, because the teen culture is saturated with sexual images, talk, and activity. However, many girls do not understand their own bodies, the responses of their bodies and hearts to sexual activity, or the lifelong consequences. They don't know how to make sense of their own stories. This chapter will help you understand your daughter's story so that in telling it with her or even for her, you can become a powerful ally in helping her write the next chapters of her life.

Just for You

Do you know your daughter's story? See how well you can answer the following questions:

1. Who does your daughter most want to be like when she "grows up"?
2. What are her top three priorities in middle school or high school?
3. What books, movies, and music have made a major impression on your daughter? Why?
4. What was your daughter's first big disillusionment in friendships? in expectations? in dating?
5. What qualities does your daughter value most in a girlfriend or boyfriend?
6. What does your daughter like about her physical appearance? What would she change if she could?
7. What is your daughter's style? What are her fashion preferences?
8. What group at school does your daughter most identify with? least identify with?
9. What is your daughter's most painful adolescent memory so far? What is her most cherished memory?
10. What does your daughter want to do with her life when she becomes an adult (e.g., career goals, dreams, etc.)?

EVERY BOY HAS A STORY TOO

The statistics about teenage boys and sex are not any more encouraging than the statistics about girls. The focus of this book is on girls, and I realize that in telling girls' stories, it may seem as if boys are the enemy. The truth is that adolescent boys live in a sex-saturated culture too. They watch Joey, the likable character on *Friends*, suggest that his M.O. is to sleep with a girl on the first date, even if he doesn't know her last name, and then to never call her again. The sitcom's prerecorded laughter suggests to boys that this is how men behave and that girls probably want them to act like this.

I have a teenage son, and I have watched him grapple with the confusing messages of the culture about what "normal" boys do and what every girl should expect. It's important to note that according to a 2003 *Seventeen* magazine survey, 33 percent of boys who engaged in sexual intercourse felt pressure from *girls* to do so.[6] We'll talk more about the rise of sexual aggression among adolescent girls later. I share this statistic here to underscore the mixed signals that teenage boys experience in our culture. Although many stories in this book will highlight the hurtful behavior of adolescent boys, they are not the enemy. They are hurting too. The by-product of a culture that believes sex is only "biology deep" is a culture that believes masculinity and femininity are only biology deep too. The sex-is-no-big deal mantra has resulted in men and women carelessly and thoughtlessly violating one another and themselves. When we all laugh at Joey on *Friends*, we send a message to boys and girls about sex that isn't the least bit funny.

THE STORY OF YOUR DAUGHTER'S BODY

Parents of teenagers often think that kids go from not thinking about sex at all to acting out sexually, seemingly overnight. This isn't true. For most teenage girls, it's a gradual process. But many parents are either unaware of their daughters' sexual development because their daughters try to hide it from them or parents may simply ignore the cues.

Barbara Strauch, medical and science editor for the *New York Times*, notes, "Maybe if we took note of these subtle markers along the way, we might not be so taken aback by puberty when it springs forth full-tilt. Perhaps we would not go through what often seems an abrupt transition, for parents anyhow, from milk and Oreos to oral sex."[7]

Developmental research has shown that between the ages of four and seven, most girls become aware of their own bodies. I remember when Kristin was four years old, she became self-conscious about her body in the presence of her three-year-old brother. One evening after Kristin screamed at him to get out of her room, he said teasingly in a singsong voice, "I've seen your private parts before." To which she replied with great angst, "Yeah, but that was before I knew I had them!"

When girls begin to notice and explore their own bodies, moms have a wonderful opportunity to marvel with them at the amazing design of the female body. This is the time to begin to talk in appropriate ways about female development and the purpose of different parts of our bodies. (The resources section at the end of this book provides a variety of resources that can help with this task.) This is the chapter in your daughter's story when she is "naked and unashamed." It is our role as mothers to begin to tell with wonder and without shame the story of how females develop sexually.

During this chapter of your daughter's story, she may begin to notice the opposite sex. Once again, this is a good time to cultivate your daughter's self-awareness in the context of acceptance and encouraging guidance. When your daughter confesses a "crush" on the boy who sits next to her in class, ask her what her body feels. Do her palms sweat? Does her heart race? The purpose of these questions is not to encourage an early romance but to acknowledge reality and begin to build a bridge between the two of you so that she knows you can be trusted with her experiences later on.

We don't have a ceremony for the first pubic hair. Well, why not?

—MARTHA MCCLINTOCK, hormone researcher, University of Chicago

---

One of the hottest trends in youth marketing is age compression—taking products and messages originally designed for adults and targeting them to children or teenagers. I am saddened when a ten-year-old girl comments on a boy's butt or wears makeup and belly-button-baring shirts. Once again, the culture acknowledges that the body is important and that relationships with the opposite sex are a big deal—it just distorts them greatly. We make a big mistake when we ignore or diminish these realities in our daughters' lives and leave the culture to fill that vacuum.

Ideally, from an early age we have the opportunity to celebrate the amazing design of the human body and the already growing longings in our daughters' hearts for relationships. But what if you missed these opportunities when your daughter was younger, and now she wants to wear clothes that you find scandalous and she seems to think about boys nonstop? It's not too late. The Just for the Two of You section that follows will give you some ideas to make up this lost ground.

JUST FOR THE TWO OF YOU

1. Schedule a special day with your daughter. Book a manicure or make reservations for a special lunch. Ask your daughter what she remembers about your talks about female development and sex. Take this time to reemphasize sexual development, the design of the female body, and your values about kissing, physical contact, and sexual intercourse. Ask your daughter about her developing values. The purpose of this time is not to lecture or judge but to communicate openly.

2. Plan a special evening with your daughter. Get out old photo albums and look at pictures of your daughter at different ages. Ask her what she thought about her growing and developing body.

3. Look together at teen magazines. Note what the magazines have to say about the body. Ask your daughter what she agrees or disagrees with.

4. Ask your daughter what she likes and dislikes about her body. What would she like to change? With all the focus on plastic surgery today, ask your daughter if she's ever thought about going to this extreme. This could be a good time to talk with your daughter about accepting and finding beauty in her unique features. You might also want to talk about the kinds of changes she can make through a healthy lifestyle.

5. Ask your daughter what style of clothes she likes. What does she think best complements her body? Perhaps a shopping trip is in order.

A Note About Body Image

Body image has a great deal to do with how girls present and protect their bodies. If a girl believes that her body is only for display or to connect with others, she may be overly sexual in dress and manner. If she is dissatisfied with her body, she may be willing to go to unhealthy lengths to prove that her body is okay. If she is ashamed of her body or afraid of her sexuality, she may obscure her body completely under extra-baggy clothes. If a girl has been sexually abused, these possibilities are intensified. According to one report, 53 percent of teenage girls are unhappy with their bodies by age thirteen, and by age seventeen, 78 percent of girls are dissatisfied with their bodies.[8] Even if your daughter has never overtly struggled with an eating disorder, I urge you to read my book *"Mom, I feel fat!"* for ideas on how to help your daughter build a healthy body image. A good body image is an essential component in holding fast to sexual purity in a culture that promotes a distorted view of girls' and women's bodies.

Girls today have an entirely different set of pressures when it comes to body image. A lot is being thrown in front of them. Sometimes it leads to eating disorders; sometimes to sexuality. But whatever it is they're dealing with, they need to start dealing with it so much earlier than they feel comfortable with.

—DANNAH GRESH, founder of Pure Freedom

MORGAN'S STORY

Morgan didn't talk to her mom about her body image or her boyfriends. She explained to me that when her parents went through their divorce, her mom cried all the time, and Morgan didn't feel as if her questions or concerns were important enough to "bother" her mom with. Sadly, Morgan's parents' divorce took place during the most critical years for Morgan in terms of her own physical and emotional development—ages thirteen and fourteen. Two years after their divorce, both parents remarried and were more involved in their new relationships than they were with Morgan. So when the boy from the mall made Morgan feel important, he filled a place in her heart that was left vacant by her parents.

I don't tell Morgan's story to pass judgment on her mother or to make moms feel guilty. I do tell it to emphasize that we have a window of time to lay a foundation for a strong relationship with our daughters that will last through their adolescent years. Unfortunately, that window is often when our daughters are at a most moody and unattractive age. Their bodies are growing like crazy, and their emotions are swirling out of control. If we withdraw from them because they aren't easy to be with or because we have our own problems, we leave them vulnerable to immature or potentially destructive relationships. We'll explore this in more depth later in the chapter.

Morgan's mom felt awful that her daughter had believed that her mom was not available to her. Both Morgan and her mom agreed to do some of the exercises in the previous Just for the Two of You section to try to regain connection regarding issues of body development and image. At this point, Morgan's mom still did not know about her daughter's heart-shattering relationship with the boy from the mall.

Morgan explained to me that she didn't talk to her mom about boys because when her mom had discovered some thong underwear in Morgan's bedroom dresser, she had snatched them up and told Morgan, "You are not going to dress like a slut!" I must confess that I don't understand thong underwear, but I do know that most girls today do not wear them to feel sexual. They wear them because "everyone else does," and they tell me that they are comfortable. I am not suggesting that you establish guidelines with regard to underwear buying in your home based on this information. That's up to you. I tell Morgan's story to emphasize that the names we call our daughters and the judgments we make have long-term effects.

I do not believe that a mother should ever call her daughter derogatory names. God highlighted the power of naming when He made it one of the defining tasks for Adam and Eve. When we "name" our children, we tell them who they are. If we tell them they are bad or dirty, they may be tempted to live up to our name for them. Or they may just disconnect from us and stop telling us their stories.

When I talked with Morgan's mom about the name-calling incident, I gently asked her what kind of relationship she would expect to have with someone who "suggested" that she was a slut. Of course, Morgan's mom was horrified. She hadn't meant to alienate Morgan by what she said, but in her passion to protect her daughter, she had unknowingly driven Morgan away.

We want to be powerful in our daughters' lives, but we cannot dismiss the power we have when we are careless or judgmental with our words. The following Just for the Two of You section will take humility and courage on our part as mothers. But it is a crucial step in becoming our daughters' allies. We cannot become their allies if they are harboring thoughts that we don't value them. How can we ask them to value themselves if we, above all people, don't show them how valuable they are to us?

Just for the Two of You

Ask your daughter the following questions. Resist the urge to defend yourself or explain your words or actions. Listen to understand and then sincerely ask for your daughter's forgiveness and for the chance to begin again.

1. Have you ever felt like you are a burden to me?
2. What do you think is most important to me?
3. What would you like me to say or do to show that you are a priority?
4. Who else in your life treats you like a priority? How does the person demonstrate this?
5. Have I ever called you names? What were they?
6. Do you think I judge you? In what ways?

THE STORY OF YOUR DAUGHTER'S SOUL

Before we discuss what it means to learn the story of your daughter's soul, let me begin with a few stories.

Jennifer's parents brought her to counseling because she and a friend had left the movies with two high-school boys. Jennifer was in the eighth grade. The boys had driven to one of their homes, and the girls had performed oral sex on the boys.

According to the 2002 National Survey of Family Growth,
55 percent of boys and 54 percent of girls ages fifteen
to nineteen admitted to engaging in oral sex.[9]

My own daughter, Kristin, had her first sexual encounter when she was fifteen. She thought she was going to the movies with a group of friends. It turned out to be one boy and her. During the movie he made a "move" to touch her inappropriately. She told him that she was sick and called me to come get her. When I suggested that she confront him about his behavior, she said, "Everyone would think I'm the biggest loser. Just drop it, Mom."

Twenty-six percent of teens "think it's embarrassing to admit being a virgin."[10]

In 2002, 34 percent of girls and 43 percent of boys had
some kind of sexual encounter at age fifteen.[11]

Sarah's mom called me, hysterical. She and her daughter had just returned from the doctor. Sarah had been diagnosed with chlamydia, the most prevalent sexually transmitted bacterial disease in the United States today. Sarah's mom didn't even know that Sarah had a boyfriend.

One study reported that one in twenty-five young people between the
ages of eighteen and twenty-six was infected with chlamydia.[12]

According to a national survey of teenage girls between the ages of
fifteen and nineteen, 10.5 percent reported having an STD.[13]

I hadn't seen Tina for more than six months. She had graduated from high school and from counseling. She showed up at my counseling office one day with two opened pregnancy tests in hand. "I think I'm pregnant," she stammered. "My mother is going to kill me."

A 2002 national survey of teenage girls found that 24 percent of fifteen- and
sixteen-year-old girls and 17 percent of seventeen- to nineteen-year-olds
did not use contraception the first time they had sexual intercourse.[14]

Jamie's parents brought her to counseling because they discovered pictures that she and a friend had taken of themselves. They were wearing only underwear and shirts. Jamie's parents asked me, "Where did she get this idea? It almost looks like pornography. Who did she take these pictures for?"

"Teenage girls as a group are fast becoming one of the most vulnerable to pornography of any category."[15]

Almost 85 percent of girls surveyed decide to have sex because their partner wanted to.[16]

I will conclude these vignettes and statistics with Morgan's story. She had sexual intercourse when she was thirteen years old. She thought that she was in love. During the entire relationship with the boy from the mall she wore the purity ring that her parents had given her.

Half of sexually active teens between the ages of fifteen and seventeen said they wish they had waited until they were older.[17]

There is no significant difference in STD rates between teens who take virginity pledges and those who don't.[18]

What makes a teenage girl kneel down in a dark basement and give a boy oral sex? How can a girl pledge to remain pure, and in a few minutes throw that promise out for the sake of a cute boy she meets at the mall? I report these stories and statistics not to scare you or disgust you but to challenge you to think about your daughter's soul.

The soul is the "seat" of our emotions—what we feel, want, dream about, and hope for. The soul is the starting place and resting place for relationships. Your daughter's soul is what allowed her to fling her arms around you when she was three years old and exclaim, "Mommy, I love you more than anybody in the whole wide world." Your daughter's soul compelled her to "ask Jesus into her heart" when she was seven years old. Your daughter's soul fuels her longings to belong, fit in, and find a best friend.

When girls engage in oral sex, they are not wanting to demean themselves.

They are wanting to connect with a boy who will want them. When teenagers are embarrassed about being virgins, they are not touting the glory of being promiscuous. They are afraid their sexual experience—or lack of experience—will reveal their relational desirability. When girls engage in unprotected sex, they are not stupid. They are willing to take risks for the chance of a relationship. When Morgan had sex with the boy from the mall, she was not a slut. She was an immature thirteen-year-old girl who wanted to be loved.

Do you think that I shall ever have a bosom friend—an intimate friend, you know—a really kindred spirit in whom I can confide my inmost soul? I've dreamed of meeting her all my life.

—ANNE in *Anne of Green Gables* by L. M. Montgomery

Am I simplifying the sexual behaviors of teenage girls? Not at all. In fact, even if what I write sounds simplistic, I cannot write eloquently or passionately enough about the realities of the soul. How old were you when you heard your first story about "falling in love and living happily ever after"? What ignited interest and passion in your heart? The castle? The beautiful dress? Or the thought of being noticed, pursued, and loved by someone forever? This is the story that most of us live by. One day someone will see me, want me, care for me, and love me for eternity.

As we talk about teenage girls and sex—as we talk about your daughter and sex—you will be detached or disgusted by the subject if you do not connect it to your daughter's heart. It is our job to guide our daughters in knowing that their private parts—their sex organs—are connected to their hearts. When a girl engages in sexual activity, she fuses her heart to another person. Then when the relationship fizzles or never materializes, her heart is torn. Today's girls who are sexually active are tearing their hearts in pieces over and over again. Pretty quickly, a girl will learn to harden her heart so that it won't hurt so much—so that relationships don't matter quite so much. And that is tragic, because it is a departure from the core design of our souls.

JUST FOR YOU

1. What were your favorite stories when you were young? What realities did they enliven in your own soul?
2. What were your daughter's favorite stories? What do they tell you about her?
3. What are your favorite stories, songs, movies today? Why?
4. What are your daughter's favorite stories, songs, movies today? What do they tell you about her longing for relationships?
5. What do you ache for, dream about, take risks for, pray to God about? How much of what is most important to your innermost being revolves around relationships?
6. What do you know about your daughter's innermost being and what is important to her?
7. Think about your first significant experiences in relationships—be they childhood, teen, romantic, or otherwise. What did they teach you about yourself and about relationships?

THE STORY OF YOUR DAUGHTER'S SPIRIT

After surveying the statistics and stories about today's teenagers and sex, it would be tempting to walk away in disgust or despair. I know that as I initially began work on this book, I felt a bit discouraged. I commented to my friends, "This is one area in our culture where the Enemy has won." My work with Morgan changed my mind.

I often watch parts of teen movies with my adolescent clients to highlight truths about teenage life. Morgan and I were watching the film *The Notebook*. This is a story about lifelong love that began as teenage romance. I was hoping that Morgan would notice the main character's interest in his girlfriend, the ways he honored her, and his willingness to wait for her. I realize that parents may find some parts of this movie objectionable, but I believe that teen stories in music and movies can be powerful tools to connect adults and adolescents. We can certainly mention or censor what is objectionable

while using resources that speak a teenager's language in order to forge a connection with our daughters.

After one tender moment in the movie, Morgan looked at me with tears
in her eyes and said, "Will I ever find someone to love me like that?"

But then something tugs at our hearts…a movie, a book, a friend,
a scripture, a child, a song…and reminds us that deep within
us is a desire for fulfilling relationships so intense that even
the daily or disappointing realities of life cannot extinguish it.

—SHARON HERSH, *Bravehearts*

Morgan's question is the question of every teenage girl engaging in
shame-filled or even proudly cavalier sex, "Will I ever find someone to love
me, fill my emptiness, make me complete?" I knew that was my question too.

I also knew what all the startling statistics and sobering stories really
reveal: not a world conquered by the Enemy but a world desperate for a
Lover. Every single one of the fifty million romance novels sold in America
every year, every song a teenager sings about love, every statistic about
teenage sex is about the greatest love story ever told. The craving in your
daughter's flesh to be with another is about a bigger story. The desire to be
with another person is a desire, a longing, and a passion deep within her very
body so that she can know and believe in the love of God.

We will look at this mystery over and over again throughout this book.
A book on sex *and* Jesus? Absolutely. Thank goodness. When I hear my
teenage clients talk about having sexual intercourse with their pants pulled
down around their ankles, their private parts hurting and bleeding, and their
hearts in a state of conflicted emotions, I initially feel anger and sorrow at a
culture that has told them that sex is just about biology. And then I feel hope,
because I know that God uses every story to romance us to His love and His
longing to fill our emptiness with love, forgiveness, and healing.

I didn't respond to Morgan's question about the movie with a sermon
about God's love. She would only have been confused. Maybe you're feeling
a bit unsettled as well. You didn't expect to find Jesus in a book about teen
sex. I urge you to read on. In the next chapter we will continue to look at this

subject of teenage girls and sex and how mothers can become powerful influences in their daughters' lives. We will also continue to consider how sex is one way that God romances us to fill our empty cravings with Himself.

In the next chapter we will continue Morgan's story. An important new chapter in Morgan's life was beginning that day in my office. I said, "Oh, Morgan, your longing to be loved by the boy from the mall is not a sign that something is wrong with you—but that something is more profoundly right with you than you have ever dared to imagine!"

Chapter 2

Sex and You

At eleven, when I finally got up the nerve to question my mother about sex, I was instantly sorry.... She led me into a room and pulled out a paper and pencil from her bedside drawer. All of a sudden she was drawing fallopian tubes and asking about follicles and menstruation. Ten diagrams, fifteen minutes, and considerable discomfort later, she asked me if I had any questions. I did...I ask[ed] whether there was any way to avoid the entire situation.

—MARTHA MANNING, *Chasing Grace*

Every mother I know can tell a story similar to the one author and counselor Martha Manning told in the opening epigraph—learning about "the birds and the bees" in awkward and sometimes funny moments with either her mother or a well-intentioned elementary-school teacher. Manning continues the story of her sex education:

> Just when I thought it couldn't get worse, the [teachers] handed out boxes to all the girls. At first I thought it would be cool stuff, like party favors, to take the sting out of the [sex education class]. I made the mistake of ripping mine open right there. It was "feminine protection": a booklet, "sanitary napkins" (a frightening phrase), and a stupid little belt. And even though they served Hawaiian Punch and Pepperidge Farm cookies, which we never had at our house, I wanted to evaporate.[1]

Talking to our daughters about sex is a task of heroic proportions—especially today when a sexualized culture compels us to know about much more than fallopian tubes and feminine protection.

Dr. Robert Blum, a professor with the University of Minnesota's Center for Adolescent Health and Development, conducted a significant study about mothers, daughters, and sex. One important conclusion of this survey of ninety thousand teenagers was that a close relationship between mother and daughter is a strong factor in influencing teenage girls to delay having sex for the first time.[2] This "connectedness" was defined as "how close teens feel to their mothers, how much they feel mother cares about them, how warm and loving mother is, how good communication is with their mother and how satisfied teens feel with their relationship with their mother."[3] The report concluded that "simply stating parents' disapproval of teen sex is not enough. Clearly, some teenagers do not get the message."[4] In an interview with CNN's Gina Greene, Blum said that "kids who are close to their moms are much more tuned in and in sync with what their moms value."[5]

What are your *values* about sex? In this chapter you will have an opportunity to develop your answer to that question. Once again we will be using story to flesh out what you really believe about sex. Your story. Your accumulated sexual experiences as well as your education and your faith have shaped your story. Many moms make the mistake of trying to separate their stories from their beliefs. When we hate, hide, or dismiss our stories, we present heartless rules and reasons to our daughters. We are, in effect, asking our daughters to form an alliance with the law. We are not authentically powerful. When we incorporate our own experiences, failures, victories, heartaches, and joys in the context of values and information, we bring more than the law to our daughters. We bring ourselves. We invite our daughters to form an alliance with *us*.

Morgan and Her Mom

Morgan and I spent several sessions talking about her relationship with the boy from the mall. We talked about her body's responses to the physical relationship, her soul's longing for connection, and the damage to body, soul, and spirit caused by this broken relationship. I thought that it was time for Morgan to tell her mom.

"Why? Why do I have to tell her? It's over. What difference will it make?" Morgan pleaded with me.

"Your mom knows things about you that I don't. She will be there for you in future relationships, and I probably won't be. She needs to be your helper, your advocate, and your support," I answered.

"But she is going to freak out!" Morgan complained.

"I promise I'll help her. Let me meet with her first," I said.

I asked Morgan's mom to come in for a session. We talked a little about Morgan's progress, and then I asked, "Have you and Morgan talked much about sex?"

I saw a flicker of fear in her eyes, and then defensiveness. "We had 'the talk' a long time ago. I've always told her that it's important to wait until she's married to have sex. Morgan is a good girl.... Why are you asking? Do you know something I don't know?"

Morgan's mom had provided the foundation of sex education that most parents offer their children—the "birds and the bees" talk and a strong admonition against premarital sex. But the law is not enough. The apostle Paul warned, "Rule-keeping does not naturally evolve into living by faith."[6] I suspected that Morgan's mom's "stiffness" with regard to sex came out of her own story.

We find ourselves involved in loyal commitments,
not needing to force our way in life, able to marshal and direct
our energies wisely. Legalism is helpless in bringing this about.

—GALATIANS 5:22–23

"What did you learn about sex when you were growing up?" I asked.

"Basically the same thing," she answered. "The school taught us about female development. My mom told me that if I had sex before marriage, I would ruin my reputation and my marriage."

The kind of sex education Morgan's mom experienced years ago is still the norm between mothers and daughters today. Interestingly, research findings on the influence of mothers on teenagers' sex lives seem to indicate that mothers talk differently with their daughters and their sons about sex. Mothers tend to warn girls about their reputations and their futures, but they warn boys about protecting themselves.[7] All three categories are important in sex education, but protection actually gets more to the heart of the matter. But protection from what and for what?

I asked Morgan's mom, "What was your sexual experience before marriage?"

"I pretty much followed my mother's rules," she answered. "I saved sex for marriage."

"And what has been your sexual experience after marriage?" I asked.

Morgan's mom looked surprised by my question. "Well…," she paused, "it's been hard. I guess right after we were married I wondered what the big deal was. It was pretty awkward and uncomfortable. In my new marriage, my husband's more interested in it now than I am."

"Did you wonder what you 'saved sex' for?" I asked.

"I saved it for my marriage," she answered defensively. "It was important to me to be a virgin when I got married. I want that for Morgan, too."

"Why?" I pressed her.

She struggled to find an answer. Finally she said, "Because that's what the Bible teaches."

"Why?" I asked again. "Why does God care about sex?"

Morgan's mom was increasingly frustrated by my questions. "I don't have an exact answer to that," she said. "I just know that it's important."

JUST FOR YOU

You can begin to discover your own story by answering the same questions Morgan's mother did:

1. What did you learn about sex while you were growing up? What do you wish you had learned?
2. What did you experience of sex before marriage? What did this teach you about yourself and about sex?
3. What have you experienced of sex after marriage? What has it taught you about yourself and about sex?
4. What do you value about sex?
5. What do you wish were true about your sexuality and your experience with sex?

Morgan's mother's story spoke volumes about the way she educated Morgan about sex. She thought sex was a big deal, but she wasn't sure why. She had saved sex for marriage, but it had been a disappointment. She believed that God cared about sex, but again, she wasn't sure why. Her discussions with Morgan about facts and rules lacked heart. Morgan's mom had disconnected her own heart from sex, and her disconnection only added to the confusion Morgan felt about sex and her fear that she had to figure this out for herself.

Teenagers are filled with a mix of emotions, and they are compelled by passion. When given a choice between rules and romance, many will forget the rules for the promise of a relationship. I handed Morgan's mom a copy of *Seventeen* magazine. I asked her to read it and come back the next week. "Write down what the culture says are its values about sex," I told her as she looked dubiously at the magazine. "Also, write down what you value about sex. It might help you to write what you wish were true about sex." Morgan's mother accepted my assignment. She didn't know it yet, but she was in the process of writing her own story.

EVERY MOTHER HAS A STORY

Everyone has a sexual history. Perhaps your story has been shaped in ignorance (I'll explain what I mean by this in the following section), as Morgan's mom's story was. Or maybe your sexual history involves foolishness—you took risks or "went further" with a boy in the heat of hormones and teenage romance than you intended. Your story might include sexual sin—experiences or promiscuity that you believe need to be kept hidden, certainly from your daughter. And I know that some of you have a sexual history that includes sexual abuse. In this chapter we will examine all four categories in order to help you know your own story. What conclusions have you come to about yourself and sex as a result of your history? We will look at ways in which you can forgive yourself for the past and arm yourself for the task at hand: being an effective ally for your daughter. With a clear mind and a calm heart, you are much better equipped to enter your daughter's world of sexual confusion and potential calamity.

SEXUAL IGNORANCE

Many well-meaning Christian families create a context of sexual ignorance when they dispense only information and rules. Your daughter may know the biological facts, and perhaps you've told her that she should save herself for marriage. But what is she saving herself for? What is the value of sex?

Morgan's mom came to her second individual counseling session with a troubled expression on her face. "I'm having a hard time writing about the value of sex," she explained. "For some reason, all I can think about is a time when I was about six years old and my mother found me touching my own body. She screamed at me, 'What is wrong with you? Do you want to grow up to be a bad girl?' I guess I've always felt like sex and sexual touch is dirty or bad."

Morgan's mother was discovering her story. Her own mother had led her to believe that the human body—especially the private parts—is a source of shame. Masturbation is a natural early childhood self-exploratory act. It can also be an exploratory act in adolescence. Child-development experts report that self-exploration normally takes place between the ages of three and six and between the ages of twelve and seventeen. Christian counselor and author Dan Allender suggests an appropriate response to a child's self-exploration: "I am delighted that you have discovered that your body can give you pleasure to various degrees. I hope you understand that that is God's design for you and your spouse." He continues, "I would not make a big deal about it and I would certainly not shame them. To shame a child over this would be sin."[8]

When I shared this with Morgan's mom, she stared at me in silence for a while. Finally she spoke: "I don't even know what to say to that. I have never been able to believe that sexual touch is good. I'm sure that I've even wrinkled my nose in disgust whenever I've talked about sex with Morgan."

I suggested that Morgan's mom pray and ask God to show her the value of sex. I also encouraged her again to write about what she wished were true for her about sex.

When a mother counsels her daughter about sex out of her own ignorance or discomfort with sex, she may suggest to her daughter that sex is dirty. This can be very confusing to a teenager. Why is sex dirty before you're married and not after? When a mother talks to her daughter about sex in only biological terms and also communicates a strong disapproval of sex, she leaves her daughter vulnerable to a culture that presents sex in a much more positive light, although without necessary guidelines about boundaries, limits, and consequences. And if her daughter likes a boy, kisses a boy, enjoys holding hands with a boy, her mother might be the last person she confides in when she needs guidance about how far to go, because she fears her mother's disapproval.

We need to teach our daughters that one purpose of sex is for meaningful enjoyment. It allows two people to be drawn into a potentially wonderful and deep expression of intimacy. We can let our daughters know that waiting for this intimacy in the context of marriage will be hard, because the body naturally longs to touch and be touched when the soul is engaged in a relationship. We must also teach our daughters that physical touch allows bodies to become symbols of something far more mystical, and that is why waiting for the commitment and communion of marriage is wise.

We will talk about this in more detail later in the book, and I'll present it in terms that an adolescent will be able to understand. But now is the time for you to examine your own beliefs about sex. Did you start out thinking of sex as something to be feared and then dreaded, or did you view it with awe and gratitude? How do you view it now? Sexual ignorance is not simply naiveté about the biological facts about sex; it is missing the mystery of sex. If you have relegated sex to mere biological realities, or rules and regulations, then you may be ignorant as to its purpose and meaning.

JUST FOR YOU

1. What messages did you receive growing up that suggested sex was dirty?
2. What messages have you given your daughter about sex being dirty?
3. What messages did you receive growing up that suggested sex was enjoyable?
4. What messages have you given your daughter about sex being enjoyable?
5. Are you afraid to talk about the pleasure involved in sex? If so, why?

SEXUAL FOOLISHNESS

I first kissed a boy when I was thirteen years old. We had just moved to a new town, and I was anxious to make friends. We moved at the beginning of the summer, and by the end of the summer I knew quite a few of the kids in my neighborhood. Much to my delight, as summer ended, I was invited to a back-to-school party by one of my new friends. This was my first boy-girl party. I didn't know what to expect, but I was thrilled at the prospect of being "in" with a group of kids before school began.

As soon as I arrived at the party, I noticed that most of the girls were paired up with boys. I observed couples holding hands and walking off into dark corners of the backyard. Pretty quickly after I arrived, the host of the party told me that my "date" for the night would be there soon. His name was John. I had no idea what was going on or what to expect. I just knew that I wanted to fit in.

When John arrived, my friend introduced us and left us standing there alone. I'm sure we made small talk, but all I can remember from that night is John taking my hand and leading me to a spot along the backyard fence. The only detail I remember vividly is that John tried to stick his tongue in my mouth, and I bit it. I had never "made out" with anyone. I didn't even know the term *french kissing*. I thought it was disgusting, but I didn't ask John to stop. I felt paralyzed.

This was the first of many make-out sessions with boys in which I went numb while I allowed the boy to do whatever he wanted. My own sexual naiveté and intense desire to be liked made me pliable to boys' roving hands and raging hormones.

When a girl doesn't know her own standards and doesn't understand her own body—much less a teenage boy's body—she is vulnerable to foolish behaviors. As my own daughter began to date, I had to examine my own foolishness during those adolescent make-out parties. I didn't technically have sex, so was what I did a big deal? Did I want my daughter to make out with her boyfriend? Should she go past "first base"? When my story collided with my daughter's story, I had to find the answers to these questions.

I wrote in chapter 1 about Kristin's first sexual encounter with a boy when she was fifteen years old. She ended up in the movies by herself with a boy she liked. Pretty quickly into the movie, he made a move to touch her breast. She stood up, announced that she was sick, and left the movie. She found the nearest pay phone and called me to come get her. When I picked her up, she was distraught. While crying inconsolably, she told me what had happened. I didn't know what to say. I just wanted to find the boy and make him pay for what he had done to my daughter.

During the sleepless night that followed Kristin's movie incident, I thought about my own story. I remembered all those moments of paralysis when I let a boy do whatever he wanted, even if I felt uncomfortable. I never talked to my mom about the experiences, but I did write about them in a journal. One day, near the end of my middle-school years, my mom found my journal and read it. I came home from school to an angry mother. She threw the diary at my feet and said, "I don't understand you at all. Why would you act like some tramp? I don't even think you're a Christian!"

Although my mother's words sounded harsh, I know now that she was parenting out of fear. She had her own story that had resulted in harsh conclusions about sex. At the time, though, her words convinced me that I could never tell her about what I liked or didn't like about those experiences. And I couldn't talk to her about the reasons I could not seem to find my own voice during these encounters.

By the end of that sleepless night, I was able to articulate what my own sexual foolishness had cost me. Every time I had allowed a boy to go a little further, my defenses were worn down for the next encounter. I foolishly told myself, "I've already let a boy touch me there, so what difference does it make if it happens again?"

As my defenses crumbled, my voice was increasingly silenced. I didn't believe that I could ask for what I wanted and keep the relationship, and I thought that making someone like me was the most important goal of all. I had sacrificed my standards, my comfort, and my self-expression—myself—to someone else. And I hadn't known that this was the foundation for an unhealthy relationship. I was stunned to see that my foolishness had set me up for later relationships when I would allow unhealthy behaviors and stay silent.

The next morning I searched the basement for my old middle-school yearbooks and asked Kristin to sit with me. We looked through the yearbooks, and I pointed out pictures of my old boyfriends. We laughed together at the thick glasses and awful haircuts. And then I told my daughter about my sexual experiences and silent paralysis. I congratulated her for standing up for herself and speaking up at the movies. We talked about healthy relationships based on mutual respect. We also talked about what happens when a boy touches a girl's breast and how her body and his body respond. I reminded Kristin that sexual pleasure between a man and woman is part of God's design for marriage, but that when it happens between teenagers, it sends the wrong message to both the boy and the girl. It communicates to the boy that he can continue to follow his hormonal urges, and it tells the girl that her body can be explored before her heart is connected in the security of a lifelong relationship.

Kristin's response to my story filled me with gratitude. She said, "Mom, I've heard kids talk about 'hooking up,' 'going to third base,' 'giving head,' and lots of other things. I wasn't sure what they were even talking about. I don't want to be stupid, but I don't want to do things I'm not comfortable with, either. I hope we can keep talking about all of these things."

Her words gave me hope that sexual ignorance and sexual foolishness will be met in Kristin's story by a relationship—our relationship—that gives her information, understanding, and a vision for *more*.

JUST FOR YOU

1. Recall the sexual foolishness in your own story—making out, petting, etc. What did these experiences teach you about sex, relationships, and yourself?

2. Were you comfortable telling a boy no? Why or why not?

3. Were you able to discuss your experiences with your mother? Why or why not?

4. What do you wish your mother had told you about kissing, petting, etc.?

5. How would you respond—or how have you responded—if your daughter told you that a boy tried to touch her inappropriately? What message do you want to send her—or did you send her—about sex, relationships, and herself?

Sexual Sin

Perhaps the story that mothers most hate and believe needs to be hidden from their daughters is a story of sexual sin or promiscuity during adolescence or their early adult years. I have heard many mothers say, "I just don't want my daughter to make the same mistakes I did." But by allowing guilt and shame to cut them off from this important part of their own story, mothers cut themselves and their daughters off from a powerful source of wisdom and guidance.

The word *promiscuous* is derived from the Latin and can simply mean "of various kinds mixed together." This definition offers the best description of a girl or woman ensnared by sexual sin. She is many things at once—afraid, taking risks, longing for love, looking for love in all the wrong places, foolish, selfish, headstrong, hurting herself, and trying to meet her deep and legitimate longing for connection.

If your story includes experiences of sex outside of marriage—maybe many such encounters—what have these experiences compelled you to believe about sex and about yourself? Sadly, many women whose story includes sexual sin believe that they are stained or second-rate. If that is what you believe, then you may communicate to your daughter that if she falls or fails, she too is stained and second-rate. To avoid disappointing you or being judged, she may hide her experiences from you, and if she feels that she has already blown it, she may continue acting out sexually.

God did not send his Son into the world to condemn
the world, but to save the world through him.

—John 3:17, niv

I understand that if sexual sin is part of your story, some scenes and memories are painful and shame-filled. I also believe that it is at those very moments that your story has the potential to become glorious. Yes, glorious! I love the words of author and storyteller Frederick Buechner: "Grace is what needn't happen and can't possibly happen because it can only impossibly happen in the dark that only just barely fails to swallow it up."[9] We can have the most profound experience of grace and forgiveness in the context of our greatest sin.

When you believe that your story must be hated and hidden because of your sin, the Enemy wins twice. If you allow God to touch these shame-filled places with His redemptive touch, then you can be a powerful presence in your daughter's life. I don't think it is an accident that the one woman mentioned by name in the faith Hall of Fame is the prostitute Rahab. In reminding us of her story, God seems to be telling us that the most shameful stories become the containers of His most glorious grace. He delights to turn weakness to strength.[10]

God's highlighting of Rahab's story challenges us to examine righteous attitudes about sexual purity that may have turned into an overly zealous message to teenagers that sexual sin is unpardonable. But the gospel proclaims that there is no sin too dark for the light of God's love. Consider the tender words of hope from the fourteenth-century writer Julian of Norwich:

> And here I understood that our Lord looks upon his servant with
> pity, not with blame. For this passing life does not ask that we live
> completely without blame and sin. He loves us endlessly, and we
> sin continually, and he shows us our sin most tenderly. And then we
> sorrow and mourn with discretion and turn to look upon his mercy,
> clinging to his love and goodness, knowing that he is our medicine.[11]

One of my clients, Karen, is a wonderful example of this mix of sorrow, joy, and clinging to God's love. Karen was in her midtwenties and still frequenting bars and clubs, meeting men, and participating in what she called "recreational sex." We spent many sessions talking about her careless attitude about herself and sex—all to no avail. But God pierced her heart with love that resulted in change.

Generous in love—God, give grace!
Huge in mercy—wipe out my bad record.
Scrub away my guilt, soak out my sins in your laundry.

—PSALM 51:1–2

She came in for a session after I had not seen her for two months. She said, "Wow, a lot has happened. Over Christmas I met a man who is different from any man I've dated. He really respects me. He's sent me flowers, is getting to know me, and he hasn't tried to have sex, even when I let him know that it would be okay." And then Karen started to cry. Her tears surprised me because Karen usually comes across as a tough party girl.

"What's wrong?" I asked.

"I didn't think it was a big deal," she sobbed.

"What was a big deal?"

"All that sex. I thought it didn't matter. But it did! Now that I've met someone who I think I love and who loves me, I know it matters. My mother told me it would. I hate to admit that she was right, but she was. What do I do?" Tears streamed down Karen's face.

My first word to Karen after her outburst was, "Welcome."

Confusion clouded Karen's face. "What do you mean?"

"Finally the real you has shown up. When you cavalierly told me that sex was no big deal, you were really saying that *you* were no big deal. You were disconnected from yourself. Now that love is knocking at your door, you are coming out of hiding and realizing that you matter. That is good news!"

I asked Karen to do the exercise in the Just for You section that follows. If sexual sin is a part of your story, I encourage you to do the exercise as well.

JUST FOR YOU

1. Write out as many details of your sexual experiences as you can recall.

2. Read the details aloud to yourself. If you know a trusted counselor or have a close-mouthed confidante, it would be beneficial to read it to that person as well. Finally, read your words aloud to God. Ask for a sense of His presence, forgiveness, and cleansing.

3. Read Psalm 51. (This is David's prayer after his own sexual sin with Bathsheba and the murder of her husband.) Take each page of your writing and burn it. While it's burning, pray again for a sense of God's forgiveness and cleansing.

4. In faith, believing in God's complete forgiveness, look at yourself in the mirror every day and say, "I forgive you for…[whatever comes to mind]."

After three weeks of doing the Just for You exercises, Karen came in for a counseling session. Her face looked radiant. She really looked different. She explained, "I know I'm forgiven. Even if this relationship doesn't work out, I know that *I matter* to God—not my sin but me, my heart matters to God. That's why careless sex is a big deal. It convinced me that I didn't matter to myself, others, or even God."

My heart thrilled to hear Karen's new understanding of God's love in the unlikely context of her sexual sin. You can believe that your story is a gift to yourself and your daughter if you receive the unconditional gift of God's forgiveness and love. Receiving His gift allows you to give to your daughter wisdom, compassion, and hope.

Everyone thinks change is based on what you're going to get,
but change has a lot to do with what you're willing to get rid of—
like a hot air balloon that goes up when you throw the sand
out of it. A lot of people don't want to throw the sand out;
they want to keep the sand and still go up.

—JOE McQ, *The Steps We Took*

SEXUAL ABUSE

Sexual abuse is the Enemy's most insidious tool in convincing girls and women that they don't matter, that others cannot be trusted, and that God is absent. When sexual abuse is part of your story and you haven't done the work to understand what it did to you, you are likely to overlook dangers in your daughter's life or to be so hypervigilant that your daughter will feel smothered and do everything she can to get away from your watchfulness and guidance.

I won't take the time here to delve into the complex damage from sexual abuse or the healing path for the woman who has been sexually abused. There are resources listed at the back of this book that can help you if this is your experience. I urge you to do the necessary work to understand the harm that sexual abuse has caused you and to embark on a path of healing—for your sake and your daughter's.

One of the most damaging results of sexual abuse is that it makes a girl or woman feel powerless. Because you were powerless to foresee or stop the sexual abuse or the agony of the aftermath of abuse, you may feel that you cannot significantly affect your life or the lives of others. A woman who has been sexually abused may believe that there is something deeply wrong with her. This tragic belief steals her sense that she has anything to offer others. She loses herself. Ironically, when a mother loses herself to her story of sexual abuse, she loses her ability to be powerful in her daughter's life with regard to sexuality.

A significant part of the damage from sexual abuse is that it stops you from asking, "Who am I on behalf of my daughter?" Once again, the Enemy wins twice. He won when the sexual abuse occurred, and he wins by keeping you locked in self-contempt, distanced from your daughter.

If you have not confronted your sexual abuse with the help of a skilled counselor, I suspect that alarms are going off in your soul right now. Maybe your heart is raging, "How can I help my daughter when I couldn't help myself?" or "How can I trust God now when He wasn't there for me during the abuse?"

I urge you again to explore the resources mentioned at the end of this book and to consider the following:

1. Find a recent picture of your daughter. Look at her. God knew your story when He entrusted this child to *you*. He knew about the sexual abuse. He knew about the sexual questions and temptations that your daughter would face. In infinite wisdom and unconditional love, He knew that *you* were the mother your daughter needed.

2. If God's wisdom and love seem far removed from your story of sexual abuse, the Enemy is continuing to abuse you with his lies. He doesn't want you to trust the great Bridegroom.[12] The Enemy wants you to believe that God is absent or missing. Your hypervigilance makes sense. The Enemy and evil men will rape you, but Jesus will never force His way into your story. He will never rape you. He stands at the door and asks your *permission* to enter your life.[13] The key to sexual healing is to surrender our shame to the Lover of our souls. And as you come out of hiding and invite Him to love you, you will be available for your daughter.

JUST FOR YOU

1. What has sexual abuse in your story led you to believe about yourself?

2. When do you feel powerless in your daughter's life? Could it be connected to your story of sexual abuse? Explain.

3. What, if any, uneasiness about situations or people in your daughter's life have you dismissed? What, if any, hurt that was inflicted on you in sexual abuse have you dismissed?

4. Are you hypervigilant with regard to your daughter? Is your vigilance a result of what happened to you?

5. Write out everything you learned as a result of your sexual abuse—potential dangers, the harm that others can inflict, damaged self-esteem, surviving suffering, etc. Take note of all you uniquely have to offer your daughter *because* of your story.

6. Are you mad at God because of the sexual abuse? It will be difficult to believe that God can be trusted with your child if you don't believe that you can trust Him. Consider praying daily, "God, I want to see Your fingerprints in my story. Help my unbelief." God is the source of faith. He can increase your faith even in the face of painful chapters in your story. "The fundamental fact of existence is that this trust in God, this faith, is the firm foundation under everything that makes life worth living. It's our handle on what we can't see."[14]

In chapter 3 we will examine how you can use your story in mothering. Even though we've covered a lot of ground in this chapter, you may not have put specific words to your unique story. Take the time now to write out your story. Use the four categories—ignorance, foolishness, sin, and abuse—to guide you. Conclude with what you believe about yourself and sex. What do you value about yourself and sex because of your story? I know that this can be hard work, but it is work well worth doing, both for your sake and your daughter's. Disconnection with your own story is a knife that severs your connection with your daughter.

Morgan's mom did the hard work. When she came into my office one day for a counseling session and announced, "Now I know what I value about myself and sex," I suspected that she had connected with her own story and was ready to connect with her daughter. We'll continue her story, along with Morgan's, in the pages that follow.

Chapter 3

Sex, You, and Your Mothering

Though I acknowledge that the culture at large plays a significant role in our view of ourselves as women, ultimately the beliefs and behavior of our individual mothers exert a far stronger influence. In most cases, she is the first to teach us the dictates of the larger culture. And if her beliefs are at odds with the dominant culture, our mother's influence almost always wins.

—CHRISTIANE NORTHRUP, *Mother-Daughter Wisdom*

I wish sex was a tender, pleasurable expression of love," Morgan's mom said wistfully. "I wish it celebrated the body, connected the soul, and reflected our commitment before God to love each other for eternity."

Before I could marvel at her words, Morgan's mom held up the copy of *Seventeen* magazine that I had given her. I had asked her to note the value that the culture places on sex. "The culture says it's fun, magical, and exciting. I wish all of that were true for me. I'm sure my husband did too."

"Do you think *you're* fun and exciting?" I asked her.

She grunted in response. I understood her incredulity. Most middle-aged moms immersed in carpools, curfews, and casseroles don't feel fun and exciting. Before I could empathize with her, Morgan's mom interjected, "I know what you're saying. My problem with sex is a problem with *me*. I've never believed that I was worthwhile, beautiful, or desirable. I wonder if Morgan feels the same way about herself?"

Now we were getting to the heart of the matter. Morgan's mom's approach to sex and sex education had been disconnected from herself. She believed, as do many well-intentioned Christian women, that saving sex for marriage would not only result in sex being wonderful, but it would make her feel wonderful about herself as well. When the results were a bit different than anticipated, she concluded that sex was a disappointment and that she was a failure, causing her to devalue herself even more.

I knew that Morgan's mom had some work to do on herself. I also knew that Morgan couldn't wait for her mother to complete weeks of therapy. She needed her now. Part of the joy of doing therapy with both mothers and daughters is that I get to see healing in both—often as the result of the daughter's "problems." God has a strange sense of humor. He often uses the "speck of sawdust" in our daughters' eyes to reveal the "plank" in our own.[1]

"What do you think Morgan believes about her self-worth?" I asked her mom.

"I don't think she's really confident, and I'm sure our divorce unsettled her," her mom answered. "And she's been so boy crazy," she added as an afterthought.

"Do you think she believes that having a boyfriend might make her feel better about herself—similar to the way you thought getting married would make you feel better about yourself?" I asked gently.

Morgan's mom was silent for a few minutes. I could almost see her mind processing the concepts we were discussing. A look of panic began to creep across her face, "Oh, my goodness! Have *I* made Morgan think that she needs a boyfriend to be okay? She's certainly seen me *not* be okay since our divorce." Quickly her mind leaped to the next thought, "Does Morgan think she needs to have sex to get a boyfriend and to feel okay about herself?"

I knew she was thinking about the messages she'd unwittingly given her daughter about self-esteem and sex as well as the messages Morgan had been getting from *Seventeen* magazine.

Morgan's mom's story was intersecting with her daughter's. She was confronting the painful truth that not valuing herself had distorted her understanding of the value of sex, and that despite all of her pleas for her daughter to remain abstinent, Morgan had inherited her mom's lack of self-worth and misunderstanding about the value of sex—in the context of a culture that suggests that the remedy for low self-esteem is found in articles with headlines like "Knockout Makeup for Making Out" and "Hooking Up—Failure-Proof Ways to Get a Guy."

"What should I do?" Morgan's mom asked. "Is it too late to help Morgan develop better self-esteem than I have had? What should I tell her about sex now?"

"Maybe you should begin by telling her *your* story," I suggested.

"I don't know how," she lamented. "I know how to lecture, nag, and plead, but I don't know how to tell my story."

I knew that her request for help would open the door for this mother and daughter to begin to connect in meaningful ways. I respect the wisdom of board-certified ob-gyn Christiane Northrup. Based on more than twenty-five years of clinical experience, she writes:

> No mother is under any obligation to share her sexual past with her daughter, of course. This is especially true when doing so would serve no purpose. What she is obligated to do, however, is make sure that she has confronted, to the best of her ability, any past sexual trauma or disappointment that may influence the legacy she passes on to her daughter. In my experience, it is not a mother's history of abuse or promiscuity that is the problem in a mother-daughter legacy; it is the fact that it is taboo that destines it to be repeated in subsequent generations, until the pattern is brought to consciousness and healed.[2]

YOUR MOTHERING STYLE

In the last chapter we examined some important categories for understanding your own sexual history. Before you can use your story powerfully on your daughter's behalf, you may need some individual counseling to better understand your own story. That does not mean, however, that you are powerless to interact with your daughter until you are healed. In fact, you can experience further healing as you interact with your daughter. I don't mean that you work out your issues *on* your daughter; I mean that you can take the information you accumulated in the last chapter and use it *in relationship with* your daughter. As you begin to treat yourself with kindness and understanding, you will be able to offer the same to your daughter. As you look at your own face in the mirror and know who you are, you will be able to look into your daughter's eyes and tell her who she is.

At the end of this chapter, we will look together at guidelines for telling your story to your daughter. But before you are ready to tell your story, you need to examine what you have already told your daughter—both spoken and unspoken messages—about you, her, and sex. When Morgan's mom disclosed that she knew how to lecture and plead but didn't know how to tell her own story, she was acknowledging her mothering style.

In this chapter we are going to look at four mothering styles. These styles are simply *postures* in parenting. Posture is what makes certain activities possible. When I stand, I can walk or run. When I sit, I can lean back and relax. When I kneel, I can pray or scrub the floor. When I lie down, I can rest or sleep. Your posture in response to your daughter's questions about herself and sex likewise yields specific results for both you and your daughter. There is no one right posture in parenting. However, your posture does determine how you tell your story.

Some mothering styles make it almost impossible for our daughters to hear anything personal about us or to tell us their stories. In this chapter you will have an opportunity to identify your primary posture in mothering and see how it helps or hinders connecting with your daughter. As we examine each mothering style, you will have a chance to link your style to your story and to identify the strengths and weaknesses of your style. The purpose of the work in this chapter is not to make you feel guilty but to guide you in transitioning to a parenting posture that allows you to use your experience powerfully in your daughter's life as well as to invite her to trust you with her experiences.

MOTHERING FROM ABOVE

DAUGHTER: Mom, I don't understand why you are making such a big deal of this. We were just sitting in the basement watching a movie.

MOM: It looked to me like you were doing a lot more than watching a movie. He was almost on top of you!

DAUGHTER: Mom, he just had his arm around me. We weren't doing anything else.

MOM: I wasn't born yesterday. I know what you were doing. Nothing good comes of sitting in a dark basement that close to a boy.

Have you forgotten everything we've taught you? Do you even
wear your purity ring anymore?

DAUGHTER: WE WERE JUST WATCHING A MOVIE! We couldn't
do anything more if we wanted to—with you coming down
every two minutes and flipping the lights on. I was so embarrassed. Do you think we were going to have sex, Mom? Is that
what you think?

MOM: I think you were asking for trouble. I'm signing you up for that
abstinence conference they talked about in church last Sunday.
You need to be reminded of how a godly girl acts. And no more
boys in the basement!

DAUGHTER: Mom, you are way overreacting!

The mom who places herself above her daughter is most comfortable
with teaching, correcting, monitoring, and enforcing rules and regulations.
Her response to her daughter's questions about sex and her interest in the
opposite sex is to try to take control. She shares facts about sex, but the information offered is not the beginning of a dialogue on the subject; it's the end.

This mothering style is most effective during our daughters' early years.
It is our responsibility to instruct our children and lay a solid foundation for
their faith and values. Young children need boundaries and careful watching.
However, as our daughters grow into adolescence, they will naturally want
greater independence. If we continue to dispense rules and try to oversee
their every move, they may rebel or hide. It is scary to acknowledge that our
daughters are in a transitional period of finding their own faith and deciding
who they are when nobody is watching.

---

*Parents can start by making every effort to see the child they have
instead of the one they think they have—or should have.*

—HARVILLE HENDRIX AND HELEN HUNT, *Giving the Love That Heals*

I'm not suggesting that you throw out all your rules and wear a blindfold.
But I am inviting you to *add* something to your parenting: curiosity and
compassion. Rather than just focusing on what you want your daughter to
know, be curious about her life. Curiosity replaces lecturing with an interest

in knowing what your daughter is thinking, wondering, and considering. Compassion makes room for her desires, mistakes, feelings, and foolishness. The mother who parents from above doesn't have much room for compassion because she is often filled with judgment. A girl who feels judged may also feel "bad." That feeling can then compel her to either come to demeaning conclusions about herself or to act "bad," since her mother thinks she is anyway.

We have a twofold longing for our daughters. First, we desire an attainment of the heart in which our children value themselves and others and integrate their faith into their conduct. Not robotic behavior just to stay out of trouble or deceptive behavior that keeps them from getting caught, but behavior that flows from heart-level convictions connected to heart-to-heart relationships with themselves, with others, and with God. No one is ever judged or nagged into an attainment of the heart. Our daughters may pull away from us if we are determined to pull them into purity. They are more likely to take our hand and walk toward sexual purity—sometimes taking two steps forward and three steps back—when they sense that we respect their questions, understand their longings, and empathize with their mistakes and confusion.

Second, we long for relationships with our daughters that invite their confidence, their listening ears, and their respectful consideration. How do you feel about people who lecture and judge you? If we want strong, life-giving relationships with our daughters, then we must be willing to put aside all we know to make room for their questions, heartaches, hopes, and hurts. A good relationship isn't one that is free from failure, struggles, and turbulence. That would be a fake relationship. A good relationship is possible *because* our daughters struggle, make mistakes, and even blow it completely.

When we mother from above, it is easy to focus on externals. Changing postures can free us to focus on the internal world of our daughters. The mother in the previous vignette might ask, "What did it feel like for your boyfriend to have his arm around you?" Or "How do you think you would have responded if he had wanted more physical contact?" Curiosity invites our daughters to tell their stories. It also frees them from shame about natural attraction and longings.

The mother might also empathize: "I know it's embarrassing to have your mother popping in the room all the time. I do remember what it's like to want to be alone with your boyfriend. I also remember what it's like to be tempted to go further physically than you intend to. Could we compromise? I'll only come down once if you keep the lights on?" Compassion invites connection. Connection opens the door for our daughters to understand that sex is sacred because they are sacred. The mom who parents from above may convey to her daughter that sex is a thing to be guarded against rather than communicating that her daughter is a glorious sexual being to be honored, enjoyed, and loved.

If you are more likely to mother from above, consider how your parenting style may be linked to your story. Perhaps, as in Morgan's mom's case, you don't really know what you value about yourself and sex. You just know that you want your daughter to stay as far away from it as possible. Mothering from above feels safe when you don't know your own story or you fear your

JUST FOR YOU

The following questions will help you identify if mothering from above is your primary parenting style:

1. As a teenager, was the desire to please your parents your primary motivation in decision making? Did you believe that obeying the family rules kept you connected to your parents?

2. If you mistook compliance for intimacy, how might that affect your relationship with your daughter?

3. As a teen, were you aware of your budding sexuality? Did you fear it or hide it? Are you afraid of your daughter's naturally developing sexuality? How might she interpret your fear?

4. What are you afraid might happen if you aren't in control of your daughter?

5. Can you recall meaningful heart-to-heart conversations with your daughter about sex? If not, why? What's missing?

6. Are you curious about your daughter's changing attitudes about boys, physical contact, and relationships? If so, how have you expressed that curiosity? If not, why not?

7. Are you compassionate toward your daughter, especially when it comes to her desires and questions about sex? If so, how have you expressed your compassion? If not, why not?

daughter's unfolding story. Maybe your past is marked by mistakes or perhaps your own mother was absent during this part of your life. Mothering from above can be fueled by a determination to keep your daughter from making the same mistakes you or even your mother made. Or maybe your story has chapters of sexual abuse. You recall these painful parts of your story and hate that you felt as if you had no control over the things that happened. Mothering from above can stem from a determination to be in control.

Whether your style of parenting is linked to your story by a history of sexual ignorance, foolishness, sin, or abuse, trying to control your daughter in this area will most certainly backfire. Even if she escapes adolescence without sexual compromise, she will miss the opportunity to develop her own values, reasons for waiting, and sense of self. You may be substituting rules for heart-to-heart conversations. Being in control can give you the illusion of connection with your daughter, but it is impossible for her to feel close to someone who is always in control. As you let go of trying to control her, you will discover that a new mothering posture is possible. Rather than feeling the relational distance that is inevitable when you mother from above, you can experience the relationship that is possible as you walk hand in hand *with* your daughter.

THE ABOVE MOTHER

Goal: Compliance with family values.

Role: Instructor, vigilant overseer, disciplinarian.

Fear: If I'm not always watching and commenting, my daughter will make bad choices.

Values About Herself and Sex: "It is my responsibility to make sure that my daughter remains a virgin." "Sex is some*thing* to be saved for marriage."

Story She Is Telling About Herself and Sex: "Sex is bad. Sexual purity is the highest ideal in life." "I am here to control you and keep you from having sex."

What Her Daughter Hears: "Sex is bad." "I am bad if I want to have any kind of physical relationship with a boy." "I can't talk honestly with my mom about this. She wouldn't understand, and she'd judge me."

MOTHERING FROM BENEATH

DAUGHTER: I don't know why you're making such a big deal out of
      this. We were just watching a movie.

MOM: I just don't want you to make the same mistakes I did.

DAUGHTER: What are you talking about? It looks to me like you
      turned out okay.

MOM: I just know what can happen, how things can get out of control.

DAUGHTER: Are you talking about sex, Mom? Do you think I'm going
      to have sex? WE WERE JUST WATCHING A MOVIE!

MOM: Okay, okay. You don't have to get upset. It's just that I've never
      had good self-esteem, and I don't want you to be like me.
      Please, just watch yourself.

DAUGHTER: I don't even know what you're talking about. You're way
      overreacting.

The mother who places herself beneath her daughter sends a strong message: "I cannot be trusted with your questions and struggles because I am deeply flawed." Furthermore, she may suggest to her daughter that her daughter's impulses and longings in relationships are so dangerous that no one can handle them. That's a heavy load for a girl to carry—"Something inside me is uncontrollable, and my primary caregiver is too weak to help." This posture in parenting rarely has a positive outcome. A girl may dismiss her mother altogether. Or she may reason that even though her mom made big mistakes, she still "turned out okay," so it really isn't a big deal if she makes risky choices as well.

The mother who places herself beneath her daughter usually hates and hides her own story. Because she is not fully available to her daughter, her daughter may withdraw into herself. Left alone with her hormonal impulses and the challenging culture of adolescence, she may construct her own rules and reasons with regard to sexuality. The mother who parents from beneath may be more lenient with her daughter because of her own self-doubt. This combination can be disastrous.

A girl who does not learn a healthy response to her own sexuality and who perceives her mother as weak and powerless may respond in one of two ways. She may misunderstand her own power and use her sexuality to control relationships, or she may feel that she too is powerless against the advances of others. The mother who parents from beneath is not in a posture to help her daughter. Unlike the mom who mothers from above, her issue is not trying to be in control; it's an abdication of her own parenting power. Left to herself, her daughter may become a victim or a perpetrator of destructive or demeaning sexual behavior.

A sense of powerlessness is most often a result of sexual sin or sexual abuse. A mother who has made sinful choices in her past may believe that she is a second-class mother, that her sin has rendered her powerless. Or a woman who has been sexually abused may understandably believe that, at her core, she is unable to affect the world around her. Powerlessness is related to a distortion of hope. Hope is what pulls us forward. Hope has to do with the person we rely on.

If you hope that you can somehow plead with your daughter to avoid sexual traps and temptation based on your own failure, you have a faulty foundation for hope and, thus, a distorted view of your power. Powerful hope is fueled by knowing that your failures are forgiven by a Power greater than yourself and that as you live free and forgiven, you know things about weakness and strength, sin and grace, power and powerlessness *because* of your failure.

When I accept in the depth of my being that the ultimate accomplishment of life is me—the person I've become and who other persons are because of me—then living in the wisdom of accepted tenderness is not a technique or craft, but a way of life, a distinctive and engaged presence to God, others, and myself.

—BRENNAN MANNING, *The Wisdom of Tenderness*

If you hope that your daughter will somehow be a better person than you, the energy of your hope is toxic. Our daughters need to know that we are stronger than they are. We can give them that confidence as we walk hand in hand with the One who "forgives [our] sins—every one" and "redeems [us] from hell."[3] Our daughters need to know that we are not afraid of their struggles, questions, and doubts and that we can offer understanding, dialogue, and compassionate guidance. We offer these things not as pitiful victims but as real women with real stories and an unshakable sense that we have been crowned "with love and compassion"[4] ourselves. That gives our daughters hope!

The mother in the previous scenario might begin by saying, "I may act overly concerned. It's just that I know what can happen when you're alone with a boy you really like and how you might feel. Let me tell you a story…"

You will be able to powerfully offer your daughter curiosity and compassion when you have offered these to yourself. Use the questions in the following Just for You section to link your story to your mothering style and then link your story to your *strength*. Instead of being in a position beneath your daughter and her questions about herself and sex, you will move to a place *beside* your daughter. You might not have a flawless past or all the answers in the present, but you will be able to give her what she needs most—*you*.

JUST FOR YOU

Use the following questions to help you determine if you are mothering from beneath as your primary parenting posture:

1. Are you afraid of your daughter? Why?
2. Are you afraid of sex? Why?
3. Do you keep your sexual history hidden from your daughter? Why?
4. Do you hate your own story? Why?
5. Do you believe that you are a victim in your story? What took away your power?
6. What experiences or events in your story keep you from believing that you can be a powerful mother?
7. What is the source of your hope for influencing your daughter?
8. Do you believe that being negative about yourself will have a positive outcome for your daughter?
9. List everything you know—good and bad—because of your past sexual experience. What keeps you from fully appreciating and respecting what you have learned from your past?
10. If you did respect your story and yourself, how would that change your mothering?

THE BENEATH MOTHER

Goal: Keep my daughter from repeating my mistakes.

Role: Victim of my own life and of my daughter's concerns and
    struggles.

Fear: "If my daughter knows about my past, she'll never listen to me,
    and she'll probably make the same choices I did." "I cannot
    handle my daughter's struggles."

Values About Herself and Sex: "I am powerless." "Sex is dangerous."

Story She Is Telling About Herself and Sex: "Don't listen to me; I can't
    help you." "Sex is uncontrollable."

What Her Daughter Hears: "I can't rely on my mother." "I must rely on
    myself." "There is something in me that is potentially dark and
    dangerous. It is certainly too much for my mother to handle."

MOTHERING FROM A DISTANCE

DAUGHTER: Mom, I don't understand why you are making such a big
    deal out of this. We were just watching a movie.

MOM: I don't know what you were doing. I just know you were in that
    dark basement with your boyfriend. I just don't want you to get
    into trouble.

DAUGHTER: What do you mean "get into trouble"? Do you think we
    were going to have sex?

MOM: It doesn't matter what I think. Just watch yourself.

DAUGHTER: Mom, I'm not stupid. WE WERE JUST WATCHING A
    MOVIE!

MOM: Okay, I'm glad you've got it all figured out.

The mother who places herself at a distance from her daughter is in a
posture to observe and disengage from her daughter's life. Knowing when to
step in or step out is a parenting skill that is developed during this transitional
stage of adolescence. Allowing our daughters to learn from their own mistakes and develop their own sexual standards is essential. However, if we are
distant from our daughters while they are in this process, they will be left
alone to develop their own rules and reasons in the midst of confusing emotions. A girl may become a law unto herself.

When a mother is disconnected from her daughter, a teenage girl often becomes disconnected from her emotions. She doesn't know how to negotiate relationships and isn't in touch with all of the emotions behind her impulses. Her mother's minimal involvement in her daughter's life (especially her internal world) may mean that her daughter will tend to act with minimal awareness of the boundaries of others or the consequences for herself.

The paradox here is that a girl desperately needs her mother's input and guidance about matters of sexuality. Rebellion against family values is often an unconscious attempt to connect. Just as heartless compliance with family rules is false intimacy, so overt rebellion against family values is a type of false intimacy. It is a reflection of a desire for some type of connection, even a negative one. A rebellious daughter's goal is to get her parent involved. Getting into trouble is a message to her mother: "Deal with me!"

Even if a girl does not act out sexually, the mother who parents from a distance leaves her daughter to try to understand and define her own sexuality. A girl who stays away from the opposite sex for whatever reason—fear, lack of opportunity, etc.—still has to negotiate her budding sexuality on her own. She may decide that she is unattractive, undesirable, or even asexual, since her mother has kept her distance from this part of her development.

A mom who mothers from a distance abandons her daughter to the guidance of peers or a reliance on herself. Either resting place for a teenage girl is fraught with potential peril and misinformation. The mother in this vignette could say, "You're right. I'm not sure what you were doing, but I do want to know how you feel about this boy. What do you like about him? What do you have in common? Let's go to Starbucks and talk. I'll even tell you about my first boyfriend."

Many mothers who parent from a distance tell me that they adopt this posture because they are afraid they'll damage their daughters. They doubt or disparage their own wisdom and guidance, perhaps due to bad choices in the past or the lack of affirmation in their own lives. Most often, a mother who parents from a distance is replicating what she experienced with her own mother. Her mother left her alone to figure out who she was, so she does the same with her own daughter.

One of the primary jobs and joys of parenting is to tell our children who they are as we see and know their weaknesses and strengths, gifts and abilities, quirks and unique ways of being in the world. You won't be able to do that if you don't trust your experience; know your strengths, weaknesses, gifts, and abilities; and feel confident in your unique way of being in the world.

Like mother, like daughter.

—Ezekiel 16:44, NIV

If you mother from a distance, it may be because you aren't sure who you are—a mother of fierce compassion, purpose, and wisdom. How do I know that's who you are? When God gifted you with your daughter, He wove into the fabric of your heart all that you need to love your child. Your job is to do all you can to uncover and develop your natural love and longing for your daughter. Use the questions in the following Just for You section to determine whether you mother from a distance. If you do, work through the suggested exercises to unlock your heart to love your daughter. Doing these exercises can make a new posture in parenting possible. Rather than standing away from you daughter, you can enter her world and be in a position to support her during some of the most crucial struggles of her life.

JUST FOR YOU

1. Do you feel that your daughter's questions about sex and relationships are a burden? If so, why?

2. Who, if anyone, taught you about sex and relationships? Or did you feel you were left alone to figure it out for yourself?

3. Do you believe that someone else is better equipped to help your daughter with her emotional and relational life? Why?

4. Do you try to avoid relational "messiness" with your daughter? Why?

5. If your mother was distant, how did her parenting posture impact what you believe about yourself and sex?

6. Whom do you rely on? If you are mostly self-reliant, why?

7. Consider praying daily that God will help you fall in love with your daughter.

8. List your unique strengths, weaknesses, gifts, and abilities. How do these equip you to mother your daughter?

9. List your daughter's strengths, weaknesses, gifts, abilities, quirks, and unique ways of being in the world. Share one of these attributes with your daughter each day.

THE DISTANT MOTHER

Goal: Provide basic needs for my daughter and minimal comment about her life. Avoid trouble.

Role: Physical provider.

Fear: "I don't have what it takes to provide for my daughter's emotional needs." "I might make things worse or get sucked into my daughter's chaos."

Values About Herself and Sex: "I am available only for physical needs." "Sex is a necessary evil."

Story She Is Telling About Herself and Sex: "You can only depend on yourself in this world." "You have to figure out sex for yourself."

What Her Daughter Hears: "I am on my own." "Whatever I discover or decide about sex is true."

MOTHERING FROM TOO CLOSE

DAUGHTER: Mom, I don't see why you are making such a big deal out of this. We were just watching a movie.

MOM: Oh, I know, honey. Don't get mad. I just don't want things to go too far with your boyfriend.

DAUGHTER: What are you talking about? Do you think we were going to have sex? WE WERE JUST WATCHING A MOVIE!

MOM: Of course not. Never mind. I'm sure I was just overreacting. I'm so glad that you have a boyfriend. Do you want to have him over next weekend? Your dad and I will stay upstairs.

The mom who mothers from too close is a "hover mother." She wants everyone to be happy. Because she's hovering, she may notice things that are troubling, but she'll be quick to dismiss them or turn them into something positive so that her daughter does not get mad at her.

The hover mother is often involved in her daughter's life, but she may approach that involvement with a desire to be more of a friend than a mother. Teenage girls need friends—their own age. They also need mothers who notice the details of their lives and aren't afraid to stir things up. The mom who parents from too close may send the message that an absence of conflict is the highest goal in relationships. This can be a dangerous message to a girl trying to navigate the world of boyfriends and heightened sexual impulses. This girl may learn—from her mother—that it's better to keep quiet than to anger or disappoint someone, a potentially disastrous conclusion when it comes to dating and developing relationships.

When a mom mothers from too close, she may lose sight of her daughter's strengths and weaknesses, struggles and successes, and thus, she may lose the ability to offer perspective. Our daughters need our input, insight, and honest evaluation. We have the opportunity to show them that relationships can have conflict, disagreements, and uneasy times and still become stronger—an important lesson for our daughters as they evaluate their own relationships.

The mom in the vignette might say, "I know this is an uncomfortable subject. I do trust you, but I also know what can happen when a girl is alone in the dark with a boy. Believe it or not, I was there once. And it's not a sign that something's wrong with you. When you like someone, natural physical impulses arise. Tell me what you like about your boyfriend? What do you like to do with him? You're welcome to bring him home. What would make your time here with him enjoyable? Oh, and there are a couple of rules: no closed doors and the lights stay on!"

A mother who parents from too close has learned somewhere in her story that the only way to keep relationships is to avoid conflict and diminish her own needs and opinions. Rather than honestly expressing herself in relationship, she has learned to anticipate what others want to hear from her in order to keep the relational waters calm.

Perhaps you grew up in a volatile family and determined never to have that kind of conflict in your own family. Or maybe you spoke up in a relationship, and that ended it. Did you learn that sex, in particular, was for men's pleasure and that you needed to avoid or deny your own feelings and desires in order to keep the relationship? This attitude toward sex, even if unspoken, will convey to your daughter that it's more important to keep everyone else happy. Use the questions in the following Just for You section to determine whether you mother from too close.

JUST FOR YOU

1. Do you avoid conflict with your daughter? Why?
2. How do you feel when your daughter is mad at you?
3. Do you deny troubling things you see in your children in order to keep the peace?
4. Have you ever lost a relationship because you voiced your needs or opinions? If so, how do you think that loss affected what you believe about yourself and relationships?
5. Have you viewed sex as being something primarily for the other person? Why?
6. Is your daughter your best friend? What kind of pressure do you think this might put on her? on you?

THE HOVER MOTHER

Goal: A "happy" family.

Role: Facilitator of peace and happiness.

Fear: "If my daughter is mad at me, she may rebel and push me away."

Values About Herself and Sex: "I am here for others." "Sex is a means to keep relationship."

Story She Is Telling About Herself and Sex: "I am here to make everyone happy." "What I want and believe about sex isn't important as long as the other person is happy."

What Her Daughter Hears: "I can get away with anything as long as I'm nice to my mom." "I need to be nice to others to make them like me."

TELLING YOUR STORY

Morgan's mom had done the hard work of linking her story to her style of mothering. "I'm ready," she said. "I want to talk to Morgan, but can we do it in your office?"

I was honored that she wanted me to be a part of their unfolding story. I shared with her three guiding principles for telling her story to Morgan. These are important guidelines for you to use when you tell your story to your daughter.

1. BE DIRECT

Perhaps you noted in all four of the vignettes in this chapter that the daughter wanted to know, "Are you afraid I'm going to have sex?" And in each scenario the mom avoided the question. The reality is, our daughters know what we are asking even if we're too afraid or conflicted to ask them directly. Unfortunately, when we beat around the bush or hope that our indirect statements or questions will lead to what we really want to know, our daughters feel manipulated. Manipulation is never the doorway to true connection.

The mothers in the vignettes would have done well to say, "Yes, I am worried that you might have sex. I know that the pressure out there is intense, and I also know what happens between a boy and girl as the relationship gets close. When you get close emotionally, it is natural to want to be close physically." Tell your daughter that you want to talk to her about sex, that you are afraid she might be pressured to have sex, or that you are wondering if she's been tempted to have sex.

Your daughter may start to squirm and feel uncomfortable. We need to know that as hard as it is for us to talk about sex, it may be even harder for our daughters to talk with us about this subject. You can dispel some uneasiness by explaining, "My questions about you and sex have made me examine my own story and think about how I've talked to you about this in the past. Are you open to hearing a little of my story?"

Pick the most comfortable setting for this conversation. Most girls want to have this conversation in their rooms—on their turf. Let your daughter know that there is a time limit for this conversation. Teenagers are afraid of being trapped in an unwelcome conversation for hours. You might say,

"Don't worry. I won't tell you my entire life history. This will take about fifteen minutes. Then we can run that errand you needed to do." Finally, make sure your daughter knows that you are asking her permission to have this conversation. Forcing a girl to talk about sex seldom has good results. Your daughter may invalidate everything you say just because she didn't want to have this conversation anyway. If your daughter says, "No, I don't want to talk about it," let her know that you will respect her wishes but that you will continue asking. You could say, "I have some things I really want to tell you. I promise I won't put you on the spot or make you talk about anything you don't want to. I can wait for you to let me know when it's a good time for you, but I won't wait forever." Wait a few days, and if your daughter does not invite the conversation, ask again.

2. TELL YOUR STORY REDEMPTIVELY

You'll know that you are ready to share your story when you understand what it has taught you. Author Frederick Buechner described his redemptive understanding of his sexual story:

> We are bodies and as bodies we need to touch and be touched by
> each other as much as we need to laugh and cry and play and talk
> and work with each other. Once they had sinned Adam and Eve tried
> to hide their nakedness from each other and from God, and to one
> degree or another we have all been hiding it ever since. I [realized]
> that sexuality is a good gift from God which as sinners we can
> nonetheless use to dehumanize both each other and ourselves.[5]

If your story is one of sexual ignorance that has unwittingly been transferred to your daughter as a detached depersonalization of sex, you can start to make amends, change how you value yourself and sex, and tenderly share your changing views with your daughter. If your story is a painful one of foolishness, sin, or abuse, you can honor your own wounds by acknowledging how you hurt yourself and others. Instead of hating your story and trying to keep it a secret, you can feel how it has impacted you and then lay it aside as you start to approach your daughter with curiosity and compassion regarding her own longings in relationships.

You tell your story redemptively when you speak more than just the headlines of your life. You have discovered the "becauses" of your story. Because you were ignorant, you failed to see the value of your own heart and the impact of sex on your body, soul, and spirit. Because you were foolish, you dismissed your deepest longings and perhaps exchanged them for a shallow substitute for connection. Because you compromised yourself in sexual sin, you believed that you no longer deserved something wonderful. Because you were sexually abused, you hated yourself, shuddered at sex, sexualized every relationship, and didn't trust anyone.

You tell your story redemptively when you can see where you have been and how it directed where you were going. Further, you understand how your story could have waylaid you completely, but how it instead filled you with wisdom, compassion, strength, and tenderness. You understand the words of the Old Testament character Joseph—a man with many pain-filled chapters in his story—who said, "Don't be afraid.... Don't you see, you planned evil against me but God used those same plans for my good." The Scriptures describe his redemptive storytelling: "He reassured [his brothers], speaking with them heart-to-heart."[6]

An important component of telling your story redemptively is to apologize for any harm that you might have done in your relationship with your daughter. Tell her how your story has influenced your mothering style and what you now see as the weaknesses of that posture of parenting. This is not the time to berate yourself and risk adopting a mothering posture that's beneath your daughter. This is the time to let up on yourself and let go of old styles of relating.

3. Invite Your Daughter to Tell Her Story

Conclude your story with an invitation to your daughter to tell her story. You can say, "You can ask me anything about my life or yours." She might not respond immediately. Give her a chance to process all you've said. She may need to simply be with you for a while to see if you are indeed changing your parenting posture. Throughout this book are many ideas for creative, courageous conversations. Don't weary of gently and creatively inviting your daughter to have conversations about you, herself, and sex. Little by little, as you share yourself, you will invite her to move the subject of sex out of the shadows and toward the light.

Morgan and her mother sat together on the couch in my office. Morgan's mom began, "I've been worried that you might be tempted to have sex, and I'm even more worried that I've given you some mixed messages about the subject."

"What do you mean?" Morgan asked.

"I'm afraid that because I haven't valued myself, I never really believed in the value of sex. I just thought it was a thing to be saved for marriage. I never knew how to enjoy it the way it is meant to be enjoyed in marriage, because I didn't enjoy myself. My mom just gave me a few facts and told me to stay away from sex, and that was it. I apologize that this is the way I've approached the subject with you too. Sex isn't the main thing I'm concerned about, Morgan. You are." Moving closer to her daughter, she said, "I want you to be able to tell me anything, and we'll figure out together what we can learn from it and how it can contribute to valuing yourself more—"

"Mom," Morgan interrupted. "There's something I need to tell you."

Chapter 4

Sex, Your Daughter, and You

Sexually healthy adolescents do not just happen. They have parents who consider educating their teens about sexuality an important responsibility, and these parents create homes where sexuality is discussed naturally and easily. Sexually healthy teenagers know that they can always come to their parents for assistance and that they are truly loved.

—DEBRA W. HAFFNER, *Beyond the Big Talk*

The room was filled with teenage girls—girls in midriff-baring tank tops, showing off their bellybutton rings; girls in oversized sweatshirts featuring the names of high-school mascots like Eagles or Grizzlies; girls with dangly earrings, pierced noses, and lips drenched in glossy colors.

When I arrived at this meeting of teenage girls, I overheard them chattering about TV shows, cars, and their Friday-night activities and escapades. I knew that this gathering was about more than adolescent superficialities, however, when the first girl began to speak.

"It's my turn to start this week," she said. "I'm supposed to talk about the first time I had sex."

No one giggled or raised an eyebrow at the introduction of the subject. Everyone looked at the speaker intently, waiting for her to continue.

A parent of one of my clients had invited me to visit this group. Every girl in the group had been in some kind of trouble—at school, with the law, or at home—that had resulted in her placement in this therapeutic "growth group" run by county social services. The parent who had invited me thought I might be interested in hearing the girls in this group talk honestly and directly about their choices so far in life and what precipitated those choices. Each week one girl took a turn telling her story and getting feedback from the group.

The girl who told her story the week I attended spoke poignantly and painfully about her first sexual experience at the age of thirteen. She spoke for thirty minutes about the following three years of considerable sexual activity. The girls listened quietly and respectfully. I was both captivated and sickened by her story. I respected her honesty and agonized over her experience. Surprisingly, her story was not the most moving part of the meeting. That moment came near the end of her time of sharing.

Twenty percent of high-school seniors have
had four or more sexual partners.

—CENTERS FOR DISEASE CONTROL AND PREVENTION,
2003 Youth Risk Behavior Surveillance Summary

The parent who had invited me to the group had explained the group protocol on our way to the meeting. The group had some good rules, such as not interrupting while someone was speaking and not talking to other group members during the speaker's time. The most interesting ritual had to do with the way group members could demonstrate support for the speaker. If a girl agreed with the speaker, she was to snap her fingers.

The girl telling her story the day I attended the group concluded by saying, "Let's see, how many boys have I had sex with? Probably four…six…no, ten… Um…let's see… Mike, Casey, Aaron… Yeah, probably like fourteen. How many do I wish I had sex with? None. *Not one of them.* I wish I had known how awful I'd feel later. I wish someone would have told me. I wish I would have listened."

One girl in a pink T-shirt that had the word *Princess* in glittery letters across the front began snapping her fingers. In what seemed like only a few seconds, every girl in the room was snapping her fingers—a room of more than twenty girls snapping their fingers to a silent song about sex and sorrow, growing up way too fast, and wishing they could turn back time.

I was moved by the story, but I was undone by the support these girls were able to demonstrate to one another.

And then I thought about mothers. Mothers who love their daughters more than their own lives, who often sacrifice their own needs and interests to care for their children, and yet who don't know how to talk to their daughters about sex in meaningful ways and don't know how to demonstrate support when the story becomes disappointing or disturbing. My heart almost burst with longing for mothers who sometimes hear the notes of their daughters' lives but don't hear the song.

---

*Eighty-five percent of parents report talking to their
kids about sex while only 41 percent of teens agree.*

—Results of a 2004 NBC/*People* magazine national poll

In this chapter we will explore how to use the knowledge you are accumulating about your own sexual history, your daughter's culture, and your love and longing for your daughter to keep communication open, honest, and meaningful about sex. In the pages that follow, you will find strategies, exercises, questions, and conversation starters to help you talk with your daughter about sex—without disgust, fear, or censorship.

But the questions and the exercises are not the most important elements for creating a relationship of trust and influence with your daughter. Just as you long for your daughter to reach an attainment of the heart with regard to her values about herself and sex, *you need an attainment of the heart* with regard to your values about yourself, your daughter, and sex. This is not a chapter about doing; it is a chapter about *being*—being an ally, a resource, and a haven for your daughter.

My hope for you and your daughter—and my daughter and me—is that no matter what her story, she will be confident that at least one person in her life will be snapping her fingers like crazy, listening and truly hearing the song in her story.

BEING AN ALLY

I recently attended a Pure by Choice rally at the Denver Coliseum. More than four thousand teens—along with their parents, counselors, and church leaders—gathered to listen to speakers plead for purity. I was struck by the power of girls banding together, pledging abstinence with their peers witnessing the event. The strength of the abstinence movement, in my opinion, is providing a context for like-minded teens to support one another—to be allies.

According to the National Longitudinal Study of Adolescent Health, 75 percent of teens who took an abstinence pledge were still virgins at age seventeen as compared with 50 percent of teens who did not take an abstinence pledge.

—FROM HANNAH BRÜCKNER AND PETER BEARMAN,
"After the Promise: The STD Consequences of Adolescent Virginity Pledges," *Journal of Adolescent Health*

As I listened to the speakers, enjoyed the skits, and watched the teenagers, I thought of other alliances teenage girls are involved in.

Not too many months before the purity rally, another gathering had taken place in the coliseum. A musical group named Incubus played to a sold-out crowd of mostly teenage boys and girls. Prior to the concert the girls were asked to mail a pair of their underwear to the band so that group members could use the clothing for a sense of "connection" with the concert attendees. I was particularly unsettled by this concert-promoting stunt because I had learned that the word *incubus* refers to a demonic spirit that has sex with women in their sleep. I couldn't sleep thinking about the countless teenage girls enticed by such a dark and dangerous alliance.

I, of course, thought about Morgan and her alliance with the boy from the mall that ended in hurt and heartbreak.

And just two weeks before the purity rally, one of my clients told me about an alliance she had formed in response to questions and concerns about sex. She was seventeen years old and had been dating a boy for more than six months—a long time for a teen. My heart fell when she told me that she and her boyfriend had "given in" and had sex. It felt as if my heart had stopped beating when she told me that they had not used any protection. She promised me that it would never happen again.

The next week she told me that she and her boyfriend had had sex four additional times, still without protection. I was almost out of my seat, ready to shake her, when she said, "Don't worry. I went to Planned Parenthood yesterday. The woman there gave me condoms. She told me that the next time we had sex without a condom, I could come in the next morning and they would give me the morning-after pill so I wouldn't get pregnant."

The percentage of teens who believe that unprotected sex is not a "big deal": 17 percent. The percentage of teens who don't think about HIV or STDs the first time they have sex: 54 percent.

—From the 2003 Kaiser Family Foundation and *Seventeen* magazine national survey of teens, "Virginity and First Time"

My client had found an ally that didn't judge her, that would provide her with information on sex, and would dispense birth control. I also knew that this ally would not be there in the middle of the night when guilt haunted my client's heart. Nor would this ally encourage her to listen to her nagging conscience reminding her of the values she had held about sex, lying, abortion, and relationships.

By this time my mind was swirling with all of the dangers that are lurking for our daughters behind what seems like every bush. But then I remembered Emily.

I met Emily at a mother-daughter seminar where I was speaking on body image. Emily provided the special music. She was young (twenty-four years old), hip, and sang edgy songs with compelling lyrics. Emily sang one song about falling in love, and then she said to the group of teenage girls, "I waited until I got married to have sex." Blushing, she continued, "I have to tell you, it's the best decision I ever made. I love sex with my husband!"

The girls in the room giggled at Emily's confession, and I knew that I wanted to talk to this young woman as soon as possible.

A few weeks after the seminar, we met in my office over coffee to talk about sex. I asked Emily, "How did you wait? Where did you learn about sex?"

Without missing a beat this young singer replied, "My mother. I credit my mom with my great sex life today!"

I laughed at Emily's exuberance, and I couldn't help but think how rare it is for someone to link her *mother* with anything positive about sex. I wanted to learn from Emily and her mother about the secrets of their powerful alliance.

"What did your mom do to earn that kind of credit?" I asked Emily, eagerly awaiting her answer.

Emily reached into an oversized denim bag. She pulled out a large scrapbook and handed it to me. I expected to see baby pictures, snapshots of family birthday parties, and school pictures, so I was completely unprepared for what I did see. I opened the scrapbook to a page somewhere near the middle. In big pink letters the page heading read, "Oral Sex." Below the heading and on the following pages were pictures, quotations, Bible verses, and statistics cut out from magazines and other sources. The following quotation was in the middle of the page:

> *Monica Lewinsky:* We didn't have sex, Linda.
> *Linda Tripp:* Well, what do you call it?
> *Lewinsky:* We fooled around.
> *Tripp:* Oh.

Along the side of one page was a column with the heading "What My Mom Thinks About Oral Sex." Along the side of the next page was another column: "What I Think About Oral Sex." I read penciled-in remarks in both columns. Emily's mother had written, "I never thought about oral sex until after I was married." Emily had written, "My friends call oral sex 'giving head.' I don't understand why a girl would want to do that."

I looked up at Emily after reading her scrapbook pages. "We had quite a few conversations about oral sex," she said, smiling. "My mom encouraged me to find articles, read them, and talk to her about them as I formulated my own opinions."

I noted the last penciled-in remark in Emily's column: "I've decided that oral sex *is* sex."

As I continued flipping through the scrapbook, I saw pages on kissing, intercourse, hooking up, sexually transmitted diseases, birth control, and married sex. I was almost speechless by the time I finished looking through this most unusual scrapbook.

"Wow" was the only thing I could say.

The percentage of fifteen- to nineteen-year-old teens who said in a 2002 survey that they had engaged in oral sex: more than 50 percent.

—2002 NATIONAL SURVEY OF FAMILY GROWTH

Emily picked up the conversation for me. "I know I had the most amazing sex education. My mom encouraged me to read about things the parents of my friends forbid them to even talk about. My mom let me form my own opinions. Once when I french-kissed a boy, I wrote about it on the 'French Kissing' page in the scrapbook. My mom read it and only asked, 'Do you have any questions for me?' My friends always wanted to look at my 'sex book.'"

Perhaps you are reading about Emily and her mom and feeling a bit incredulous that you and your daughter could have such a relationship. Maybe you fear that your daughter won't engage with you in the same manner that Emily did with her mother, but I do not know a teenage girl who would not be intrigued and interested by such an effort from her mother. Your daughter might roll her eyes or refuse to contribute to the book, but you would have her attention!

Perhaps you're afraid that such open communication will encourage bad behavior. I've read many of the studies about sex education and abstinence-only education. Both groups have compelling statistics to support their programs. A majority of teens report, at the very least, delaying having sex for an average of eighteen months after taking an abstinence pledge. The problem is that of those teens who break their pledge, a majority are less likely than other teens to use contraception when they start having sex.[1] These statistics might answer the question puzzled parents often ask me: "Why does it seem like it is the good Christian girls who make a mistake and have sex once and get pregnant?"

I'm not taking sides in this abstinence-only-versus-sex-education debate. *But I am suggesting an alternative.* As powerful as peers can be in encouraging abstinence, and as necessary as sex education has become in this sexually saturated culture, nothing is more powerful or more necessary than forming a mother-daughter alliance to confront sexual questions and challenges. If we believe that our daughters are "safe" because they have a purity ring and a promise or because they've successfully completed a sex-education course, we are naive. *Our daughters need us* not only to help them navigate this sexually complicated and dangerous world but also to help them prepare for a sacred sexual relationship in the future.

Eighty-eight percent of teens ages twelve to nineteen
say that they would find it easier to postpone sexual
activity if conversations with their parents
about sex were more open and honest.

—2003 NATIONAL CAMPAIGN TO PREVENT TEEN PREGNANCY SURVEY,
"The Parent Gap: Teen Pregnancy and Parental Influence"

The Just for You and Just for the Two of You sections on pages 77 and 78 will help you evaluate what may be getting in the way of forming an alliance with your daughter and will give you ideas to help you get started in forming an alliance. I tell Emily's story not to make you feel guilty about your own mothering but to encourage you that mothers can make a difference. Emily was a normal teenager who made her own decisions about her sexual values. She made mistakes as well. Both Emily's response to her mistakes as well as the development of her sexual values were formed in a creative, committed relationship with her mother.

Emily laughed when she told me about her husband's response to her scrapbook. He said, "I guess I owe your mother a great big 'thank you'!"

I think we can all learn from Emily and her mother. It was not merely waiting until marriage to have sex that protected and nurtured Emily's future sex life—it was the countless conversations between Emily and her mother, the open exchange of ideas and information, and the give-and-take circle of trust they shared. The amazing alliance between Emily and her mom, cemented by the subject of sex, produced a bond described by poet Adrienne Rich as "the knowledge flowing between two alike bodies, one of which had spent nine months inside the other."[2]

JUST FOR YOU

Before you try some of the ideas in the Just for the Two of You section, answer the following questions to see what might be preventing you from forming an alliance with your daughter.

1. Do you respect your knowledge about sex? Why or why not?
2. Make a list of the subjects you feel knowledgeable about as well as a list of subjects you feel unknowledgeable about. What steps will you take to learn about the areas in which you lack knowledge?
3. Do you respect your daughter? Why or why not?
4. Make a list of things you respect about your daughter. What can you do to communicate your respect for her?
5. Do you trust your daughter? Why or why not?
6. Make a list of what you can trust about your daughter. How can you communicate your trust to her? Make a list of what you can't trust. Commit to pray for your daughter in these areas.
7. Does your daughter trust you with questions and concerns about sex? Why or why not?
8. When you talk with your daughter, how often are you thinking about your next point while she is talking?
9. Do you believe that it's too late to form an alliance with your daughter? If so, why?
10. Do you believe that your daughter's choices about sex represent something she is "doing to you"? If so, why?
11. Are you afraid to talk to your daughter about sex? Why?
12. Will you commit to praying that God will increase your courage as you continue to think and learn about your daughter and sex?
13. Do you wish that someone else would take responsibility for your daughter and for what she learns and believes about sex? If so, why?

JUST FOR THE TWO OF YOU

1. Consider making a scrapbook like Emily's. You don't have to tackle every sexual subject at once. Start with one or two topics. Ask your daughter to make a page or two.

2. Keep a stack of teen magazines for the scrapbook. You can also do the following:

    • Ask your daughter to look through a magazine, pick out every reference to sex or sexuality, and then mark those things she thinks you will agree or disagree with. While she is looking through one magazine, you look through another and pick the pages, pictures, or articles you think your daughter will agree or disagree with. Compare and discuss the items you both picked out.

    • Look for examples of mixed messages or hypocrisy in the magazines. For example, you might discover an article on one page about sexually transmitted diseases followed by a story about teenagers "hooking up."

    • If possible, find some magazines from the time period when you were a teenager. Look at these together, noting the different messages about sex.

3. If your daughter watches TV programs for teens, watch them with her. Inevitably (like every ten minutes) the characters will be talking about sex. During commercial breaks, ask your daughter what she thinks the character should do and why.

4. How many of the folowing topics do you think you have talked about with your daughter? Ask her. Compare your answers.

Dating/Romance	Sexual Intercourse	STDs
Faith and Dating	Alcohol, Drugs, and	Condoms
Married Sex	Sex	Contraception
Sexual Limits	Date Rape	Kissing
Media and Sex	Your Sexual History	Sexual Pleasure
God and Sex	Abstinence	Making Out
Sexual Harassment	Oral Sex	Sexual Orientation
Abortion	HIV/AIDS	Pregnancy

BEING A RESOURCE

I was going to meet my boyfriend at his place of employment—a hot-tub store. I was sixteen years old at the time, and hot tubs were a big deal. (Now I've given away how old I really am!) Only the rich and famous actually owned hot tubs. My boyfriend had gotten permission for us to go into the store after hours and get in a display hot tub—just the two of us. We met at the store, changed into our swimsuits, and climbed into the steamy, bubbling water. It didn't take very long for the novelty of the hot tub to be eclipsed by something much more enticing. Within a few minutes we were out of the hot tub and passionately making out. Wearing just our swimsuits, I had never been so physically close to a boy before. I was acutely aware of his body and my own—and I was scared to death.

We did not have sex, but I wasn't sure of that. We kept our swimsuits on, but I wondered if you could have sex *through* a swimsuit. It sure felt like something different had gone on. Now you can smile at my naiveté, and if you read this story to your daughter, she'll probably roll her eyes and scoff: "And that woman is writing a book on sex?"

I grew up in a sexually ignorant home. My mom did not seek to create an alliance with me cemented by the subject of sex. For reasons of her own, she hated sex and shuddered at the thought of it. Even right before I got married, my mom's words to me were few: "You know," she said, "he's going to want to have sex."

---

*The percentage of teens ages fifteen to seventeen
who said that their decision not to have sex was
influenced by their parents: 91 percent.*

—KAISER FAMILY FOUNDATION AND *SEVENTEEN* MAGAZINE
NATIONAL SURVEY, "Virginity and the First Time"

My own sexual ignorance left me confused, vulnerable, afraid, and lonely. After the hot-tub encounter, I worried for weeks that I might be pregnant. I had no one to talk to about my experience or my fears. From that day on I determined to be more educated about the subject of sex. Some of my friends were reading the book *Valley of the Dolls,* so I asked one friend if I could borrow her copy. For a few nights, by the light of a flashlight, I read this story about the sexual revolution and then hid the book under my pillow. Unfortunately, my mom found the book when she was changing my sheets, threw it away, and grounded me for two weeks. It was really okay, because the story of these California socialites using drugs and sleeping around didn't really help me make sense of my own story.

During my teenage years I was desperate to find any resource on sex. But today's teenage girls have a lot more resources available to them than I did. Television programs, however, portray the risk or responsibility for sexual activity only 14 percent of the time.[3] Perhaps the most striking finding in the analysis of programs most popular with teens is that 8 percent of these shows, roughly one in twelve, include a portrayal of sexual intercourse.[4] Teens also have access to unlimited information about sex on the Internet. This resource, however, can quickly turn dangerous and even deadly. According to a study conducted in 1999, one in five children between the ages of ten and seventeen were solicited or approached about sex on the Internet, and one in four teens reported being exposed to unwanted sexual material.[5]

The percentage of parents who understand
"chatlingo": less than 1 percent.

—2004 survey conducted by
Dr. Parry Aftab of WiredSafety.org

I'm not sure which is worse—the absence of resources I experienced or the abundance of unreliable and even dangerous resources our daughters can access. What is certain is that our teenagers need resources today about sex. My challenge to you—and to myself—is to be that resource. Use the list of subjects from the previous Just for the Two of You section to begin to accumulate information. Watch movies, read magazines, immerse yourself in your daughter's culture so you will understand the challenges and ideas she is confronted with.

As we educate ourselves about the resources on sex that are available to our teens, we may be tempted to feel overwhelmed by, angry with, or even disgusted with today's culture. And with good reason. Youth specialist Tom Piotrowski reminds us that we should "never discount the *relational* factor that many young people have with the media they consume, whether it is music, TV, film or print" (emphasis added).[6] If we feel the resources of the culture are pulling our daughters away from us, *we* must do the work of creating a relationship that offers our daughters more than the culture offers them.

In sifting and sorting through all of the materials available on the subject of sex, I have read a lot of books I don't agree with and watched or listened to media that I certainly don't endorse. As I've negotiated this maze of resources, I have found the following principles very helpful in categorizing the information I uncover so that I keep what I agree with, learn from what I don't understand, confront what I disagree with, and consider all that my daughter faces in her world.

PRINCIPLE ONE: GOD'S VIEW OF SEX IS DIFFERENT FROM "HOOKING UP"

God intended sex to be for our pleasure and for procreation in the context of marriage. "Making love" is an outward act that represents an inner reality. It is an extension of an emotional and spiritual bond. Today's teenagers refer to sex as "hooking up." Sex in uncommitted, loveless relationships is presented as the norm, whether on popular television or in mainstream high schools.

In his book *Hooking Up,* novelist Tom Wolfe describes today's teenagers' progressively casual attitude toward sex:

> Only yesterday boys and girls spoke of embracing and kissing (necking) as getting to first base. Second base was deep kissing, plus groping and fondling.... Third base was oral sex. Home plate was going all the way. That was yesterday. [Today] boys and girls have never heard of anything that dainty. Today's first base is deep kissing, now known as tonsil hockey, plus groping and fondling.... Second base is oral sex. Third base is going all the way. Home plate is learning each other's names.[7]

Author and counselor Dan Allender describes a different view of sex:

Deep body-and-soul intimacy with another person is rare. We all
desire it. We yearn for someone to know us and then desire to know
even more. We long for someone to know us beyond the perceptible
to the depths of what even we do not comprehend. We want a person
with whom we can be "naked," a person who will not judge us and
who will find in our presence an unreserved delight.... God gave us
sex to arouse and satisfy a hunger for intimacy.[8]

PRINCIPLE TWO: NOT EVERYONE IS "DOING IT"

If the statistics are correct that 50 percent of high-school students will engage
in sexual activity this year, then that also means that 50 percent will not.

My daughter recently went to the gynecologist for an exam. She wanted
me to be with her. After the doctor asked her if she was sexually active and
Kristin said no, the physician asked me to leave the room. Kristin told me
later that the doctor asked her three additional times, "Are you certain that
you are not sexually active?"

In the face of all the statistics and stories we have considered, it is difficult for some to believe that a beautiful, passionate young woman is not sexually active. As mothers we need to remember that many teenagers are
choosing to remain abstinent. We need to be on the lookout for these teens,
who are role models in their culture, and applaud them and our daughters
for their choices.

Kristin said to me after her gynecology appointment, "I felt like there was
something wrong with me because she kept asking me if I was sure that I was
not having sex."

We need to be a persistent, passionate, positive voice in our daughters'
lives, reminding them that their choice not to have sex is an indication that
something is profoundly right with them!

PRINCIPLE THREE: SEX HAS A PRICE TAG

Regret is the single greatest common denominator among teenagers who
have had sex—regret that they felt forced, that they weren't in love, that they
were under the influence of drugs or alcohol, or that they didn't plan on hav-

ing sex. When we become allies with our daughters in engaging with the culture, we must look past the shiny, glossy, and seductive images and remind our children that there is a cost to sex—physically, emotionally, and spiritually.

In 2000, 9.1 million young people between the ages of fifteen and twenty-four were infected with an STD. This averages out to about 25,000 young people a day who contract an STD.

—FROM HILLARD WEINSTOCK, STUART BERMAN,
AND WILLARD CATES JR., "Sexually Transmitted
Diseases Among American Youth"

I collect statistics about teen pregnancy and sexually transmitted diseases. I remember stories from girls who have been sexually active and ended up with broken hearts—or worse. As a therapist, I have also received a painful education in the school of suffering from the girls I have worked with. I know that whether a girl chooses to have sex or is forced to have sex, in almost all cases *she will pay.*

PRINCIPLE FOUR: THERE ARE REWARDS FOR WAITING
I am privileged to know many young women—including my own daughter—who have decided to wait to have sex and who have fought to honor that decision. It's not easy. I'll never forget picking Kristin up from school one day during her sophomore year of high school. She was only fifteen and wasn't driving yet. When she got into the car, she burst into tears.

"What wrong?" I asked.

"I just am so tired of it," she answered.

"Tired of what?" I imagined homework, mean girls, or bad food in the cafeteria.

"Tired of all the talk about sex." She surprised me. "It's all anyone talks about. If you're not hooking up or talking about it, you're lame [a teenage euphemism for 'not cool']. Everyone thinks it's a big joke. Mom, what's wrong with me?"

I knew that Kristin wasn't asking me to tell her what was wrong with her for not having sex. She needed to be reminded of why she took it so seriously, why the angst and not fitting in were worth it, and how she could navigate through hundreds more days like this one.

I reminded Kristin, "Honey, you value your body, you're guarding your heart, you're waiting for an amazing relationship in the future. That's hard. Waiting is one of the hardest experiences in life. If you don't remember what you're waiting for, you'll give in or feel stupid for waiting."

I knew that Kristin wasn't in the mood for a prolonged pep talk. We'd had hours of conversations laying the foundation for her values and her willingness to wait. She needed an ally in waiting, a resource who would hold in remembrance all the conversations we'd shared and every dream she had for the future. I also knew she needed a break from the pressure, profaneness, and challenges of her world.

"Let's take a 'ditch day' tomorrow," I suggested. "Let's sleep in, get a manicure, and find the best chocolate dessert in town!"

PRINCIPLE FIVE: THERE IS GRACE FOR SEXUAL SIN AND FOOLISHNESS
I am perhaps most passionate about this principle. As mothers we need to remember that as passionately as we long for sexual purity for our teenage daughters, we must also passionately believe in God's grace and redemption. I ask every sexually active teenage girl I work with, "What would your mother say if she knew what you were doing?"

Without exception, girls fear that their mothers will freak out. That's understandable. Almost every girl tells me she knows that her mother will still love her. That's reassuring. But I have never heard a girl say, "I know my mom will still believe in me."

For love is but the heart's immortal thirst to be
completely known and all forgiven.

—HENRY VAN DYKE

We need to believe—for ourselves and for our daughters—that sexual sin and foolishness provide a context for God to shower us with His love *and* to redeem us for glorious purposes. When a girl goes too far in making out, gets a sexually transmitted disease, becomes pregnant, or gets an abortion, there is a great cost to her body, soul, and spirit. When she believes she must hide her sin and/or foolishness, there is an even greater cost. When she believes that her life is over, there can be a tragic cost. When we convey to our daughters that their sin is the end of the world, we compel them to hide the very part of their lives that most needs a redemptive touch.

Even if you've fallen, even if you've failed, even if everyone else has rejected you, Christ will not turn away from you. He came first and foremost to those who have no hope. He goes to those no one else would go to and says, "I'll give you eternity."

—MAX LUCADO, *Walking with the Savior*

Are you afraid that if you are soft on sin, you will encourage your daughter to continue making bad choices? God does not need you to convict your daughter of sin. That's His job. God does, however, invite us to be messengers of His grace: "We're not keeping this quiet, not on your life.... And what we believe is that the One who raised up the Master Jesus will just as certainly raise us up with you, alive. *Every detail works to your advantage and to God's glory:* more and more grace."[9]

JUST FOR YOU

The following questions will help you develop guiding principles for becoming a resource for your daughter.

1. Write a brief summary of your view of sex compared to the culture's. Do you think your view is compelling or attractive to your daughter? Why or why not? Can you rewrite your summary to be more compelling or attractive to her?

2. List several female role models (friends, family, or girls/women from the pop culture) who are sexually abstinent or who remained sexually abstinent before marriage. Brainstorm ways you can affirm and applaud your daughter for her choices about sex.

3. List every cost you can think of that comes from being sexually active before marriage. Document statistics and stories about broken hearts, sexually transmitted diseases, and painful relationships.

4. List the rewards for waiting to have sex. Are these rewards compelling or attractive? Why or why not? What can you add to your list to make it more compelling or attractive?

5. Recall a time when you experienced God's grace after you sinned or failed. Do you believe that sexual sin negates God's grace and redemption? Why or why not?

BEING A HAVEN

As your daughter's ally and a resource for her questions and concerns about sex, you will be a haven for her from the sexually crazed and confused world. I love this Irish proverb: "It is in the shelter of each other we were meant to live." Does your daughter know that she can ask you anything? tell you everything? count on your support no matter what? As you work to become an ally and a resource, your daughter will be able to answer "Yes!" to these questions.

You cannot keep her from the world out there. You cannot control her every thought and action. You cannot protect her from the harmful actions of others. *But you can be there for her.* A boy from the mall, misinformed and misguided peers, Planned Parenthood, and seductive cultural heroes may offer her refuge or support, but their shelter is about as trustworthy as a paper tent in the middle of a hurricane. And our daughters are in a hurricane. Perhaps you feel ill equipped for the storm or in need of a haven yourself from all the challenges of mothering. Do not neglect your own needs for rest, support, and solace. Talk to other mothers, pray, and rely on the words of the One who promises to be our ally and resource: "[I] will be a shelter and shade from the heat of the day, and a refuge and hiding place from the storm and rain."[10]

On the day Kristin and I played hooky, we both wore sweats and no makeup. I complimented Kristin on her natural beauty and said, "I love it best when you're 'unarmored.'"

Her response was a gift I will treasure forever. She said, "You are the one place I can take off my armor."

JUST FOR THE TWO OF YOU

Brainstorm ways you can provide a haven for your daughter. Here are a few ideas to get you started:

- Create a sacred space where the two of you hang out, look at magazines, watch movies, or just talk.
- Create a safe zone where your daughter can ask you anything about sex and you won't jump to conclusions or hold it against her later.
- Plan a spa day together.
- Keep a list of things you would like to do when you and your daughter feel the need to play hooky.
- Surprise your daughter with a day off and see how many of the things on your list you can do together.
- Model nurturing behavior for your daughter by taking time for yourself to read, take a nap, indulge in a bubble bath, or meet girlfriends for coffee.

Part II

Building a Bridge Between Your Worlds

If you're a mother of a teenage girl who is on the verge or already is out of control, or if your relationship with your daughter is on the rocks, there are steps you can take to bridge the widening gulf between you. However, before you decide what action to take, it helps to understand how you got to this point in the first place. Out-of-control behavior is a symptom of deeper problems. If you treat just the symptoms, the underlying trouble will still be there and will eventually erupt again. By discovering its roots, you can repair the unseen damage and reestablish a healthy and satisfying relationship.

—JUDY FORD AND AMANDA FORD, *Between Mother and Daughter*

Chapter 5

"Mom, It's Not the Same as When You Were a Teenager!"

During the late 1950s, 8 percent of girls had had intercourse by age sixteen. In the early 1970s, 9 percent of sixteen-year-old girls had had sexual intercourse. In the mid-1980s, 21 percent of sixteen-year-old girls had had sexual intercourse. In 2003, 43 percent of tenth-grade girls had had sexual intercourse.

—Statistics from the Alan Guttmacher Institute, "Sex and America's Teenagers" and the 2003 CDC Youth Risk Behavior Survey[1]

Look at this! Just look at this!" Allie's mom, Laura, handed me a piece of paper. Her hands were shaking. She was the mother of one of my seventeen-year-old clients. I glanced at the obviously disturbing piece of paper. It appeared to be a printout from the Internet. I recognized the format as being the text from an instant message (IM). It read:

suzygurl111: so how was friday night? did you do it?

kickinit: yeah…it was coooool. how r u?

suzygurl111: you gotta say more than that!!! what happened???

kickinit: i don't know…we just did it…he didn't bust in me. it was kinda weird.

suzygurl111: that sux…so will you do it again?

kickinit: yeah, we're hooking up on Saturday. i gotta do homework. cya tomorrow…lol.

I looked up at Laura after reading the printout and was met with an expression that appeared to be a mix of rage (at whoever kickinit "did it" with) and horror.

"Tell me that's not what I think it is," she said. "Is Allie talking about having sex?"

Laura's question put me in an awkward position. I was her daughter's counselor, but I make it clear when I begin to work with an adolescent girl that I want her mom to be involved in the therapy. I ask the mothers of the girls I work with to let me know what is going on at home so that I can use their perspective in helping my clients. I also tell my adolescent clients that everything they tell me is confidential—unless they are doing something illegal or life threatening. I knew that Laura's daughter Allie had been having sex with her boyfriend for the past month. I felt caught between the confidential nature of my relationship with Allie and her mother's direct question.

Allie and I had spent the past three counseling sessions talking about her relationship with her boyfriend, her questions about sex, and my fears and concerns for her. When I repeatedly suggested that we talk with her mother, Allie's immediate response was, "No way! She'll just freak out and make me break up with T. J.!" So every time I thought about Allie, I prayed that somehow her mother could be brought into this process. The instant-message transcript was an answer to my prayers.

"I think we should meet with Allie," I suggested to her mom, "and you can ask her about this."

"I can't talk to her about this!" Laura said forcefully. "I'm so mad at her and so disappointed. I didn't want her to make the same mistakes I did. If we talk about this, I'll just get mad and cry, and it will cause a big fight. And then what am I going to do? Am I going to lock her in her room, or should I just go out and buy a pack of condoms and tell her, 'Good luck. Don't come crying to me when you get pregnant!' I can't talk to her! Look at this e-mail. I'm not even sure what she's talking about—things are so different today than when I was a teenager. We don't even speak the same language!"

Laura's words did not surprise me. Her anger and fear were understandable. I have learned that when I work with parents, I am working with some of the most pained people on earth. As parents we feel more passion—both good and bad—about our children than about anything else in life.

I know. I have had intense joy with my own children—inexpressible intimacy and wonder. And yet the opposite is also true. They have hurt me and confused me. I have also seen my own sin more starkly with them than with anyone else. To see our sin intertwined in our children's lives is heart-wrenching.

In a burst of frustration, Laura expressed the agony of living in a very fallen world and the anguish of her own brokenness and inability to help her daughter navigate this world. It is humbling to acknowledge that our children come to us with no baggage. Who they become reflects a combination of their experience in this world and our influence on them—both good and bad. The Book of Wisdom in the Old Testament says that children who go astray break their parents' hearts and bring them shame.[2] *It is meant to be that way.* Our brokenness compels us to seek healing—both for our children and ourselves—and hopefully leads us to the Healer who forgives our sins,

Just for You

1. If your daughter told you that she held hands with a boy, what would you say?

2. Did you ever talk to your mom about this aspect of a physical relationship? If so, what did she say? What do you wish she would have said?

3. If your daughter told you she liked kissing, what would you say?

4. Did you ever talk to your mom about kissing? If so, what did she say? What do you wish she had said?

5. If your daughter came home with a hickey on her neck, what would you say?

6. Did you ever come home with a hickey? If so, what did your mom say? What do you wish she would have said?

7. How would you respond if you learned that your daughter had sex? (Or how did you respond when you learned this?) Would you want her to talk to you about it? Why or why not?

8. What good things can you imagine coming out of these kinds of experiences in terms of potential conversations with your daughter and the possibility of transformation in your relationship?

9. What are you most afraid of when you think about these frank and open conversations with your daughter?

restores our souls, and directs our paths. Struggling, hurting parents need God more than they need success, accolades, and material wealth. Struggling, hurting children need us more than they need achievements, praise, and material security. Our children and their struggles can be the gifts that bring us Home.

I knew that in the words of Allie's instant message, Laura had received a gift that cut her hands and heart and made her bleed as she opened the message. I also knew from experience, both professional and personal, that it was a gift that would open the door to a deeper sense of forgiveness and love and would link her to her daughter in meaningful ways. We scheduled an appointment for Laura and her daughter, Allie.

LIKE MOTHER, LIKE DAUGHTER

I had been working with Allie for two years. From the time she was fifteen, I had seen her on and off again for struggles in school and conflicts at home. During the time I'd known her, she had had three different boyfriends. Her first two relationships were more casual. She spent a lot of time "talking" to the boys on the Internet. They were together in group settings, and, as Allie put it, "We barely went past kissing."

While she was involved in these relationships, Allie and I talked about the drama of who liked whom first, what to talk about on the telephone, and what to wear to the school dance—the whole wonderful, awful soap opera of teenage romance. During each relationship we talked about the physical relationship—the thrill of holding hands, the awkwardness of kissing, the shame of a hickey. Now, you might wonder why I didn't sit this girl down and tell her that holding hands, kissing, and, certainly, hickeys lead to sex, so she should keep twelve inches between herself and her boyfriend at all times. I certainly wanted to, but I knew if I started lecturing, she would stop listening.

I do wish that my adolescent clients (and my own children) would reserve as much physical contact as possible for later years and marriage. I long for my clients (and my children) to be protected from the heartbreak that can come when they prematurely give themselves—body and soul—to another. I want them to grow up, be emotionally mature, and be spiritually sound enough to make wise and thoughtful choices about their physical relationships. But I also don't want them to be alone in their experiences.

While half of teens interviewed said they never talked with a parent about sex or birth control, 80 percent said that their decisions about sex were influenced by the information their parents provided.

—2003 Kaiser Family Foundation and
Seventeen Magazine SexSmarts Survey

I have discovered that there is an epidemic of noncommunication about sex in well-meaning families. It could be based in denial, or it could be fueled by fear. Whatever the cause, noncommunication is not a good idea. My aspiration as I talk with my clients (and my children) about holding hands, kissing, and hickeys is that I will be able to help them develop their own values about sex before they find themselves needing to make a snap decision in the dark corner of a basement or the backseat of a car. But if that doesn't work (as it didn't with Allie), I hope at least to have created a framework that allows for honest conversation and a persistent message that past mistakes do not need to determine future behavior.

I remember one of my early conversations with Kristin about these matters. She was going to a party with friends from school. While she was focusing on what she was going to wear, I was remembering the make-out parties I'd attended in middle school. I told Kristin about one party when my boyfriend had started to make a move I was uncomfortable with. When I pulled back, he told me that his last girlfriend had liked it when he made that move. I felt stupid and afraid. I never talked about it to anyone. I was afraid my friends would think I was a prude, and I was afraid my mother would think I was a slut.

I asked Kristin, "When you're with a boy, how far do you want to go?" She answered, "I'm never going to feel pressured to do something I don't want to." I hoped she was right, but I feared that she would have experiences that would sway her differently. After telling her my story, I listened to her perspective and gave her permission to talk to me if anything ever happened. My goal for her (and for my clients) is not to get them to reach "the right decision" but to show them that there are decisions they *will* have to make about sex.

One day during a counseling session with Allie, she told me that she had had sex with her current boyfriend. She simply stated, "T. J. and I had sex."

In previous sessions she had told me that they were struggling with their physical relationship, but she had assured me (and I think that she was trying to convince herself) that she had things under control.

After breaking the news about having sex, Allie waited for me to respond. I wanted to shout, "No!" I wanted to call T. J. and tell him that *he* needed to come in for counseling. I wanted to keep Allie locked in my basement. I wanted to tell her mother. But instead I asked, "What are you feeling about having had sex?"

Allie answered, "I don't really know what I feel. By the time we were finished, I was crying, and I don't even know why."

"Do you have any questions?" I asked.

"Is it supposed to hurt?" she said. "I mean way up here." She pointed to the middle of her stomach.

We talked about some of the mechanics of sex, and then I asked a question that made my heart beat faster and my palms start sweating. "Did you use a condom?"

Allie looked at the ground. "No," she whispered. "T. J. didn't have one, but he didn't bust inside of me."

Twenty-six percent of girls between the ages of fifteen and nineteen did not use any contraception when they first had sex. This percentage increased to 35 percent for girls who first had sex at age fourteen or younger.

—2002 NATIONAL SURVEY OF FAMILY GROWTH

"Do you mean he didn't ejaculate?" I asked. It's important—whether with young children or teenagers—to use the correct words to describe sexual acts and body parts. When a teenager uses slang, it allows her to distance herself from the reality.

Allie blinked and answered, "Yeah, he didn't…um…ejaculate. Can I still get pregnant?" I told Allie that she could, and we talked about precaution and protection.

Our hour together went by way too quickly. "Before you leave, is there anything else you want to ask me?" I asked Allie.

"Well, there is one more thing. Um…I mean…um…could you tell me how you know if you have a sexually transmitted disease?"

My heart nearly broke for this way-too-young teenage girl who was experiencing way too much way too soon. I handed Allie a pamphlet on sexually transmitted diseases. She folded it so that she could hide it in her purse.

"What do you think about talking to your mother about this?" I asked as she was closing her purse.

"Forget it! She doesn't get that things are different today than when she was a teenager. She'll just be furious and insist that T. J. and I break up immediately. I can *never* talk to her about this!" Allie's voice became more panicked as she talked.

I spoke calmly. "Allie, I'm honored that you told me. Thank you."

As soon as she left, I burst into tears and prayed with all my might that God would protect Allie, provide a way for her mom to know and to move toward Allie, and give them both confidence in each other that this storm could carry them to a place of greater wisdom, grace, and love.

When it came to sex, Allie wasn't much different from her mother. They both didn't want to talk about it. They didn't trust themselves or each other. They both were afraid that talking about it would make things worse. They both were locked in a dark place of isolation, judgment, and fear. But they were both right about one thing: today's teenagers face very different challenges than teenagers did twenty or thirty years ago.

In the rest of this chapter, we will look at what is different today for teenagers when it comes to sex. It will become clear that it is virtually impossible for parents to keep up with all the sexual realities and risks that teenagers face today. Knowing the facts is important, but it is not what is *most* important. We will also look at what is the same today for your daughter as it was for you: the longing for love and the importance of relationships. That's what is most important.

One thing is certain, as you pay attention to the changing world your daughter lives in, you, too, will change. You are both in the process of learning about sex and love, and of becoming *more* in a world that tempts you to be less.

REAL SEX

Today's teenagers are engaging in more sex and different kinds of sex at earlier ages. One thirteen-year-old girl summarized the realities in her world on a 2002 HBO special: "I think we're just more of a generation that sex is being introduced to us at a younger age, and that's why we're, like, eager to start it.… You know, my mom wasn't really into the whole sex scene when she was thirteen years old. And we are."[3]

Sex for today's teenagers includes oral-sex parties, multiple partners, and sex games that encourage sexual activity for everyone to watch. According to the 2003 Youth Risk Behavior Survey, 14 percent of high-school students had intercourse with four or more different partners, and 7 percent reported that they first had sex before the age of thirteen.[4]

A study of urban high-school students found that one-third of 9th through 12th graders who considered themselves virgins had engaged in some type of genital contact.

—FROM M. A. SCHUSTER, R. M. BELL, AND
D. E. KANOUSE, "Sexual Practices of Adolescent Virgins,"
American Journal of Public Health

And sexual intercourse is not all that is going on. In 2002, more than 60 percent of teenagers between the ages of fifteen and nineteen reported having some kind of sexual contact with the opposite sex, including oral and anal sex.[5] Fifty-five percent of boys and 54 percent of girls between the ages of fifteen and nineteen indicated they had oral sex.[6] It is my experience that teenagers often don't consider this sex, don't report it as such on sex surveys, and don't think this activity poses any real risks. The body of research on sexual activity between same-gender teens is limited at this time, but according to the 2002 National Survey of Family Growth, approximately 11 percent of fifteen- to nineteen-year-old girls indicated that they had sexual contact with another female.[7]

One by-product of this sexually saturated culture is that both girls and boys have become more sexually aggressive. Girls today are as likely as boys to initiate and engage in sexual activity without relational commitment. Teens have an almost innocent-sounding phrase to describe this activity: "friends with benefits."

Sharon Lamb reported on this significant change in adolescent sexual dynamics in her book *The Secret Lives of Girls*:

Teenage girls today engage in sex earlier and speak more freely about their sexual exploits.... Girls, like boys, are deeply sexual, deeply sexually aggressive creatures.[8]

When Allie IM'd (instant-messaged) her friend that she and her boyfriend were "hooking up" on Saturday, what did she mean? *Hooking up* means to teens today what *sleeping with* meant to us. It really covers the whole gamut of sexual activity and, depending on the teenager, could mean making out and petting, oral sex, or sexual intercourse. Some teens use "hooking up" to mean a casual, no-strings-attached one-night stand, and others use the phrase to imply that they are getting together for the purpose of sexual activity.

Twenty-one percent of teens say they have looked at something on the Internet that they wouldn't want their parents to know about.

—From a 2000 *Newsweek* poll

Girls who are not so sexually savvy or who want to learn more about sex can find anything on the Internet. If your daughter has access to the Internet and has an ounce of curiosity about sex, she will probably find her way to a porn site. Girls may use the images on a porn site as models for their own behavior. Several of my adolescent clients have taken pictures of themselves— using porn pictures as examples—to give to their boyfriends. Of course, I am shocked and saddened, but this becomes an important opportunity to talk about the harm that pornography does to women. Naomi Wolf summarizes this brilliantly in "The Porn Myth":

> Here is what young women tell me on college campuses when the subject comes up: They can't compete, and they know it. For how can a real woman—with pores and her own breasts…possibly compete with a cybervision of perfection, downloadable and extinguishable at will.[9]

Even if your daughter manages to avoid learning about sex on the Internet, she will hear about it from her peers and be convinced by the media that she is the one who is not normal. All you have to do is read the following statistics that summarize today's media messages to know that the influences on your daughter are much different than they were when you were a teenager. Even if you have five or six meaningful conversations with your adolescent about sex, the culture will have had countless more interactions with your daughter about sex this year alone!

- Seventy-seven percent of prime-time broadcast television programs during the 2005 season showed sexual content.[10]
- Soap operas show almost five scenes per hour that contain sexual content.[11]
- Forty percent of teenagers have gotten ideas for how to talk to their boyfriends and girlfriends about sexual issues from moves or TV shows.[12]
- According to a 2004 NBC/*People* magazine poll, fifty-one percent of teens between the ages of thirteen and sixteen get "a lot" or "some" information about sexuality and sexual health from TV shows and movies. Forty-one percent said that magazines have provided them with "a lot" or "some" information.[13]

Just for the Two of You

Ask your daughter what she knows about the facts and statistics I've presented. You can begin the conversation by asking some of the following questions. If you're reluctant to have such a conversation, why? What are you afraid of?

1. What do you know about _____ (oral sex, pornography, etc.)?
2. What do your friends think about _____?
3. Do you have any questions about _____?
4. If you were pressured to _____, what would you say or do?
5. If you did _____, how do you think I would respond? How would you want me to respond?
6. How do you feel about talking to me about _____? What are you afraid of?

Real Risk

When Allie asked me about the symptoms of sexually transmitted diseases, I knew that she was somewhat aware of the risks. Sex-education classes, abstinence programs, parents, and even the media are pretty vocal about the risks of teen pregnancy, disease, date rape, and sexual predators lurking on the Internet. All of this real sex that teenagers are engaging in or considering comes with very real risks:

- In 2004 it was estimated that 2.2 million teens under the age of fifteen were living with HIV.[14]
- In the United States, chlamydia is the most commonly reported infectious disease, with an estimated 2.8 million new cases every year.[15]
- In 2004, the chlamydia rate for females was 3.3 times higher than the rate for males. Chlamydia rates are highest among teenage girls between the ages of fifteen and nineteen.[16]
- In a national survey, more than 18 percent of teens who had sex at or before age fourteen reported that it was not voluntary.[17]

- One in five children ages ten through seventeen have received a sexual solicitation over the Internet, and one in thirty-three children were "aggressively" solicited by someone who pressured them to meet, contacted them by telephone, or regularly sent them mail, gifts, or money.[18]
- According to the 2002 National Survey of Family Growth, more than 80 percent of pregnancies among girls age seventeen and under were unplanned. When asked how they would feel if they found out they were pregnant, almost 70 percent of girls said they would be "very upset."[19]

Having sex can lead to creating life, and it was meant to be that way. Your daughter's budding sexuality and growing interest in sex are also signs of life, hinting at the day and time when she will establish a life of her own—a life, you hope and pray, that will surpass your deepest longings and wildest dreams for your daughter. Tragically, today's "sex is no big deal" culture has distorted this means to life, transforming it into a means to death through the loss of innocence, physical and emotional health, and even hope for the future. According to the National Longitudinal Survey of Adolescent Health, teenage girls are three times more likely to attempt suicide if they are sexually active.[20]

Allie's mom had good reason to come to me full of fear and dread after she read her daughter's conversation on the Internet. Real sex has real risks.

JUST FOR THE TWO OF YOU

1. Go with your daughter to the gynecologist or an alternative pregnancy center. Call ahead and ask for an appointment to be educated about sexual health, sexually transmitted diseases, teen pregnancy, and birth control. You can interview the doctor or nurse before the appointment to make sure you are comfortable with the way the material will be presented. Sex education alone does not prevent sexual activity. The risks may seem worth it to teens when they're caught up in the moment of raging passions and hormones. But sex education can help your daughter decide in advance that the risks are too

great and that she won't put herself in a position of making a spur-of-the-moment decision that has lifelong consequences.

Does the idea of getting sex education make you uncomfortable? Why? What are you afraid of? Ask your daughter the same questions.

2. Find stories about the consequences of sexual activity outside of marriage to share with your daughter. I watch the movie *Riding in Cars with Boys* with my older adolescent clients. Although there is objectionable material in this movie, it is a realistic portrayal of teen pregnancy and of being a teenage mother.

3. If you experienced consequences due to your own sexual behavior, consider telling this part of your story to your daughter. Sharing your experience establishes open communication and reduces the chance that your daughter will view you as uninformed or judgmental.

Does the idea of having this conversation with your daughter make you uncomfortable? Why? What are you afraid of? Ask your daughter the same questions.

REAL SECURITY

Although the realities and the risks of teenage sexual behavior today are different than they were when we were teenagers, some things remain the same. Your daughter has the same core needs you did. She needs to know that she is safe and loved. For a teenager, growing in independence is as necessary as food and water. In fact, gaining independence is one of the primary developmental tasks of the teenage years. Your daughter needs to know that she can make more of her own choices, trust her developing intuition, and find her own way in the world. But she needs to know that she is developing this independence in a context of safety and protection. When teenagers believe that they are free to do whatever they want without any consequences, they will inevitably make foolish choices and ultimately be filled with rage because they feel unprotected and unloved.

Do you remember the thrill of getting more privileges when you got your driver's license or your first paycheck? We were designed to grow into a sense of personal power. Sexual behavior feels powerful. Girls learn that they have the power to attract a boy's attention, arouse his desire, and make him want them. When girls use this power too young and without guidance, they may become hardened and manipulative. They desperately need to understand their sexual power, and we, as females and mothers, are the ideal source of that information.

JUST FOR YOU

1. Recall when you first learned that you had sexual power. Who taught you how to use this power? If no one did, what did you believe about your own sexual power?

2. In the home you grew up in, did you feel safe talking about sexual development and the sexual sparks that go off between teenage boys and girls? If not, why not?

   Do you think your home today is a safe place for your children to talk about sex? Why or why not? When you talk about this sexual tension—the sexual sparks that go off between teenage boys and girls—how is it viewed? Disgusting? Normal? Humorous? What, if anything, are you afraid of?

3. Remember your first intimate (not necessarily romantic) relationship. (I define *intimacy* as a mutual relationship in which each person is known and loved.) What do you think made your relationship intimate? How do you think it influenced what you believe now about intimacy and relationships?

4. Do you think that the relationships in the home you grew up in were intimate? Why or why not?

5. Is your relationship with your daughter today one of growing intimacy? Why or why not?

Home should be the place where sex is talked about freely in age-appropriate ways. Home is the place where your daughter needs to learn about her developing sexuality and how it can be used and abused in relationships. Home is the place where your daughter needs to feel safe to ask questions, admit her mistakes, and test out her ideas. Home is also the place where your daughter needs to know that she will be told no, given boundaries, and experience consequences. Hopefully, throughout this book you will get ideas for how this can practically take place.

Budding adolescent sexuality is powerful. As we've briefly discussed earlier, our sexually saturated culture is powerful as well. But your daughter needs to know that you are *more* powerful. Your daughter will *feel* safe when she knows that you will say yes to some of her requests and plans and no to others. Trust develops in your relationship with your daughter as she experiences both your creative help in helping her become more independent and your tender authority in protecting her from the real risks of sexual behavior.

Just for the Two of You

Ask your daughter the following questions. Don't listen in order to debate her or defend yourself. Listen to understand and learn how you might give your daughter a greater sense of safety and protection.

1. Do you feel that it's safe to be honest with me about sex? Why or why not?
2. Do you feel safe telling me about what is going on with your friends? Why or why not?
3. Tell me about a time when you felt safe talking to me, and a time when you felt unsafe.
4. How often do you think I say yes to you?
5. Do you think I help you brainstorm ways to be with your friends?
6. How often do you think I say no to you?
7. Do you think I'm tender and compassionate when I say no? If not, what do you feel from me?
8. Do you feel independent? What would make you feel more independent?

During a counseling session with Allie, she disclosed to her mom the sexual relationship she had with her boyfriend. I had met individually with Allie's mom to prepare her to listen to her daughter with understanding rather than judgment or condemnation and to build a bridge for further con-versations. I assured Allie that her mom was ready to listen and would not "freak out." Nevertheless, it was a tearful hour. At the end of our time, Allie's mom sighed, "I don't know what to do."

"Neither do I," Allie whispered.

Allie's mom and I met the following week to begin to formulate a response to the question of what to do next. I suggested that she enforce some consequences for her daughter's underlying deceit. Allie admitted that she'd lied to her mother on several occasions about where she was and what she was doing.

Although I do believe that Allie's pattern of lying had the potential of becoming as dangerous as her sexual choices—if not more so—my sugges-tion of grounding Allie from contact with T. J. for a month was really not about punishing her. I wanted Allie to have some time away from her boyfriend to hopefully gain a little clarity.

When a girl is having sex with her boyfriend, it becomes almost impos-sible for her to see the truth about the relationship. She may feel desperate to hang on to the relationship at any cost because she's given so much of her-self to it. She may also feel pressured to continue having sex to keep the relationship.

When Allie's mom enforced the consequence we discussed, initially Allie was furious. But as time passed, she began to more calmly evaluate her rela-tionship and to question whether she really wanted to have sex at this time in her life. I suggested to Allie that she write out why it was okay for her to have had sex with her boyfriend and under what circumstances she thought that it would be okay again.

Her mother was terrified of this exercise because she was afraid that it would encourage Allie to have sex. But based on the many conversations I had had with Allie over the years about her vision for love, romance, and sex-ual expression in marriage, I felt I could trust her with the exercise. Allie really believed that sex and marriage matter. But even "good" girls make bad choices and get caught up in the whirlwind of hormones. The greater tragedy is that when a girl processes those experiences in isolation, she often comes to the conclusion that there's no going back to what she really believed and wanted. I knew that although Allie might not articulate her parents' values exactly with regard to sex, she knew that sex matters. I hoped the exercise would lead her to the conclusion that *she* matters and that her sexual choices were not adequately protecting herself—body, soul, and spirit.

Allie has given me permission to share one of the things she wrote about:

> I guess what I am realizing is that the biggest disappointment in this is that sex was not as special as I thought it would be. It hurt the first time. Although it got easier after that, it got even less special. We had sex once while I was talking on the phone and once in a park when there were other kids not that far away from us. Yuk! I wonder if I'm that special to T. J. I thought I was because we were having sex, but now that I think about it, I'm scared.

Allie's writings led to many meaningful conversations with her mom. Laura told Allie about a time as a teenager when she felt forced to have sex and how she believed that she would never be special to anyone after that. Laura and Allie also went to an alternative pregnancy center together and learned about sexually transmitted diseases and pregnancy. As their relationship became more intimate, their fear of talking together about sex was slowly slipping away.

Eventually, Allie's month-long hiatus from her boyfriend came to an end.

"Now what do we do?" Laura asked me during a counseling session. "I don't want to go back to where we were a month ago."

"Neither do I!" Allie insisted. "But I don't want to break up with T. J.!"

I suggested that Allie's family invite T. J. over for dessert. "You all need to talk about sex," I said.

"No way!" Allie cried. "He'll freak out!"

"I'm not sure that's a good idea," Laura agreed. Allie's parents were divorced, and I knew that Laura was feeling overwhelmed at the idea of doing this all by herself.

"Allie," I continued, "T. J. needs to take responsibility for his part in the way your relationship was going, and he needs to express his intentions."

"We're not going to do it ever again—I promise," Allie said pleadingly.

"Then you and T. J. need to talk with your mom about how she can help you keep your promise." I wanted to encourage Laura to continue offering her daughter a safe place with secure boundaries.

Most often when I suggest that a girl's boyfriend participate in a conversation about sex, he fades into the landscape, and the relationship withers away. This is a heartbreaking experience for a girl, but it provides a context for her mother to talk with her about the dangers of giving herself away in risky relationships. I have discovered that broken hearts are very receptive to a mom's advice and TLC. Although heartbreak is not something we want our daughters to experience, it is a powerful opportunity for us to minister lovingly to our wounded daughters.

I encourage parents in Laura's position to require a conversation with their daughter's boyfriend before the relationship can continue. Why don't I suggest that they kick the boyfriend to the curb and banish their daughter from ever seeing him again? Because, in most cases, the boyfriend is not the enemy. Both teenagers are participants. I have observed too many times that when parents lower the boom on the boyfriend, their daughter joins the boyfriend to fight harder against her parents. Rebellion is a destructive reason to have sex. Parents who rely on power plays to keep the upper hand lose opportunities for open, honest, and meaningful conversations. When it comes to parenting teenagers, we need to discern where we can give up some power in order to gain it. For example, by not prohibiting the relationship their daughter has with her boyfriend, parents can then enforce other boundaries and limitations on social activities.

In Allie's case, T. J. rose to the occasion and came over for cookies and conversation. He assured Laura that he didn't want to have sex with Allie again either. He expressed fear that his parents would punish him and be disappointed in his behavior if they found out. He told Allie and her mom that he really wanted to keep the relationship and that he was willing to do whatever they wanted so that he could still be with Allie.

It is a myth that sex is all teenage boys want. Many adolescent boys want relationships as much as girls do. Yes, they are pretty controlled by testosterone, but they certainly have the ability, when given guidance and motivation, to make good choices. Allie and T. J. agreed to be in each other's homes only when a parent was around and to go on dates to places where they were surrounded by other people. Allie agreed to talk to her mom if things were starting to get out of hand physically.

Now, all of this may seem a little unrealistic to you. You need to know that both Allie and T. J. were desperate to get back together and were willing to agree to anything. Could it all happen again? Absolutely. But Laura's mom had offered a clearer sense to her daughter that she would be watching her, that she was available for questions and support, and that she would not hesitate to step in if things looked questionable.

Authoritative parents make their expectations clear to their kids, but they also listen carefully to what they say about the rules, giving them a voice in important matters and a certain degree of independence. It is reasonable to expect that authoritatively reared kids' high self-esteem and ability to negotiate conflicts would serve them well in romantic and sexual relationships.

—JUSTIN RICHARDSON AND MARK SCHUSTER, *Everything You Never Wanted Your Kids to Know About Sex (But Were Afraid They'd Ask)*

That's about as much safety as we can provide for our teenagers. Meeting their need to be safe does not mean that we can protect them from all harm or keep them from sin or foolishness. Even God doesn't do that for us. We are not immune from our own mistakes or the sins of others. That's why safety is not all we need.

REAL LOVE

It is possible for teenagers to feel safe in their home and still leave home with gaping holes in their hearts. Growing children don't need only safety; they also need love. They need strength, but they also need tenderness. Several studies indicate that teenagers who feel connected to their parents, who feel loved and cared for at home, tend to have intercourse later than adolescents who are not as well connected to their parents.[21]

Kindness, compassion, and tenderness are qualities that are easy to lose when we are angry and afraid because of the choices our children make. How can we keep our hearts alive with love for our daughters while we are in the midst of negotiating curfews, looking for warning signs, and enforcing boundaries? It requires intentionality. We need to pull back from the challenge of the moment to view the bigger picture.

Perhaps one way to stay focused—looking at your daughter through a lens of love—is to think back to when you were a teenager. How loved did you feel? When you got into trouble, what did you feel from your parents? Anger? Disappointment? Condemnation? Or compassion and tenderness?

I told you earlier about a time when my mother found my diary detailing the make-out parties I was going to in middle school. She flung the diary at me in disgust and called me a slut. I know now that she was afraid. I know now that she loved me. But when I was thirteen years old, I really believed I had done something so bad that I'd made my mother stop loving me. So I determined to find someone else who would. That's a dangerous and scary place for a thirteen-year-old to be.

[This] is why I loved you—not because you swam in the space below my heart; or because one day you might take care of me when I couldn't take care of myself. Love is not an equation.... It's not a contract, and it's not a happy ending. It is the slate under the chalk and the ground buildings rise from and the oxygen in the air. It is the place I come back to, no matter where I've been headed. I loved you, my daughter, because you were the one relationship I never had to earn. You arrived in this world loving me more, even when I did not deserve it.

—JODI PICOULT, *Vanishing Acts*

I wonder what it would have felt like if my mother had gently confronted me about the diary and said, "I know that all these things you've written are about one thing: you want to belong and be loved. But you're looking for that love in unsafe places. What would make you feel more loved by me?"

Of course this response would not have eliminated my boy-crazy brain, but it would have communicated that I could talk to my mom about all that I was wanting, feeling, and experiencing. I might have asked her to stop reading my diary, but I would have known in the depths of my heart that I could trust her in the future with my questions and mistakes. I might have continued to fly off from the nest into risky relationships, but I would have known that she was a safe place to land. We both would have felt less alone during those tumultuous years of my adolescence.

Fear is the primary obstacle to love. Fear turns us moms into shrieking or shrinking caricatures of ourselves. The New Testament says that "love banishes fear."[22] Practically speaking, what does that mean? It means that even though the challenges and temptations your daughter experiences are more pervasive and risky than they were for you—even though you yourself may have blown it as a teenager or even though you're a single mother or even though you feel tongue-tied and scared or even though you're angry and confused—you can go into the hidden places of sexual sin and foolishness and ask her questions, offer kindness, set boundaries, and invite further relationship. Like Allie's mom did.

Allie is still dating T. J. Laura still worries and gets scared. But she also asks questions, checks up on her daughter and her boyfriend, and takes them out for ice cream to talk about dating and sex.

Just a few weeks ago, I had an experience that reminded me of Allie and Laura and underscored how we can banish fear with love. I was invited to dinner by dear friends who have four young children under the age of ten. While their mother was making dinner, I offered to play with the kids. They wanted to play Sardines. I didn't know what Sardines was, so they instructed me in this version of hide-and-seek. In this game, one person hides, and everyone looks for that one person. As each person finds the hidden player, the "finder" hides with the "hider." By the end of the game, everyone is hiding—waiting for the last person to find them.

The ten-year-old offered to hide first. By the time I found him, two of his siblings were already in the hiding place. We squeezed into the dark cabinet in the basement and waited for the last seeker. We poked each other and giggled and tried to be quiet. The last person to look for us was the youngest—three years old. One of the siblings whispered to me as we heard the little sister come down the basement stairs, "She's afraid of the basement. She's afraid of the dark. She's afraid of everything!"

We waited as we heard her little voice. "Are you down here?" She walked tentatively toward the hiding place, talking to herself. "I don't like it down here. I'm scared, but I'm a big girl."

We waited together, each of us trying to hold our breath and not move. Finally she clumsily opened the cupboard, and we burst out upon her. She gleefully exclaimed, "Everything I'm looking for is here!"[23]

I believe that everything we want most is often found within and beyond our deepest fears. Throughout this chapter I've asked you what you are most afraid of. Could it be that everything you are looking for is found in your fears? I don't mean that that is where you'll find the rules to keep your daughter from sex and make her conform to your agenda. But perhaps in the midst of this scary subject is everything that we and our daughters are longing for most: a mutual relationship where we are known and loved.

Chapter 6

"Mom, We're Not Having Sex!"

The whole idea is that [oral sex] is the risk-free way to have sex, or nonsex. No pregnancies. No STDs (or so they think). They don't even have to take their clothes off. Just step into the bathroom or behind the garage…and back to the party. Sounds like what making out used to be…. If your teenager is not sure what sex is, what about abstinence?

—JUSTIN RICHARDSON AND MARK A. SCHUSTER, *Everything You Never Wanted Your Kids to Know About Sex (But Were Afraid They'd Ask)*

I'm in big trouble," Britlee sighed. "I'm in counseling because I'm in big trouble."

I tried not to smile at Britlee's pitiful confession. I was meeting with her for the first time and wanted to know why she thought her parents had insisted that she see me.

"What kind of trouble?" I asked.

"Well, I was supposed to be at the movies with my friend, but you know how it is at the movies. Everyone just meets up and talks and stuff…and my parents just don't understand…but anyway we met these two guys…and there really wasn't anything good showing anyway…and we got into a car with them and I know I'm not supposed to do that…but I didn't think it was a big deal…and we went to one of their houses…and we…um…we, like, we…did stuff."

"Stuff?" I waited for Britlee to continue.

"Well, I don't know how my mom found out, but I gave one of the guys a blow job. I'd never done it before… I don't know what the big deal is… It

isn't like we had sex or anything… But my mom is all freaking out and acting like I'm some kind of a slut!" Britlee looked me right in the eyes and then
quickly looked out the window. I suspected that she thought I would probably agree with her mom.

"You've been through a lot in the last few days," I said kindly. "You've had
an experience with a boy probably unlike any you've had before, and you've
had a major conflict with your parents. I bet you just want all of this to go
away."

"Yeah," Britlee closed her eyes and leaned back on the couch in my office.

"If what you experienced with the boy from the movies wasn't sex, what
was it?" I asked.

Britlee gave me the most popular response I hear in my office: "I don't
know." Then she added, "But it wasn't sex. I'm not going to have sex. My
mom probably thinks kissing is having sex."

Britlee had just described the dilemma mothers and daughters face in
defining not only sex but abstinence. Sex, it seems, is not easily defined by
today's teenagers. Teenagers who grow up in religious homes or homes where
abstinence is stressed are often confused about what exactly they should
abstain from. Parents are hesitant to talk about specific sexual behavior.
(The emphasis we sometimes put on virginity may be destructive. When
we organize everything around virginity, we limit the definition of sex and
miss the point of what really matters in sexual relationships—which, hopefully, is the point of this chapter.) Lauren Winner, in her thoughtful book
Real Sex: The Naked Truth About Chastity, explains her confusion as a well-
read, conscientious young adult. It doesn't take much thought to imagine the
confusion for a teenager.

> I knew, dimly, that Christianity didn't look kindly on premarital sex,
> but I couldn't have told you very much about where Christian teach-
> ings about sex came from. I did read the letters of Paul, but to tell you
> the truth, I wasn't entirely sure what "fornication" meant, or how
> much leeway I had in interpreting it. In fact, I'd never even actually
> heard the word "fornication" before reading the New Testament.… I
> knew it had something to do with illicit sex, but I wasn't sure exactly

what constituted illicit sex...which left me with the ill-defined sense that the Christian God cared somehow about how people ordered their sex lives.[1]

According to the *American Heritage Stedman's Medical Dictionary*, sex is "the sexual urge or instinct as it manifests itself in behavior—sexual intercourse or genital contact." In other words, the *medical* definition of sex is any genital contact at all, whether hand to genital, mouth to genital, or genital to genital. I realize that some may disagree with this definition, but that isn't my primary concern. As parents, we need to help our children understand and define sex for themselves. Sexual contact between teenagers often leaves them feeling confused, ashamed, excited, embarrassed. They want to know what it all means. Our culture has told them that it doesn't mean anything more than an opportunity to experience pleasure, but their hearts are telling them that it means *more*. Our job is to help put words to the "more."

Which brings me back to the conversation with my confused young client Britlee. "What if I told you," I asked, "that I think sex is having any genital contact?"

Britlee's face turned red, and she was quiet for what seemed like a long time. Then she almost whispered her question, "Does that mean I'm not a virgin?"

"Is being a virgin important to you?" I answered her question with a question.

Once again she was quiet. Finally she sighed and said, "I'm not sure what's important."

What *Really* Matters to You Speaks Louder Than Words

Britlee's honest conclusion gets to the heart of the matter regarding teenage girls, mothers of teenage girls, and sex. *What really matters—and why?* If we define sex as *any* genital contact (the medical definition), then we must be prepared to answer why genital contact matters. And even if we narrow the definition of sex to include only sexual intercourse, we still need to answer why genital contact, sexual arousal, and fondling a girl's breasts matter. This is where the task becomes more difficult—and more personal. To communicate effectively with our daughters and guide them in developing a sexual ethic that will shape their lives, we must have a sexual ethic that shapes our lives. I have discovered that we too often say one thing to our children but practice another.

Let me explain what I mean. This week I met with a couple seeking marriage counseling. They have been married almost twenty years and have two teenage daughters. Their marriage has been good and bad, wonderful and difficult. Recently they have wisely recognized that their relationship is drifting toward deadness. They live more as roommates than lovers—understandable with all the tasks involved in supporting a family.

We began to talk about their nonexistent sex life, and this honest wife summarized her position: "Sex is just not important to me. I know this may sound awful, but I wouldn't care if we never had sex again."

My mind immediately went to this book about teenagers and sex. "Isn't it interesting (and convicting)," I said, "that you are telling your teenage daughters that sex is so important that they should do everything possible to wait until marriage but that after almost twenty years of marriage, it's not that important anymore?"

My client's response was, once again, honest: "I know it's important for my daughters to wait to have sex, but I'm not sure why it's important for me to have sex with my husband now."

My client's confusion highlights why I believe we are often ineffective in talking to teenagers about sex. *We* don't know why sex is important. There can be many reasons why a married couple isn't enjoying a healthy sex life, but when a couple concludes that sex is just not that important, they are most likely missing the meaning of sex. They may need to work on their *emotional* intercourse or there may be physical challenges, but they still need to know the meaning of sex—that what we do with ourselves, others, and God in a sexual relationship matters. We can lecture our daughters about the sins of sex and scare them with the possible consequences, but these methods are not effective motivators and the results will likely be short-lived. We must hold something up to them that's worth waiting for. And we can't do that if we don't know—I mean *really know*—why sex is important. When we can answer this question in meaningful ways, we will be able to tell our daughters why abstinence is important (a task we will tackle in chapter 7).

JUST FOR YOU

1. If you had genital contact before you were married, did you think it was a big deal? Why or why not?
2. What is your definition of *abstinence?*
3. Why is sex important to you?
4. If you are a single mom, should sex still be important to you? Why or why not? Does your single status give you something unique to say to your daughter about abstinence?
5. Why should sex be important to your daughter?

If you had trouble coming up with articulate, compelling answers to the questions in the Just for You section, don't feel bad. In my own informal survey of mothers, only one in ten had a fully formed answer to these questions. When I asked, "Why is sex important to you?" most answered, after hemming and hawing, "It just is." If this is the only answer we can give our daughters, then they won't be too motivated to wait for something so blah. Another problem with not knowing why sex is important is that in deadening our desire for "more" with our husbands (even if "more" might never happen), we cannot help but deaden our desire to be pursued by, loved by, and penetrated by God. Hopefully, by the end of the chapter you will have a few more ideas about why we should care about sex in the first place.

WHAT WE DO WITH OUR BODIES MATTERS

When I was a teenager, oral sex was not standard adolescent practice. That doesn't mean we were any clearer about sex than teenagers are today. Rather than using words like "hooking up" and "blow job," we used words like "second base" or "outercourse." In the make-out parties I participated in, we had sexual contact just as surely as teenagers today have sex during oral-sex par-ties. Like teenagers today, we didn't spend a lot of time thinking about why genital contact or other sexual experiences might be important. In fact, we thought about it so little that many mothers today tell themselves and their daughters that they didn't have sex before they got married because they didn't have sexual intercourse. In so doing, I believe we not only lessen our effectiveness in talking to our daughters about sex, but we also keep from considering why sexual contact impacts us. We deny our bodily experience and that it mattered.

I did not acknowledge the truth about this part of my story until I heard the story of one of my fifteen-year-old clients. Her parents had caught her having oral sex with a boy in their garage, and they sent her to see me. We spent a few sessions talking about her experience, but we seemed to be get-ting nowhere. This brave girl decided to help me help her, and so she brought in a poem that she had written. I share this with her permission:

> I heard you fighting and so I left.
> I camped out in an alleyway.
> One month later I came back.
> You were still fighting—
> wanting your dinner,
> wanting an apology.
> Did you see my soul go out the door again?

My client waited expectantly for me to finish reading the poem. I con-gratulated her on her writing. I wasn't getting it—how this poem connected with her sexual exploits. She guided me further into her world when she said, "That's how I do it."

"Do what?" I asked.

She sighed heavily. "A blow job. I just leave. I'm not really there—like when my parents fight. My body is there, but I go someplace else."

Tears welled up in my eyes as I looked at my wise client who was teach-ing me not only about her but also about myself.

I suddenly remembered all of those make-out parties. My body felt tingly and sweaty, awkward and aroused. I felt pleasure and even some pain. I also felt confused, happy, ashamed, desirable, and guilty. In the midst of all those feelings, I disconnected from my body. This happened when I was engaged in sexual activity, even when there wasn't genital contact. My body became separate from me. This separation, at a formative time in my physical and emotional development, set me up for a distorted view of my body, which of course meant a distorted view of myself. I thought of my body as

- an object to be decorated or dieted away to conform to others' standards
- a tool to make others happy
- a necessary but insignificant trapping
- a source of conflicting emotions

This body-soul separation made me more vulnerable to an eating disorder and substance abuse by teaching me that I could harm my body and simply dissociate from any emotional consequences. The disconnection also set me up for unhealthy relationships. I did not know how to rest in a physical relationship with another person—even a righteous relationship. I habitually disconnected my emotions from my body, making true intimacy impossible. Premarital sex often forms in us destructive habits that ultimately make their way into marital sex.

Perhaps there's one more reason why I was able to sever the connection between body and soul so easily. I learned from the earliest days in Sunday school that the body is bad. I knew that the body was the source of my aroused desires and the temptation to make out in backyard parties with a boy. I knew that my body was what drew a boy's attention and attracted his roving fingers. I knew that even if I willed myself to "be good," my body could betray me at the slightest touch—arousing desires in me that I both wanted to act on and didn't want to act on. My bodily experience told me that sexual contact felt good, but all of my other experiences told me that sex was bad. I could live with myself only if I cut off my inner life from my outer life. During my middle school make-out parties, I became like a sleepwalker going through a routine. Later, when I let myself think about what was happening, my body became my enemy. These realities—disconnecting my heart from sex, being uncomfortable with myself as a sexual being, and hating my body—have haunted me all my life.

God created our bodies, and He said that they were good.[2] He connected our genitals to our hearts, designing our bodies to be aroused so that our flesh would connect with another person to form a union that nothing can tear apart.[3] When our bodies are aroused to connect our flesh with another person in a fleeting or casual union, something in us is torn when the relationship is over. Many girls and women tear their bodies from their hearts in an attempt to make sense of all the inevitable conflicting emotions. Or they harden their hearts completely. The more naked they get physically, the less naked they become emotionally.

In sexual sin we violate the sacredness of our own bodies,
these bodies that were made for…"becoming one" with another.

—1 CORINTHIANS 6:18

It's no wonder that most adult women seeking sex therapy complain that they have a lack of sexual desire. Many of us have learned that bodily sexual desire is connected with guilt and shame, so we've learned to disconnect from our desire. This can be true whether or not we've been sexually active before marriage. Christian sex therapist Douglas E. Rosenau explains in *A Celebration of Sex for Newlyweds,*

> You have so carefully guarded your sexuality and set such rigid boundaries that you have repressed your sexual feelings…. Nudity and sexual activity may be scary or even repulsive at first.[4]

I'm afraid that we conclude that sexual struggles in marriage are most often linked to premarital sex when they may be more accurately linked to a premarital disdain or disconnection from the body.

Tell your daughter that her body was designed to develop sexually and to be aroused sexually. Let her know that even holding a boy's hand will arouse her body. God intended it to be that way, not so that we automatically follow the body's leading, but so that we pay attention to its cues. Physical arousal is a cue to pay attention to what is going on and to choose whether to keep going or to stop and save further physical pleasure for later.

Physical arousal is a sign that something is natural and right. We can best teach our daughters to honor these cues when we teach them that these cues are honorable.

JUST FOR THE TWO OF YOU

1. Recall your earliest experiences in a physical relationship. What did you believe about your body's arousal? What did your mother tell you? If you didn't talk with her about it, why not?

2. How do you feel about your body? Have any of these feelings come from your sexual experiences? How have these feelings impacted your sex life?

3. If you have felt critical or contemptuous of your body, consider reading a book on body image. (See the resources section for a list of resources on this topic.) For now, read Psalm 139. Meditate on God's view of your body.

4. Consider sharing part of this story with your daughter. Ask her the following questions, but make sure you've answered them for yourself first:
   • Have you ever felt sexual arousal?
   • Did you think it was good or bad?
   • Why do you think God made our bodies to be sexually aroused?
   • Why do you think God made our genitals?

WHAT WE DO WITH OTHERS MATTERS

According to a 2004 NBC/*People* magazine poll, "eight percent of 13- to 16-year-olds, which amounts to roughly half of young teens who have had oral sex or sexual intercourse, have been involved in a casual sexual relationship."[5] Of these casual relationships, 78 percent involve oral sex and 79 percent involve sexual intercourse. The top reason teens gave for engaging in a casual sexual relationship was that they wanted to satisfy a sexual desire.[6]

The idea that sex can be casual is probably one of the most powerful lies that dominate our sexual culture. In fact, popular culture has gone so far as to say that sex is just another recreational activity. In one episode of *Friends,* Monica asked her new sexual partner, "So, we can still be friends and have sex?" He replied, "Sure. It'll be something we do together, like racquetball."

Even if sex is viewed as a form of entertainment, even if it is considered meaningless, even if it is enjoyed by two consenting people, *it is never casual.* The apostle Paul wrote, "There's more to sex than mere skin on skin…. [Our bodies] were made for God-given and God-modeled love, for 'becoming one' with another"[7] Sex is *uniting* with another person—becoming one. This is not what it only "seems" to be or what only conservative Christians think it is; *this is what it actually is.* Ethicist Lewis Smedes wrote, "It does not matter what the two people have in mind…. [Sex] unites them in that strange, impossible to pinpoint sense of 'one flesh.'"[8]

Sometimes my teenage clients and I watch a scene from a popular movie that surprisingly conveys this theological message in modern language. In *Vanilla Sky,* Tom Cruise plays a character who has a casual view of sex and relationships. At one point a woman hurt by his cavalier attitude confronts him: "Don't you know that when you sleep with someone, your body makes a promise whether you do or not?"[9]

Although there is much that is objectionable in this film, this one scene is powerful in summarizing that what we do with our bodies when it comes to other people matters. God intended sex to be powerful, not just in physical arousal and release, but in emotional arousal and release. Sex is to be the place where we surrender to another person. Whom you become "one" with matters. At some level teenagers know this. I sometimes ask them the following questions. (I use the word *boyfriend* here, but if the girl has had sex outside of a relationship—like Britlee and the boy from the movies, I will substitute the appropriate descriptive phrase.)

- Would it be a big deal to you if your dad had oral sex with someone other than your mom? Why?
- Would it matter if your mom "fooled around" with another man in the same manner that you do with your boyfriend? Why?
- Would you be okay with your parents having sex with other people if they were not serious about those relationships?

After answering these questions, adolescent girls are more open to acknowledging the significance of what happens between two people during sex.

In sex we surrender our nakedness to another person. God intended that our nakedness be enjoyed, honored, and protected. Sadly, this is seldom the experience of teenage sex that I hear about in my counseling office. Girls often tell me about crude remarks that immature boys make about their bodies—remarks that they will carry with them and wonder about all their lives. Teenagers often have sex in the backseat of cars, in a dark, cold basement, or in semipublic places. Honoring nakedness is something that teenagers are too embarrassed, rushed, or childish to think about.

[Sex] is like, when you go to a party and get drunk,
you get horny. That is just what happens, and you
hook up with people…you have sex.

—PATRICIA HERSCH, *A Tribe Apart*

In sex we surrender our differences to another person. God intended sex to join together male and female as they surrender their differences to each other. "Therefore a man leaves his father and mother and embraces his wife. They become one flesh. The two of them, the Man and his Wife, were naked, but they felt no shame"[10] This surrender is most easily understood in terms of physical differences, but I think the metaphorical reality is most important. When I surrender my differences to another, I no longer must think only of myself. I can focus on the other person.

Much teenage sex is based in self-centered, immediate gratification. Helen Fisher, an anthropologist at Rutgers University who has studied the teenage brain for years, explains that adolescents have "strong [sexual] drives, but not the brain power or the experience to go with them."[11]

I help girls identify the self-absorbed focus of their relationships by asking the following questions:

1. Does your boyfriend know your favorite color?
2. What is his vision for your future?
3. Would your boyfriend stand up for you in front of his friends?

4. What has your boyfriend done to make you feel special?

5. Does your boyfriend know what you are really good at?

6. Can he describe your best day ever? your worst day?

7. Can you talk to him about your faith?

8. Does your boyfriend like your friends?

9. Are there things you can't talk to him about? Why?

10. Does your boyfriend watch you/cheer for you at your sporting events/choir concerts/school plays?

These questions can help a girl uncover whether her boyfriend is really interested in *her*. Of course, having a "good" boyfriend doesn't mean that sex is then okay, but as we talk to our daughters about sex, we must connect those conversations to real relationships, giving our daughters a picture of what type of relationship to hope for when they are ready to make a commitment.

The entertainment media has done us a terrible disservice by portraying sex as a carefree, wild, heated, and frenzied encounter, but we parents are not very good about offering an alternative. I fear that even Christian parents sometimes think that the moments of passion we see on the big screen are what we should seek in our relationships. Perhaps that is why a *Christianity Today* survey found that more than 40 percent of respondents who were married at the time of the survey had had premarital sex, 14 percent said they'd been unfaithful to their spouses, and 75 percent of those who were unfaithful said they were Christians at the time of their infidelity.[12]

The most meaningful sex is found in a relationship of mutual care, interest, respect, and enjoyment where the differences of the other person are acknowledged, encouraged, and honored. I believe that is why some studies indicate that married women experience the most satisfying sexual relationships.[13] I love the way Lauren Winner describes this reality:

Passion and desire situated within the household are transformed into emotional manifestations of the strength, resiliency, and commitment that mark the best moments of human cooperation.[14]

Sadly, many married women don't feel this way and may believe that something is wrong with *them* or with sex. A closer look at their marriages will most likely reveal areas in their relationships that have been neglected, abused, or eroded and in need of work. It's likely that nothing is wrong with them; their relationship may just not be as healthy as it could be—which is a subject for another book.

When I share with my adolescent clients my view about God's intention for a sexual relationship, more than a few of them exclaim, "That sure doesn't describe my parents' sex life!" And as I share with adolescent girls my views of why sex is important, they often echo one of the top "excuses" teenagers give for why it is okay for them to have sex.

The statistics on marriage and sexual behavior for adults are not any brighter than adolescent statistics:

- Approximately 50 percent of marriages in America are said to end in divorce.[15]
- Data from a national social survey showed that 22 percent of married men and almost 12 percent of married women commit adultery.[16]
- One of my clients expressed her cynicism poignantly:

I don't understand why anyone would want to fall in love when you see people get heartbroken all the time. Like, is it really any better to date someone for eight months and then have to break up than to just meet him at a party and then have sex with him?

What's your answer? Perhaps your sex life has been difficult or disappointing. Maybe your marriage, like mine, has fallen apart. These realities certainly confirm that what we do with other people matters—it could break our hearts.

In sex we surrender our shame to another person. This aspect of sex is most important to me and has caused the most wounding in my own life. In the physical act of sexual intimacy, there are awkward, embarrassing, and humorous moments. Unlike the carefully scripted and rehearsed scenes in the movies, real sex is full of human mistakes, smells, and sounds. (I read one interview in which an actress reported that to get the sex scene in the movie "right," they needed forty-two different takes!) God did not intend sex to be the perfect, passionate moment that is so often portrayed in the media. He intended it to be an act in which we lovingly cover one another's shame.

Sex becomes a way for two people to engage and honor not only each other's strengths but each other's weaknesses. Sexual intimacy is to represent a daily relational intimacy in which we offer forgiveness, acceptance, and grace to each other.

Many teenage girls tell me that after having sex with a boy, they are either discarded or "graded" on their performance. Teenagers have a lot to learn in general about offering grace and forgiveness—about covering another's shame. When it comes to teenage sexual activity, these concepts are miles away from entering the picture.

One of my clients came to her appointment with a face ravaged by tears and sadness. She asked me if we could go to her school, so I drove her to a high school just a few miles from my home. When we got there, a custodian was painting the door to the girls' locker room, but enough words were still visible on the door to tell me why my client was so upset. Scrawled across the door were girls' names with letter grades beside their names. My client told me that her "grade" has been a D-minus. In the car on the ride back to my office, she sobbed, "No guy will ever ask me out again. Everyone knows I'm a D-minus!" My heart broke as she continued to cry, "I don't even know what I did wrong."

As I thought about the custodian covering the names with gray paint, I prayed that my client would wait for a relationship that would cover her rather than risking this cruel exposure again. And that's where marriage comes in. Although marriage is certainly not perfect and is populated by imperfect people, it is the only relationship God designed for sex. "And because of this, a man leaves father and mother and is firmly bonded to his wife, becoming one flesh—no longer two bodies but one. Because God created this organic union of the two sexes, no one should desecrate his art by cutting them apart."[17] God's design for marriage is not so much a command but a protection. Marriage is the best chance we have, humanly speaking, of experiencing what God intended for us in a sexual relationship.

Author and psychologist Dan Allender describes sex as "a physical reflection of what takes place on the level of the human soul. It intimately unites two bodies as a reflection of the union of two human souls. This level of union and vulnerability can be entrusted only to people who are committed to each other for the duration of life."[18] A lifelong, committed relationship is the place where we can grow to be fully ourselves with another person, who is likewise growing to be himself. It is the place God intended for us to risk being naked, being different, being human. God's design invites us to sexual pleasure and sexual connectedness in a mutual relationship of care and commitment—a relationship that gives us the opportunity to become who we are meant to be.

But what do we tell our daughters about all those statistics about failed marriages? What do I tell my daughter? What do we say to girls who see the realities of the difficulties in marriage? What do you say to your daughter?

When we talk with our daughters about sex, we want them to know that what they do with their own bodies and with other people matters, but our final answer to these questions, especially in the midst of failure and heartache, is that what we do with God matters most of all.

What We Do with God Matters

Sex was intended to be pleasurable and procreational, a surrender of our nakedness, differences, and shame to another person in a lifelong, committed, growing relationship. But it doesn't always turn out that way. It didn't for me. Nevertheless, I still believe what I have written about sex in this chapter. I believe it even more passionately than I did before my marriage was broken.

In the most masterful sermon I have ever heard preached, Peter Hiett described marriage:

> The marriage covenant and the sacrament of that covenant takes two different, incomplete, sinful people and binds them together in nakedness, despite the shame, as a picture of Christ and His church.…
> What sheer and absolute insanity to vow yourself unconditionally to another fallen, sinful, needy person! You'd have to be crazy to get married! Yet Jesus is married.… Is He crazy? Yes! That's the point. He's crazy in love with you, and He is bound and determined to show you. He's bound Himself to us fallen people in an eternal covenant, knowing full well what He's doing. He's crazy in love with you, "Bone of His bones and flesh of His flesh."[19]

No other reality reveals our failures and our foibles, our goodness and our brokenness, our passion and our self-interest like sex. I'm not talking exclusively about teenagers. I'm also talking about us—the mothers of teenagers. Our bodies are, at times, out of control. We enter into relationships foolishly, and we get out of relationships foolishly as well. We hurt people, and we ourselves get hurt. We are naked when we shouldn't be, and we hide when we shouldn't. We desperately long for someone to heal us from our sexual brokenness.

That's where we get into trouble. A teenage girl thinks that if she has sex with *this* boy, he will love her and soothe the pain from the last boy. A mother of a teenager thinks that if she can get her husband to read one more book, he will heal the pain she feels from years of disappointment. A teenage girl hardens her hearts and hates boys, believing that is the only way to deal with the pain of the boy who had sex with her and never called again. A mother of a teenager agrees that men are the enemy and vows never to risk in relationship again.

Sex understood through the lens of God's Word is a mirror in which we see what we were made for and how far we fall short of that in human experience. Sex—our longing for intimacy and our hurts and hopes along the way—can lead us to the One who invites us to be one with Him. "His purpose was to create in himself one…out of the two, thus making peace, and in this one body to reconcile [us] to God through the cross."[20] And in this relationship that matters most, we can surrender our nakedness, our differences, and our shame to the One who is completely trustworthy. He is faithful when we are faithless. He won't forsake us, even if we commit adultery. He hung stripped and naked on a cross to cover our sin. As Peter Hiett states,

> [God] is not bound by the covenant of the law but by His own
> covenant of grace. That is, He's bound by His own eternal nature,
> nothing exterior to Himself. He is unrelenting love; it's His nature
> to choose to save at any cost.[21]

Whew! We have covered a lot in this chapter. Understanding and explaining to our daughters why sex matters are crucial in helping them develop a sexual ethic. Entire books and even series of books are devoted to this topic. The subject of sex provokes questions, shame, memories—both good and bad—and a greater sense of our emptiness as human beings. We are left a bit empty even in the best relationships. We are left with gaping holes in relationships that violate or hurt us. There's something about looking at this subject honestly and thoughtfully that leaves us wanting tender, loving care. That's because sex is all about desire—and letting unfulfilled desire take us to God. Sexual confusion, loneliness, pain, and frustration are powerful, and they will either lead us to numb ourselves, demean ourselves, and rage at others and God, or they will lead us to surrender to Him.

I pray that this chapter has challenged you to develop your own reasons for why sex is important so that you can translate them into relationship with your daughter and make God's presence more meaningful and real to both of you.

JUST FOR YOU

1. Have you been able to surrender your nakedness in your marriage (not just physically but emotionally)? If not, how has this affected what you believe about sex?

2. Have you been able to surrender your differences to your spouse? Explain.

3. Have you been able to surrender your shame to your spouse? How has this impacted your sex life?

4. Think about sharing some of these realities with your daughter. What would you be able to tell her about sex and why it matters to you?

5. Read Ephesians 5:29–32. If there is brokenness and hurt in this area of your life, in what ways does this passage help you think of Christ as your husband/lover?

6. If you are single or in a difficult marriage, in what ways is sex important to you? Consider the following statements:
   - When I am most lonely, I recognize my dependence on God most clearly.
   - God desires my whole person (including my body) more than any man ever will.
   - My emptiness reveals a greater "vacancy" for God.
   - Stripped of my most essential relationship, I know more about who I am and who I was meant to be.

Chapter 7

"But Mom, I Love Him!"

Someday my prince will come.

—CINDERELLA

Imagine walking through Toys "R" Us with your six-year-old daughter. As you meander down aisles and aisles of shiny, new, promising toys, your little girl runs to one spot in an aisle. She cries in delight, "Oh, Mommy, look! It's My Little Pony Celebration Castle with Pink Sunsparkle Pony! You know I've been wanting this forever!"

"Yes, honey, I know."

Your daughter runs ahead of you down the next aisle, and you can hear her jumping up and down. "Mommy, Mommy! They have it! They have the Dora the Explorer Magic Hair Fairytale Princess Dora Doll! Do we have enough money for it, Mommy?"

"Yes, sweetheart, we have enough money for it, but let's keep looking."

Your six-year-old carefully places Dora the Explorer back on the shelf and runs ahead of you again. This time she stops by a toy and waits patiently for you to catch up with her. "Mommy, look at this Wiggles Guitar. This would be good to get, wouldn't it? It's even educational!"

"Yes, honey, that looks like a great toy, and—"

Before you can finish your sentence your daughter spots one last toy. She gasps, grabs your hand, and pulls you to the shelf. "Look, Mommy, I can't believe it's here! It's the Barbie VideoCam Wireless Video Camera. I want it, Mommy. I love it! Oh, Mommy, if I got that, I would never want anything new again!"

She looks at you with bright, pleading eyes, and you calmly answer, "The

Barbie VideoCam looks wonderful. I promise I'll get you just the right toy at just the right time. Wait and see."

"Okay, Mommy." Your daughter grabs your hand and together you happily and serenely walk out of Toys "R" Us.

For most of us, this little vignette sounds like a fairy tale. No temper tantrums? No bribes to get out of the store without a scene? No box of candy at the checkout line to keep things under control? It is difficult to imagine a six-year-old with such trust in her mother that she can wait.

In light of all the statistics about teenagers and sex, the statement I most often hear from teenagers and parents alike is, "It's difficult to imagine a sixteen-year-old who waits."

Don't worry. This chapter is not intended to make you feel guilty because you have impatient children. Rather, its purpose is to suggest that the six-year-old and maybe even the sixteen-year-old play out to an extreme what we all experience. We aren't fully confident that God will give us what we need, and we don't want to wait very long for it.

The patient, trusting six-year-old and the disciplined, trusting sixteen-year-old are difficult to imagine because none of us is very good at waiting. In *When the Heart Waits,* Sue Monk Kidd writes, "We live in an age of acceleration, in an era so seduced by instantaneous that we're in grave danger of losing our ability to wait."[1] It's startling to consider that Kidd wrote these words in 1990 *before* Internet access was available on your telephone, at the mall, and in your favorite coffee shop.

Most teenagers I talk to know that their parents want them to wait to have sex. Some of the teenagers themselves even want to wait. The best answer I can get from them as to why waiting is a good thing is "Because it is." The best answer I have been able to get from parents as to why waiting is a good thing is "Because God says it is." So let me ask the question again: why is waiting a good thing?

We have spent some time considering why not waiting is risky. Fear works as a motivator for a while, but eventually most teenagers want *more*— a more compelling reason for waiting. They want to know that they are moving toward something positive, not just away from something negative. In fact, researchers have indicated that adolescence is a time when, biologically, "passions are ignited, [including] strong desires to achieve certain kinds of goals."[2] When everything biologically and culturally is telling teens to have sex, they need passionate reasons for waiting that will lead them to positive goals. When they have the passion and the power to pick any and every toy in the toy store, they need something extraordinary to compel them to wait.

In this chapter we are going to consider why waiting is a good thing. Not just why it's a good thing for your teenager to wait to have sex, but why it's also a good thing for *you* to wait for your marriage to heal, for a broken friendship to be restored, or for your daughter to trust in a relationship with you and with God. We will be powerful in influencing our daughters to wait to the degree that we believe that waiting is not only a good thing to happen to us but perhaps the best thing!

I didn't expect writing this chapter to be so transformational in my own life, but it forced me to confront not only my fear of waiting but my hatred of waiting. I want things to be quick and easy, to keep moving, and to satisfy immediately. I discovered that what has mattered most to me is avoiding the misery of waiting. I had to admit that a God for whom a day is like a thousand years[3] seems like a lunatic to me, the queen of speed. I confess this to you to challenge you to look within at your own restless, impatient heart. When a teenage girl sees love, acceptance, and power within her reach—all through sexual activity—she needs more than the lip-service reasons "Waiting is good" and "God says waiting is good." She needs a heartfelt exclamation: "Waiting is good. *I know it's good.* Watch me, wait, and you'll see!"

I hope this chapter will produce upheaval in your heart that results in transformational growth, and I hope it produces powerful answers to your daughter's exclamations:

"No one else is waiting, why should I?"

"If I wait, I might miss my chance!"

"But Mom, I love him!"

TEENAGE FAIRY TALES

Right now I have forty-six books on my office floor that reference teenagers and sex. If I were to list all the reasons teenagers, parents, and "experts" give for why teenagers don't wait to have sex, they could be summarized in two sentiments:

1. "We are in love."
2. "We should be able to make our own choices about sex."

Love and power. Most teenage girls engage in sexual activity because it promises acceptance, belonging, and relationship or because they have learned that sex is one area in which they have power not only to make their own choices but to allure boys to make choices *for them.* In the next chapter we will look at the allure of power in sexual activity for teenage girls, but in this chapter we will focus primarily on their longing for love.

In her modern-day fairy tale *Prep,* best-selling author Curtis Sittenfeld describes how sex answers a girl's longing for love and power in relationships. First she describes the loneliness and powerlessness of adolescence:

> At soccer practice, I worried that I would miss the ball, when we boarded the bus for games at other schools, I worried that I would take a seat by someone who didn't want to sit next to me, in class I worried that I would say a wrong or foolish thing. I worried that I took too much food at meals, or that I did not disdain the food you were supposed to disdain.... I always worried someone would notice me, and then when no one did, I felt lonely.[4]

The main character in the novel, Lee Fiora, is seventeen years old when she begins to have sex with her boyfriend. She describes how it changes her life:

> [After sex] I was the person [he] told things to. [He] thought I was pretty. [He] missed me when we were apart. After lying in bed, he couldn't imagine anywhere better than to be with me. It seemed to me...that this was what it was like to love a boy—to feel consumed.... I loved him so much![5]

We as mothers make a big mistake if in response to our daughters' expressed experience of love and/or power in teen romance we dismiss their feelings or become disgusted by their behavior. We pretty much guarantee that our daughters won't continue coming to us with their questions or problems about relationships if we tell them they're mistaken or wrong about what they are feeling. When we tell our daughters that they are not old enough to understand love, we are really trying to soothe ourselves. We are telling ourselves that our daughters are not old enough to experience romance. This makes us feel more in control.

Face it: girls are raised from the time they are toddlers to believe that love is magical, fantastical, and totally out of their control. If they are lucky, a wonderful prince will sweep them up, put a cheap plastic shoe on their foot, take them out of their dingy home where they are misunderstood, and underappreciated, and gallop away with them into a wonderful future.

—JILL MURRAY, *But I Love Him*

I agree with Dr. Jill Murray in her excellent book on detecting abusive relationships and protecting your daughter from them. She writes, "It is my opinion that a fifteen-year-old understands as much about love as you do… for her age and level of experience."[6]

Think back to your first experiences in romantic relationships. The thrill, the anticipation, the heart-pounding, palm-sweating longing for love was *real.* Here is a journal entry from one of my high-school diaries shortly after I began dating a boy on the debate team:

Waiting must be one of life's greatest frustrations…waiting for a phone call, waiting for a date, waiting for him to hold my hand, waiting for the right time and right place…always waiting and wondering if waiting is the right thing to do.

As you recall your own longing for love and the first hint that you might get what you longed for, remember that your daughter is no different from you. She might dress differently than you did. Her boyfriend might have a pierced eyebrow or a tattoo. You may fear that much more is at stake in teen romances today than when you were a teen. But the feelings are just as real.

MOTHERS HAVE LOVE STORIES TOO

Honoring your daughter's expressed emotions about her romantic relationships or longed-for romantic relationships will not only encourage her to continue talking with you about this important area of her life, but it will remind you that she is looking for role models for love. Your life of love *will* be a source of information to her about relationships. Does she see you involved in growing, mutual, vibrant relationships? Even if you are no longer married, does she see you pursuing healthy relationships? Whether you are married or single, does your daughter see you patiently waiting and trusting God for what you long for in your life? I am certainly not suggesting that you have to have everything "together" in your relationships. Acknowledging that some things are lacking or need work in your relationships allows your daughter to be more honest about the deficiencies in her own relationships. What you do after the romance has faded speaks volumes to your daughter about the work of real relationships. (The resources section of this book offers some excellent resources for working on your own relationships.)

Do not view your daughter's relationships as trivial or meaningless. View them as you view your own relationships. If you want your daughter to leave behind childish fairy tales or to discard the stories of people in today's culture as models for love, you must provide her with another story. How about your own? I suspect that if you shake your head and shudder at the thought of holding up your own story as a model for your daughter, your reluctance has something to do with what you believe about waiting. If you are waiting to live happily ever after before you consider your story a model for relationships, consider this: you just might be missing an opportunity to invite your daughter to see a relationship that not only models joy and sorrow, victory and failure, anticipation and dread but also shows her that you are resting in a relationship with a Lover who never fails, betrays, or condemns but is always romancing you to deeper love and greater joy.

In the novel *Prep*, the main character describes her realization that her romantic sexual relationship was a fairy tale:

> On the bed was a sleeping bag and I lay on it, and then I sat up and
> reached for [him] and he was on top of me again, his khaki pants and

belt buckle, the buttons down his shirt, my face at the side of his neck, just below his left ear, his stubble and how good he smelled and how warm he always was and how much I liked to be with him. I already recognized, even then, the sadness of another person lying on top of you. They will always leave.... You can always feel the imminent loss.[7]

How your story intersects with your daughter's story will determine whether she looks to you for cues about how to love and live with disappointment and difficulty in relationships or whether she turns to fairy tales and the stories of the culture. In the rest of this chapter, we will examine what it might look like for your two stories to form a greater story about an unshakable relationship in the midst of the inevitable stormy weather of relationships.

Just for You

1. Recall your first "crush." How did this experience impact you and what you believe about yourself and romantic relationships?

2. Remember what it was like to wait for a boyfriend. Pull out old photo albums or diaries and remember your adolescent angst.

3. When your daughter tells you that she is in love, what is your first response? Why?

4. If your response is negative, what are you most afraid of? What if she really does love her boyfriend?

5. When you were a teenager, who did you look to as role models for what it means to be in love? Who are your daughter's models?

6. What about your relationships right now would you like your daughter to emulate in her relationships? What are you afraid she will emulate?

7. List some things that you are waiting for right now in your relationships. Are you good at waiting? Why or why not?

If our daughters are truly in love—or long to be in love—and have desires as real as those in our hearts, how do we influence them to wait to have sex? Simply put, we must be passionate and purposeful in *showing* them that waiting is for their protection, that it is a discipline, and that it is a gift. As a mother who believes in the discipline and protection of waiting, I have encouraged my daughter to wait, but I have also been inconsistent in *showing* her the gifts that come from waiting. I'm talking here not about waiting to have sex but about waiting for the deeper desires of our hearts for relationships to be clarified or fulfilled. We cannot separate waiting to have sex from waiting for all that we long for in relationships. If we want our daughters to wait for all they long for in relationships—including a sexual relationship—we must model with grace and faith what it means to wait in the midst of difficult or disappointing relationships.

It is a testimony to her own character and to God's grace that my daughter, Kristin, has continued to wait to have sexual relationships despite my flawed model of waiting for God to supply, sustain, or reshape all that I long for in relationships. It is my fervent prayer and hope that in the days ahead we will both wait for honorable relationships that will not only fulfill our desires but will enable us to give and receive love with greater joy because we are coming to understand the gift of waiting.

THE PROTECTION OF WAITING

Kristin was not one of those girls who leaped into adolescence with both feet. She walked, somewhat timidly and reluctantly, into being a teenager. When we had "the talk" about sex, Kristin didn't have any questions. She wanted the conversation to be over with as soon as possible. She nodded intently at my warnings about sexual predators, hormonally charged boys, and all the risks of sexual behavior during adolescence. She wanted protection.

As Kristin waded deeper into adolescence, she grew more confident of herself and needed fewer reminders and advice from me. Instead of nodding intently at my warnings, she shooed me away with "I know, Mom. I know." Nevertheless, I continued to remind her of the risks and consequences of not waiting to have sex. I will never forget the conversation we had during Kristin's junior year of high school, which let me know how limited I had been in talking about the protection of waiting.

One of Kristin's best friends called her at 2:00 a.m. from a party and told Kristin that she was in trouble. So Kristin awakened me from a deep sleep to ask if she could go pick up her friend. Feeling slightly annoyed that my good night of sleep was forever gone, I told Kristin that she could pick her up and bring her straight to our home. The next morning I heard the story of Kristin's friend's partying—a loss of inhibition that led to unprotected sex with a new boyfriend. Kristin's friend was terrified that she might get pregnant and wanted Kristin to go with her to Planned Parenthood to get the morning-after pill.

Apart from everything I believed about teenage drinking, sex outside of marriage, and Planned Parenthood, I felt compassion for Kristin's friend, who was experiencing firsthand the trauma of not waiting to have sex. After a lot of persuading, Kristin's friend agreed to call her mother and let her participate in the decision. After Kristin's friend and her mother left, I breathed a deep sigh of relief and said, "Honey, I'm so grateful for you and your values about sex. I hope that you see that you are protecting yourself from all this pain and fear."

Kristin was quiet for a moment and then asked, "But what am I protecting myself *for?*"

I resisted the urge to tell her a fairy tale—that someday her prince would come. Instead, I answered honestly, "I'm not sure I have a great answer to that question. Will you give me some time? I promise we'll talk about this again soon."

Kristin shrugged her shoulders and probably didn't expect any further conversation. But I spent quite a bit of time praying and walking, praying and driving, and praying and talking to others before answering my daughter's question.

My answer took shape over the next few days and solidified when Kristin came home and told me more about the aftermath of her friend's night of partying and sex with her boyfriend. Her friend had gone to Planned Parenthood and had taken the morning-after pill. She told Kristin that she was haunted by memories of taking the pill and wondered if it had killed a baby already growing inside her. She saw her boyfriend in the hall and worried about what they had done and what he thought of her. She suspected that he and his friends looked at her differently. She was afraid to go to another party—afraid of what her boyfriend might expect and afraid of her own lack of willpower.

Kristin showed me a note her friend had written to Kristin during their second-period government class: "I don't think having sex really changed me. It just made me unsure of myself and everyone else."

"That's it," I told Kristin. "That's what you're protecting yourself for—to keep your sense of self growing in strength, confidence, and peace. To know that who you are is a goal worth pursuing with all your heart, no matter what anyone else says or does."

In the months ahead I worked hard to note things Kristin did or said that revealed who she was. When she made a card for a friend going through difficulties, I said, "You are a loyal, thoughtful friend." When she finished the season in gymnastics, even though she didn't like the coach, I said, "You are conscientious—able to do hard things." And when she decided to break up with a boyfriend because she knew they did not share the same values, I said, "You are courageous and full of integrity."

By the time Kristin was ready to graduate from high school, she learned that a few boys had made a bet on who might be able to persuade her to have sex before they finished their senior year. I was shocked and angered by this wager, but Kristin took it in stride. She explained to me, "It's really just a joke, Mom. They know that's not who I am."

I asked [this mother] to become a detective, looking for clues to the girl she knew was there, trapped in that adolescent body. I reminded her that she was up to the task because no one knew her daughter like she did (at this point, not even her daughter knew herself like her mother did), and no one loved her more fiercely.

—SHARON HERSH, *Bravehearts*

Waiting to have sex protects our daughters not just *from* disease, pregnancy, and heartbreak; it protects them *for* the sake of developing a sense of self. The very act of sex is a surrender of yourself to another person. The main character in the novel *Prep* described it as a "consuming" of herself. When a developing adolescent girl has sex, she loses herself, and that can have lifelong consequences. She loses herself before she really knows who she is. She loses herself before she accumulates positive choices and experiences that tell her who she is. She is at risk for thinking that she is stupid, an object, inferior, or desirable only for her body parts.

When your daughter graduates from high school, her greatest accomplishment will not be her diploma, her awards, or her achievements. It will be her *self*. Waiting to have sex protects her developing self. It allows her to know who she is regardless of what everyone else is doing or saying. It means that she regards her whole self—body, soul, and spirit—as worth working on, noticing, and desiring. Your job—while she waits—is to notice, enjoy, compliment, respect, affirm, and remember who she is.

What if your daughter fails or falters? Once again, Kristin showed me the way. During the summer months before she left for college, Kristin and the friend I mentioned earlier were sorting through stacks and stacks of pictures from their high-school days. I overheard them laughing, moaning, and remembering many high-school experiences. I don't know how they got on the subject of sex, but I heard Kristin say, "I always imagined myself as the girl who waited until she got married to have sex."

Her friend responded, "I guess I imagined myself as the stupid girl who had sex and then worried about being pregnant or getting dumped by the guy she had sex with."

Just for the Two of You

1. Tell your daughter about a time when you waited or were forced to wait—whether it was waiting for sex or waiting on God's timing in relationships—but recognized later on that God was protecting you.
2. Talk about a time when you didn't wait. What were the consequences of not waiting?
3. Look together at photographs of your daughter's childhood. Recall stories about your daughter and what they reveal about who she is.
4. List everything your daughter will protect—body, soul, and spirit—if she waits to have sex.
5. Brainstorm about other ways you and your daughter can protect and care for yourselves—body, soul, and spirit.

Kristin wisely said to her friend, "Oh, that's just the girl you thought you were. You're not her anymore."

Kristin was pulling her friend forward by seeing what was most true about her, not just her mistakes. If your daughter has blown it or made mistakes, it's not too late to look for clues that tell who she really is. And as you see her through the lens of love and envision her as she was meant to be, she will begin to see herself as someone worth protecting.

WAITING IS A DISCIPLINE

There's no way around it. Waiting is hard work. It's hard to say no when everyone else is saying yes. It's hard to remember what you're waiting for. It's especially hard when your relationship feels like love.

During Kristin's senior year of high school, she had a boyfriend. In fact, they dated almost six months, which, as I mentioned earlier, is a long time for teenagers. I had my reservations about this boy and occasionally mentioned my concerns to Kristin. She replied, "I know, Mom. It's okay. You don't know him like I do."

I honored my daughter's feelings and knowledge of this boy, but I still prayed like crazy. Every once in a while I'd ask, "What's happening in your physical relationship?"

Most of the time Kristin would sigh and say, "I told him when we started dating that kissing was as far as I would go. I remind him of that when I need to. It's under control, Mom." Every once in a while Kristin would really sigh and say, "I tell him no, and he takes no for an answer."

Still, I worried about their relationship. Although I believed in my daughter, I knew too many stories about out-of-control moments that resulted in a lifetime of consequences or about out-of-control boys who wouldn't take no for an answer. I also knew that Kristin's continued need to say no revealed some things about her boyfriend that I didn't like. Boys who continue to try are really not taking no for an answer, and not taking no for an answer can lead to serious harm in relationships. (We'll talk more about this in chapter 9.)

I was surprised when Kristin came home from school one day and announced, "I broke up with my boyfriend today."

"Why?" I asked.

"I just know I can't be with him, and it's not fair to stay together," she explained.

"What do you mean?" I wanted to know more.

"We just don't want the same things, and even though I keep telling him no, I make it all confusing for him by staying with him, and I just don't want to make a big mistake," my wise daughter concluded.

Kristin was talking about discipline. Disciplines are things we practice. Waiting to have sex is a practice of saying no, remembering who you are, and protecting yourself from people and situations that might get you in trouble. In his masterful work *The Spirit of the Disciplines,* Dallas Willard reminds us that discipline "molds and shapes" who we are.[8] The apostle Paul described discipline this way: "Take your everyday, ordinary life—your sleeping, eating, going-to-work, and walking-around life—and place it before God as an offering."[9]

When Kristin announced at the beginning of her relationship that she drew the line at kissing, she was practicing waiting. Every time she said no, she was practicing this discipline. And when she wisely broke up with this boyfriend, she was taking the discipline of waiting seriously. Not too long after she broke up with her boyfriend, I found Kristin crying in her bedroom. She choked out her words, "Oh, Mom, I know it was right to break up with him, but it still hurts. What if there isn't anyone else?"

Kristin was asking the question about discipline that we've all probably asked at one time or another:

- Why wait if there are only more difficulties ahead?
- Why hope for a good man when I have been hurt by not-so-good men?
- What's the point of living right if it doesn't get you anywhere?
- Isn't it better to settle for a sure thing than to wait for something or someone that might never come?

The next weekend was the state basketball tournament. Kristin was a cheerleader and took her place in front of the stands. The game was tied with only ten seconds remaining. During the time-out, the cheerleaders from the other team began to taunt our cheerleaders. This resulted in a competition to see who could cheer and yell the loudest. As part of the competition, the other team's cheerleaders did back handsprings across the floor to our side of the gym. Kristin was the only cheerleader from our school who could do the back handsprings. She started out by herself down the court to answer their gesture. As she continued down the entire basketball court, the whole gym got to its feet and started yelling wildly to cheer her on. When she finished, I saw her look for me in the stands. Our eyes met, and Kristin's face burst into the most beautiful, most alive smile I'd ever seen.

On the way home Kristin confirmed my description. She said, "Mom, I felt so alive!" Although I didn't mention it to her at the time, we did talk later about what allows us to feel fully alive. The Bible is clear that God longs for us to practice disciplines, not to keep us repressed in our choir robes and tight-fitting Sunday shoes, but to lead us into full lives in which our bodies, souls, and spirits are fully present. As the apostle Paul wrote to the church in Corinth, "Dear, dear Corinthians, I can't tell you how much I long for you to enter this wide-open, spacious life. We didn't fence you in. The smallness you feel comes from within you. Your lives aren't small, but you're living them in a small way.... Open up your lives. Live openly and expansively."[10]

In her book *Real Sex,* Lauren Winner writes, "[Disciplines] are ways we orient our whole selves—our bodies and minds and hearts...of being in the world—toward God."[11]

Waiting is the in-between time. It calls us to be in this moment, this season, without leaning so far into the future that we tear our roots from the present. When we learn to wait, we experience where we are as what is truly substantial and precious in life.

—SUE MONK KIDD, *When the Heart Waits*

I have been intrigued that the greatest single deterrent to teenage girls having sex before marriage is not parental pressure, teaching from the church, or signing an abstinence pledge; it's sports.[12] *Why?* I wondered. I think the answer can be found in the novel *Prep.* The young character Lee says, "Sports contained the truth.... They rewarded effortlessness and unself-consciousness.... They showed the best things in the world to be were young and strong and fast. To play a great game of high school basketball...made you know what it was to be alive."[13]

Sometimes girls get involved in sexual relationships because they think it makes them feel more alive. However, as Kristin's girlfriend experienced, sex blurs and numbs other areas of life, including one's sense of self, when it does not take place in the context of a committed covenant relationship. Teenage girls need to feel alive. Our job is to encourage their involvement in activities and practices that make them feel alive.

We will be most powerful in talking to our daughters about the discipline of waiting if we also know—heart and soul—that there are rewards for waiting. Discipline allows us to protect and nourish our whole selves, and the reward is being more fully alive. When I exercise, my body feels more alive. When I read the Bible, meditate, and pray, my spirit feels more connected to God's Spirit. When I take deep breaths in and out, I feel alive on the inside and outside. My inside catches up with my outside. When our daughters wait to have sex, they know at a biological, cellular level that they were made to connect physically with another person. They are alive to that possibility.

In *Real Sex,* Lauren Winner uses the analogy of the discipline of fasting. She concludes,

> I'm beginning to understand some of the benefits of fasting. I'm beginning to see that I recognize my dependence on God more clearly when I'm hungry; I'm beginning to chip away at some of the stupor that comes with always being sated.[14]

Being more fully alive ultimately means being alive to God—dependent on Him to satisfy our deepest desires. This is where we can begin talking about the gift of waiting (yes, I mean *gift*). But before we get there, it might be good to ponder the disciplines in our lives. We will be able to encourage our daughters in the discipline of waiting if we believe that practicing disciplines is joy rather than drudgery, because it makes us fully alive.

JUST FOR YOU

1. List the disciplines that you currently practice in your life. What are the rewards to practicing these disciplines?

2. What disciplines do you neglect? Why?

3. How much does your daughter know about the disciplines in your life? By watching you, would she know about your practice of these disciplines? Explain.

4. How often do you talk to your daughter about her romantic relationships and the value these relationships place on sex? Are you *disciplined* in talking to her about this part of her life? Is it a duty or a pleasure for you?

5. Talk about the extent to which you feel alive in body, soul, and spirit. What disciplines are lacking in the areas in which you feel less alive?

6. Recall a time when you felt fully alive. What was going on?

7. Now that you have worked to become more aware of when you feel most alive and when you feel less alive, take note of moments when your daughter is fully alive—laughing hilariously, sobbing over a sad movie, fighting fiercely with her brother, worshiping during a church service, and so on. Talk with your daughter about what it feels like to be fully present in the moment.

WAITING IS A GIFT

Kristin is now a freshman in college. If all the stories and statistics about sex in this book were magnified one hundred times, that would give us an idea of the sexual climate of college campuses today. Kristin summed it up for me recently while talking about a Friday night on campus. One of her friends in her dorm came to her room and asked if he could hang out for a while. Kristin asked what was going on in his room. He replied, "My roommate is having sex with his girlfriend. I mean, this *is* college."

Now that Kristin is in college, I've wondered how her values about sex will hold up when no one is looking. Will she still believe in the protection of waiting and be disciplined, no matter what everyone else is doing? Not too long ago I asked her those very questions. Her response was like an arrow shot straight to my heart.

"I still believe the same things, Mom, but I'm wondering what the point is sometimes. I mean, you say all the time that you love God, but look at your life."

"What do you mean," I asked tentatively.

"Well, your marriage fell apart. Here you are alone and sad all the time and worried about the future. What is the point of doing things God's way if there's no guarantee that it will all work out? What are *you* waiting for, Mom?"

Kristin's observations and questions left me speechless. But as I thought about her insights, I had to admit that I've been a bit hypocritical. I've encouraged her to wait—because God has something for her. And yet as I wait for answers, fulfillment, and understanding of my own longings in relationships, I don't often wait happily, expecting good things from God.

I thought of a married couple I counsel who is having trouble in their sex life. I suggested that they spend some time cuddling. His response was, "I can't do that. Once we start cuddling, I have to have sex." We encourage our teenagers to discipline themselves, but we don't practice that waiting in our own lives.

I also thought of a dear friend who had suffered for years in an emotionally and sexually abusive marriage. She is now in a relationship with another woman. This is her rationale: "In God's name, my husband inflicted pain and suffering on me. I'm not waiting for another man. I'm not interested in another man. I'm not going to be hurt like that again."

I thought of another client, a woman who has been single all her life. She finally met someone over the Internet. When he expressed a desire for a sexual relationship, she said, "Doing things God's way hasn't gotten me anywhere. I'm tired of waiting."

Before we express our dismay and disgust at a generation of teenagers who will not wait to have sex, we need to look inside at our own unwillingness to wait with joyful or at least peaceful expectancy for all the good things we long for in relationships.

After all, sex is a deeply spiritual issue. As we discussed earlier, it is a joining of our private parts, connected to our hearts, to another's private parts, connected to his heart. It is an expression of our deep desire, at a cellular level, to be known, accepted, and loved forever. Sex is a taste, in human relationships, of a banquet we will eat in heaven with the perfect Lover of our souls—the One who knows us fully, accepts us unconditionally, and loves us eternally. Scripture calls this banquet a "marriage supper," when we will be joined to our Groom, Jesus.[15] Of course, when our sex lives are frustrated, violated, or betrayed, we wonder about the love of God. Why would He create us for something so integral to who we are and allow it to be a disappointment or to be damaged over and over again? How can He expect us to believe in a love life with Him when our love life down here is so difficult and disappointing?

We make a mistake when we talk to teenagers about sex only on a fleshly or material level. That's exactly what their culture does. But teenagers are deeply spiritual. According to a 2000 *Newsweek* poll, 43 percent of teens reported that faith was very important in their lives.[16] In a national survey conducted by the Barna Research Group, 64 percent of teens said they were "religious," and 60 percent (three of five teens) described themselves as "spiritual."[17] We parent our whole child when we appeal to the whole person—body, soul, and spirit. My pastor says it this way:

> Do you see why God is so continually concerned with our sexuality?
> And do you see why Satan continually tries to desecrate it? Because it
> is God's premier reference to His relationship with us—His delight in
> us, how He bears fruits through us, communion in the sanctuary of
> the eternal covenant of grace.[18]

The Enemy wants to distort this reference point so that we think sex is no big deal, and then maybe we'll think that an intimate, passionate relationship with God is no big deal, either. Satan wants to take our broken, abusive, disappointing relationships and turn them into our reference point so that we will think that our relationship with God will be broken, abusive, or disappointing.

My daughter has seen me hurt in relationships—in all kinds of relationships—especially in the heart-wrenching divorce that left us all reeling. She saw me struggle with despair and fear and wondered why she should wait on a God who seems to treat people so carelessly. And in response she translated her experience with flawed human relationships onto her relationship with God. What I had neglected to do was to show her the fruits of waiting that had nourished and sustained me in the midst of disappointment and heartache.

- She didn't know I'd heard God whisper, "Sharon, *I* understand," when I feared that no one really understood what I was going through.
- She didn't know about the Valentine's Day when, during the benediction at church, my pastor had prayed that we would know that "He watches us while we sleep. He listens to us breathe. He sings over us, 'Beautiful one, I love.... Beautiful one, I adore.'"[19] I knew his words had been just for me.
- I never mentioned to her the agony I'd experienced over decisions about her and her brother as well as my daily, desperate prayers for guidance, and then the peaceful *knowing* of God's leading.
- Of course, she didn't see the mornings I woke up feeling afraid and lonely, pulled out my Bible, and hung on every word I read.
- I didn't confess to her all my failures in relationships—not just in my marriage but in other relationships—that seemed to collapse on me at times, leaving me feeling shame and self-contempt, or that at these times I heard anew His words, "I forgive your sins—every one. I heal your diseases—every one. I redeem you from hell and save your life! I crown you with love and mercy—a paradise crown. I wrap you in goodness—beauty eternal."[20]
- I didn't tell her about the times I went to church or other functions feeling ashamed because of my divorced status but then felt God's presence surround me and carry me through the event.
- And I never told her about my recurring dream. I've had this dream that I'm in heaven trying desperately to get through the throngs of people. I finally make it through the crowd and see the One who is the object of everyone's attention. He holds out His arms to me, and I fall into Love. I exclaim over and over, "This is real. This is real."

• I didn't tell Kristin—and I don't think I even acknowledged it to myself—that in the midst of waiting on God to help me sort out the longings of my heart in human relationships, I was developing an *intimate* relationship with Jesus. Jesus was becoming more real to me than the disappointment, sadness, and fear I'd experienced in all my relationships. He was becoming the Substance of my faith. That was the *gift* of waiting.

Since my conversation with Kristin about sex and college, I have begun to share more with her about my own experience of waiting—not just the sadness and frustration but the joy and peace of developing an intimate relationship with God. What I realize is that far more than wanting my daughter to find a handsome prince and live happily ever after, I long for her to be in an intimate relationship with God. In fact, far more than wanting her to stay sexually pure and hold fast to her values, I long for her to be in meaningful and passionate *relationship* with Jesus. My responsibility as a parent is not to have a storybook marriage or to do and say everything right. My responsibility is to model to Kristin a love affair with Jesus—a love affair that is possible because I am in a season of waiting. This season of waiting does not mean that my life is on hold or that I'm in a state of paralysis. Rather, I am waiting for God to heal the wounds of relationships and to lead me boldly into a life of love in all kinds of relationships that is more fully a reflection of my love life with Him—a love affair with Him that is characterized by my trusting that He will provide what I need when I need it.

[Your circumstances are] under the direction of a wise and faithful love, which is educating you for a glorious destiny. Believe only that your circumstances are those most suited to develop your character. They have been selected out of all possible combinations of events and conditions in order to effect in you the highest finish of usefulness and beauty. They would have been the ones selected by you, if all the wide range of omniscient knowledge had been within your reach.

—F. B. MEYER, *Elijah and the Secret of His Power*

Rather than daydreaming and imagining a six-year-old trusting her mother in a toy store, I am imagining a mother, sometimes tired and afraid, trusting that God is romancing both her and her daughter to intimacy with Him, because He knows what we sometimes lose sight of in our hurry-up, human world: intimacy with Him is the greatest gift of all.

Just for the Two of You

1. List some things you and your daughter are each waiting for. Does this waiting make you seek out God and depend on Him more? Why or why not?

2. Talk about the discipline involved in waiting. Tell your daughter about some of your practices of discipline and what you're waiting for. Brainstorm about ways she can practice the discipline of waiting to have sex.

3. Ask your daughter (now this takes courage) what kind of relationship she thinks you have with God. Ask her to explain.

4. Describe the kind of relationship you want to have with God. What is getting in the way of your developing that kind of relationship?

5. Ask your daughter what she thinks you want for her most. Have you conveyed to her that you want her to have a growing relationship with God?

6. Have you been waiting to live "happily ever after"? What is keeping you from being happy right now? What does a lack of happiness reveal about your relationship with God?

7. Ask your daughter, "If you were your only role model, would you want a relationship with God? Why or why not?"

Chapter 8

"Mom, It's *My* Body!"

By keeping her heart protected
She'd never feel rejected

—KELLY CLARKSON, "Miss Independent"

My cell phone rang at 2:00 a.m. I groggily reached for it and mumbled, "Hello."

"Sharon, it's me, Georgia. I didn't mean for this to happen." She choked out her words between nearly hysterical sobs. "I can't believe it. I feel so awful. I'm so sorry."

"Georgia, take a deep breath. What are you talking about?" I asked.

"It's Daniel. I broke up with him on Friday at school. I knew that he was upset, but I never thought he'd go this far. Sharon, he tried to kill himself. He took a bunch of sleeping pills, and he's at the emergency room right now. I feel so terrible. Is this all my fault?" Georgia's voice broke again, and she began to sob into the telephone.

I tried to calm Georgia, and I assured her that I would meet with her first thing the next morning. I also encouraged her to get some sleep. But after our conversation, I found that I could not get back to sleep. My mind was filled with other conversations Georgia and I had had during the past three weeks. My heart was filled with compassion for Georgia and for Daniel, two seventeen-year-olds who were sure they each knew what they were doing and never anticipated the possible price they would pay.

I was surprised by the candor Georgia and her mother displayed when they had first come to see me for counseling. Georgia's mom explained that she and Georgia's father wanted Georgia in counseling because she was promiscuous. I quickly glanced at Georgia's face to see her response to her mother's characterization. Her face was blank.

"Do you know what your mom means by *promiscuous?*" I asked Georgia.

"She means that I'm having sex, but it's just with one guy—my boyfriend, Daniel. We've been dating for six months. I think this is my choice. It's my relationship, and it's my body." Georgia spoke matter-of-factly, as if she were telling me that she liked ice cream and had the right to eat it whenever she wanted to.

Georgia's mom looked at me and shrugged her shoulders as if to say, "I don't know what to do about this. *You* do something."

I certainly did not have a plan for what I would do, but I was curious. I do not believe that any teenage girl chooses to be sexually active without reasons. She may not even be aware of the reasons herself, but the reasons that led her to those choices are rooted within her story. One of the worst mistakes a mother can make after learning of her daughter's sexual activity is to conclude that her daughter is simply bad, a slut, loose, or cheap. When we place our daughters in that box, they will in turn place us in the box of judging and shaming them rather than trying to understand them.

GIRL POWER

When a girl says, "It's my choice! It's my body! I can do what I want!" she is crying out to be powerful. We were made to have an impact. As a girl approaches adolescence, a restlessness begins in her spirit that is supported by her developing brain. She wants more independence. She's searching for her own identity. She is testing and developing her own values. She longs for her own intimate relationships. In fact, these very activities were identified in 1948 by psychologist Robert Havighurst as the "developmental tasks of adolescence." Havighurst theorized that in order for an adolescent to be ready for adulthood with a healthy sense of self and well-developed emotions, he or she needed to complete several developmental tasks, including developing intellect, achieving independence, forming identity, developing integrity, and achieving relational intimacy.[1]

Unfortunately, many of today's teenage girls use sex and sexual activity as the launching pad for these developmental tasks. Why? First of all, sex *is* powerful. It releases feelings that can be consuming. It links people in a bond that feels special and superior to other types of relationships. Second, as we have already seen in previous stories and statistics, sex is everywhere in the adolescent world. As I came to understand Georgia's story (and I will share more of it with you in this chapter), I was haunted by her words, "I wasn't that good in school or at sports. I tried out for cheerleader, but I didn't make it. But I was good at sex." Finally, despite all the rhetoric of the feminist movement, powerful women (and teens) are depicted in our culture as sexually active. In her comprehensive look at today's media, Jean Kilbourne writes about the messages our culture sends to today's girls about themselves and sex:

> The emphasis for girls and women is always on being desirable, not
> on experiencing desire. Girls who want to be sexually active instead
> of being the objects of male desire are given only one model to follow,
> that of exploitive male sexuality. It seems that advertisers can't conceive
> of a kind of power that isn't manipulative and exploitive.[2]

In this chapter we will consider the developmental tasks of adolescence, how they are distorted by sexual activity, and how we can help our daughters experience authentic power by accomplishing these tasks.

INTELLECT

The first developmental task of adolescence is developing intellect. As teens begin puberty, their thinking shifts from concrete thinking to abstract thinking. A teenager starts to realize that there is a world larger than home, there is a future away from Mom and Dad, and they can have their own lives apart from their parents.

The tasks of developing intellect and achieving independence overlap because shifting from concrete thinking to abstract thinking leads an adolescent to want to live outside the box of current ways of being in the world and interacting with others. Intellectual development always results in behavioral changes. These changes, in the best of worlds, lead a teen to experience healthy independence while remaining in an interdependent relationship with Mom and Dad.

Georgia's experience with this developmental task echoes that of most teenage girls. As Georgia began to develop abstract thinking, she started hearing "music" that spoke her language. Her beautifully designed brain was firing messages back and forth like crazy about who she wanted to be, how she wanted to present herself, and what new choices she wanted to make to step outside the box of her childhood. Friends, family members, and the nightly news told her that the world was a scary, confusing place, but Georgia's view of the world was broadening, and she wanted to live in a way that reflected this new perspective. As her developing intellect collided with her parents' rules, she became frustrated that she could not find a way to use her intellect to achieve greater independence.

During one session Georgia described her early adolescence as one power struggle after another with her parents. "They would let me listen only to Christian music. I couldn't watch any movies that weren't rated G or PG. My mom told me what kind of underwear I had to buy. She even told me when to take my shower. I wanted to shower at night, but she made me take a shower in the morning. And whenever she fixed food I didn't like, she made me sit at the table until I ate it. *I was fourteen years old!*"

Georgia's brain was telling her that a whole world was out there waiting for her to explore, but her parents were telling her, "Stay home. It's not safe out there. We'll tell you what to listen to, watch, wear, and eat." Georgia's brain was also telling her that she had certain preferences and could choose for herself. Her parents were telling her, "We'll choose for you. What you want is wrong."

Now, I understand Georgia's parents. Making the transition from parenting a child to parenting an adolescent is not always easy. We do know more than they do. We are aware of dangers they don't even know about. We can keep them safe. Or can we? The teenage years are an opportunity to acknowledge that we aren't in control. We have to begin to let go and let our daughters go through the mix of experiences, temptations, dangers, and choices that are part of growing up. In fact, not letting go will do far more harm than good.

A teenager who isn't allowed to make her own choices about lesser temptations, such as music, movies, and underwear, will have trouble thinking through the potential consequences of greater temptations like sex. A girl who can't express herself about distasteful foods will have trouble talking with her mom about the consequences of oral sex, her values about kissing and making out, or how she should negotiate physical limits with a boyfriend. An adolescent who can't make her own choices about when to take a shower may grab onto a choice to have sex as if her life depends on it.

Georgia told me about her first sexual encounter at fourteen years of age. "I couldn't listen to the radio or go see a PG-13 movie. My parents made me sit at the dinner table and eat fish, even though the smell of it made me want to throw up. I went to a slumber party for one of the girls in my youth group, and we snuck out to meet some boys at a park. This one boy and I started to kiss. He told me that I was a good kisser. He asked me to give him a blow job. I'd never done that before, but I'd talked about it with friends. I did it, and he said I was great!" Georgia looked me straight in the eyes, almost daring me to chastise her: "It felt great! I felt like I was finally free."

Georgia's path to promiscuity was paved with a natural longing to have something of her own—music, recreation, relationships, preferences, and routines. Unfortunately, her parents did not know that keeping Georgia powerless in many of her choices heightened the appeal of the power that comes from being sexually active.

If we want to be good parents, we must learn to read our children.
And that requires learning how to listen to our children—one
of life's most difficult, most demanding tasks.

—Dan Allender, *How Children Raise Parents*

In the Just for the Two of You section that follows, you will have the opportunity to evaluate how you are doing at letting your daughter develop a life of her own. I understand the fear that if you let go, she may make the wrong choices or move away from you completely. The opposite is actually true. If you hang on, she won't have the experience of making her own choices while under your protection and guidance, and she may go underground to develop a secret life that is completely separate from you. It's never too late to begin to let go. If your daughter is in later adolescence and you've been too controlling, ask for her forgiveness and, little by little, begin to let go. If your daughter is in early adolescence, now is the time to present her with all kinds of choices and to start talking with her about the possible consequences.

JUST FOR THE TWO OF YOU

1. Ask your daughter how much freedom she thinks she has in making choices about entertainment or recreation. If she feels that she has freedom, talk about what she's learned about herself through her various choices. If she doesn't feel free to choose, ask her what changes she'd like to see.

2. Ask your daughter how free she feels to make her own choices about clothes. If she is making her own choices, ask what she's learned about herself and her style. If she doesn't feel free to choose, ask what changes she'd like to see.

3. Ask your daughter what changes she'd like to see in any of the routines at home.

4. Discuss some possible scenarios in which she might need to make a choice about sex. For example:
   - If your boyfriend is pressuring you to move beyond kissing, what would you say?
   - If your best friend tells you that she had oral sex with her boyfriend, what would you say to her?
   - If you're at a party and everyone is making out with someone, would you pair up with someone? Why or why not?
   - If you went further sexually than you wanted to, would you be able to talk to me about it? If not, why not?

INDEPENDENCE

By the end of adolescence, your child will need to be independent. The *Oxford Desk Dictionary and Thesaurus* defines *independence* as "self-governing." Practically speaking, we tend to think that independence is when our children become emotionally, psychologically, and financially able to stand on their own two feet. Does this mean that your daughter—even at the age of twelve or thirteen—needs to start pulling away from you? Not necessarily. It does mean that she needs to pull away from the kind of relationship she had with you during childhood and hopefully move toward a different, developing relationship that encourages *interdependence* during the adolescent years.

Interdependence means depending on each other. You want your daughter to depend on you for feedback, advice, consolation, and guidance. You want to depend on your daughter to be open and honest with you, to be willing to listen, and, at times, to accept your guidelines. When Kristin and I experience conflict over values or choices, I remind myself, "This is good. She needs to develop her own reasons and learn to deal with the consequences. She needs to do this."

Interdependence means being able to hold on to yourself and still be in relationship. It is crucial to note that if your daughter does not learn to do this with you, she probably won't learn to do it in other relationships, either. Georgia explained to me that she learned from her first experience with the boy in the park that she could do something to keep boys in relationship. She poignantly offered, "I didn't always want to do it, but I kind of became the girl who did whatever boys wanted. And then when I didn't want to do it anymore, I broke up with them. I was in charge."

The contradiction in Georgia's words was obvious to me. She gave up herself in order to gain relationships, and then she felt she recovered herself when she broke away from relationships. Sadly, Georgia had learned this dynamic with her parents. If she gave up what she liked and wanted, her parents would be happy. To gain what she wanted, Georgia believed that she had to lie and disconnect from her parents completely.

When girls use sex to gain a sense of independence, freedom, and being in control, it becomes a means to an end rather than a sacred expression within a relationship. In her book *Can't Buy My Love,* Jean Kilbourne explains:

Women who are "powerful" in advertising are uncommitted. They treat men like sex objects. "If I want a man to see my bra, I take him home," says an androgynous young woman. They are elusive and distant: "She is the first woman who refused to take your phone call," says one ad. As if it were a good thing to be rude and inconsiderate.... In adolescence girls are told that they have to give up much of what they know about relationships and intimacy if they want to attract men.[3]

How good are you at facilitating a growing interdependence between you and your daughter? In the next Just for You section, you will have the opportunity to evaluate whether you are transitioning from the season of parenting when your daughter was dependent on you to a season when you are showing your daughter that she can make her own choices and still be in a close, growing relationship with you. As Debra Haffner wisely reminds parents, "It is fine for the child to walk away from the parent—you are preparing them for a life on their own. You must assure them that you won't walk away from them."[4]

JUST FOR YOU

1. When your daughter disagrees with you, do you listen, lecture, or get mad?

2. List the ways your daughter is different from you. Do you see these as good things or as threats? Think about ways you can affirm your daughter's uniqueness.

3. After an argument with your daughter, do you withdraw, give her the silent treatment, apologize, or invite her to spend time with you? Explain.

4. When your daughter makes a foolish or bad choice, do you punish her, lecture her, or talk through the choice and its consequences? Explain.

5. Do you applaud your daughter for making her own choices? If not, why not?

6. Have you ever lost yourself in a relationship? If so, why?

7. Have you been in a difficult relationship with conflicts and tension but continued to work through things? What did this teach you about yourself and relationships?

8. Do you let your daughter know that she can be different from you and still be in a good relationship with you? If so, how do you do this? If not, why not?
9. Are you threatened by your daughter's relationships? If so, why?
10. What do you depend on your daughter for? What does she depend on you for? Are these dependencies healthy? Why or why not?

IDENTITY

Adolescence is a crucial time for forming identity. Renowned developmental theorist Erik Erikson once said that the combination of physical growth, emotional maturity, and social interactions in adolescence causes a teenager to ask "Who am I?"[5] I think it's more than that. I believe that God plants within us a continuing need to ask "Who am I?" so that we might ultimately acknowledge who He is. Am I good enough? Am I accepted? Am I desirable? Am I special? Am I worth thinking about? Am I lovable? All of these questions can eventually lead us to the great "I AM," who accepts us, desires us, loves us, thinks about us, tells us that we are special in His sight and clothed in His righteousness.

But a teenager might not look to God immediately for her identity. Even most adults fall short of that. A teenage girl looks to her parents and her peers to tell her who she is. When Georgia discovered that she was "good at sex," her peers started to tell her that she was hot, a "good lay," fun, and sexy. She showed me her eleventh-grade yearbook, pointing out what many of her classmates wrote: "To a sexy girl." Georgia developed an identity influenced by her understanding of what it meant to be female in her relationship to males. When her parents told her that she was promiscuous, Georgia incorporated being "bad" into her identity.

INTEGRITY

Integrity is living in sync with your values—what is personally right for you. Identity collides with integrity during the adolescent years. When Georgia accepted her identity as a "sexy, bad" girl, she began to live with integrity. She lived in harmony with her identity. In the three counseling sessions before Georgia's late-night call to me, she told me many stories that confirmed her identity. I have learned that when teenagers confess their misadventures with a hint of pride, they are not boasting about their sinfulness. They are proud that they are being true to who they are—or to who they think they are.

Georgia told me about one relationship after another in which she called the shots. She had learned to flirt, to "reel a boy in," to have fun with him, and then to move on to the next boy. She told me, "After we have sex, a boy almost always tells me that he loves me. But I don't always say it back. It depends what I want out of the relationship."

I sensed a bit that Georgia wanted to shock me with her cavalier, callous attitude toward boys and sex. But I knew that mostly she was disclosing her perceived identity and how she was living true to who she believed she was.

So, for all the attention paid to girls in recent years, what girls are offered most by the popular culture is a superficial toughness, an "attitude," exemplified by smoking, drinking, and engaging in casual sex—all behaviors that harm themselves.

—JEAN KILBOURNE, *Can't Buy My Love*

I was praying about ways in which I might help Georgia dismantle her perceived identity and begin to see who she could be—a girl of passion, compassion, tenderness, strength, wit, and wisdom—all in the context of relationships that brought out the best in her. I wanted Georgia to know that it wasn't too late to "try on" different values and live in harmony with them. And then came the night of her boyfriend's suicide attempt.

When Georgia came in to see me after that horrible night, she was pretty shaken. "Did *I* do this to him?" she asked. "If I did, that's pretty lame. What is his problem?"

"I guess you knew that you were pretty powerful, didn't you?" I asked gently.

"I don't want *that* kind of power," Georgia replied quickly. "I just wanted to do what I wanted to do when I wanted to do it."

"But we can't escape from the reality that we impact other people," I said, and then I went out on a limb. "It's not all about you."

Georgia was quiet. I said something that she had probably heard before from her parents. I had said something that she might find offensive. But I suspected that in the context of her concerns about Daniel, she would listen to me.

Just for the Two of You

1. What do you think is your daughter's identity?
2. Ask your daughter to define her identity.
3. In what ways do your perceptions differ? Why do you think that is?
4. If your daughter were to live in harmony with your sense of her identity, how would she live? What would it look like?
5. If your daughter were living in harmony with *her* sense of her identity, how would she live? What would it look like?
6. Ask your daughter what kind of person she wants to be. In other words, what qualities and characteristics would she want to define her identity? What can you do to facilitate the development of your daughter's identity? What behaviors and traits can you identify that are in harmony with who she wants to be?
7. Ask your daughter about her values with regard to sex. Does she live in sync with these values? In what ways is she out of sync with them?
8. Ask your daughter what you can do to support her efforts to live with integrity.
9. If you disagree with her values, ask your daughter if she is open to hear why you disagree. If she's not, tell her that you are willing to talk whenever she is. If she is open, share with her some creative stories that illustrate and support your values. For example, one mom I know told her daughter how she and her boyfriend struggled to hold on to their values in their physical relationship. They decided not to do anything they wouldn't do on the front steps of her parents' house. This mother then told her daughter, "Sometimes when things started to get out of control, one of us would picture us on the front steps of my house and start laughing!"

A tear trickled down Georgia's face. "But if I don't take care of myself, no one will."

"How well do you think you're doing caring for yourself?" I asked. "Do you feel protected, honored, good about yourself?"

Georgia was quiet for several minutes. I could tell she was wrestling with something.

"It's a little late for that, don't you think?" Her words were drenched in sarcasm and sorrow.

I was quiet, praying about what direction to take with this young woman who thought she was in charge but was on the brink of acknowledging that she was completely out of control.

I handed Georgia a DVD. Yes, a movie. "Take this," I said as I handed her a copy of the popular Hollywood hit *Bruce Almighty.* "Watch it," I continued. "Ask your mom to watch it before you both come in for your next session."

Georgia sighed. "Whoa, that isn't what I expected at all," she said.

"Exactly," I replied and smiled.

INTIMACY

During adolescence, girls develop a capacity for intimacy. When sex is the starting point or the glue in a relationship, girls learn to mistake sex for intimacy. Unfortunately, for many teens sexual intercourse is seen as the only sign of a healthy relationship. Emotional intercourse and spiritual connection are not even categories for consideration. The sexualization of intimacy can have significant ramifications later in life. Girls may enter marriage on the basis of a sexual relationship without any other foundation for the marriage. They may believe that all they have to offer in a relationship has to do with sex.

The good news (yes, there is good news) in the foolish and harmful choices teenage girls make about sex is that in understanding those choices and the consequences, girls have the opportunity to really understand intimacy. I am saddened by parents who write their daughter off once she has sex or who determine to get her back into the fold without getting to the heart of what has happened to her.

That's why I wanted Georgia and her parents to watch *Bruce Almighty*. Bruce is a character whose life is not going too well. He wants a sign for what he should do next, but when he gets signs, he can't read them. During the story God shows up as a beggar, but each time He shows up, He's holding a different sign. In fact, the first sign He shows Bruce is "You are blind." The point of the sign was to show Bruce that he's using his girlfriend, Grace. He wants her body, but he's blind to her heart. Bruce is so wrapped up in himself that he is miserable.[6]

When Georgia and her mother came in for their appointment the following week, Georgia handed me the movie. "I suppose you think I'm like Bruce," she said.

"What makes you think that?" I asked, although I was glad that Georgia (like most teenagers) was not blind to the meaning of the story.

"I'm selfish and think everything is about me. Isn't that what you said?" she volleyed back to me.

I left her question hanging and said, "Actually, I wanted you and your mom to watch the movie because I think that you are both missing some important signs in your life."

"Do you mean like Daniel trying to commit suicide?" Georgia asked.

"Not exactly, although that could be a sign. I mean like your choices about sex," I said.

"What kind of sign is that?" Georgia's mom could not hide the disgust in her voice.

"I'm afraid you've thought it's a sign that Georgia is bad. And Georgia, I think you've thought it's a sign that you're desirable or in control," I paused and let them both digest my words.

"It's really a sign of your wonderful need to be loved and connected to another person and to have impact on others," I continued.

"Yeah, that's what I think," Georgia nodded, hopeful that I was taking her side.

"In *Bruce Almighty*, Bruce gets almighty and gets miserable. He has all God's power, but he doesn't have God's heart," I explained.

"Wow, you got a lot from that movie," Georgia said. "I guess you think I'm in control, but I don't have a heart. I know Daniel thinks I'm a heartbreaker."

I continued, "Remember in the movie that Bruce used his power to tap into some of Grace's prayers. They're all for him. Grace is brokenhearted for Bruce, and when he sees that, he breaks."

"I remember," Georgia sounded uncertain. "Then Bruce prayed for Grace. Remember, Mom? That's when we both started crying."

"Yes, he prayed that Grace would be happy and loved by someone the way she deserved to be loved. Why do you think you both started crying at that point in the movie?" I asked.

"I don't know," Georgia responded quickly.

"I think that's God's heart for you right now. He wants you to be loved by someone the way you deserve to be loved. He wants you to give and receive real love. That's intimacy. You both cried because deep within that's how we all want to be prayed for, cared for, and thought about."

Georgia looked at her mom. "You think it's too late for that for me, don't you, Mom?"

"Of course not," her mom replied a little too quickly.

"Right!" Georgia's cynicism returned.

"Let me just wrap this up," I said. "Bruce dies in the movie, but a transfusion of donated blood brings him back. He returns to his old life with a 'new' heart and marries Grace. Now he can read the signs. Everywhere he sees grace."

"So what exactly are you saying?" Georgia asked.

"I see grace everywhere in your life, Georgia. It's grace that you haven't gotten a sexually transmitted disease or ended up pregnant. It's grace that Daniel did not kill himself. It's grace that your parents brought you to see me. It's grace that you started crying during the movie at the thought of being really loved. But you have to die to your old life of being a sexy teenage girl who gets boys to like her and then dumps them." I quickly turned to talk to Georgia's mother.

"And you need to see Georgia as God sees her," I said to Georgia's mom.

"What do you mean?" Georgia interrupted.

"God sees you as a beautiful girl, without any sin, ready to love and to be loved," I said passionately.

Georgia and her mom stared at me in silence. "Just think about it," I said as we ended our session.

I got all of this from a silly movie? I hoped that *Bruce Almighty* would bring home a greater truth to Georgia and her mother. Mothers need to know that scary, shocking teenage behavior is a sign. We get so worried about the signs that we can't read them. When teenagers become sexually active or experiment with sex, we have to look for the meaning or we'll cave in to judgment and fear. When we read the signs and see the meaning, we know that, ultimately, our daughters' sexual identity will be answered by a Lover who sees, accepts, forgives, and invites them to an unconditional relationship. We can find gospel meaning in our daughters' outlandish or foolish behavior. We *must* find gospel meaning in it or our influence in their lives will be relegated to meaninglessness.

If you are engaged in a power struggle with your daughter or have given up because her behavior does not conform to your values, then you need to take a lesson from Bruce. True power comes when we conform ourselves to the heart of God. And the heart of God is Jesus, broken and bleeding for you. You may be brokenhearted for your daughter and bleed when she throws daggers of contempt or disregard your way. But as you entrust your daughter to God's care and remember that she is His beloved, you will begin to believe that her sexual sins and foolishness are opportunities for moments of grace—moments when God invites her to know Him more intimately. Regardless of what your daughter does, God is wondrously capable of making her His.

But, really, how do you communicate all of that to your sullen, headstrong, rebellious (not to mention hurting, confused, and afraid) daughter? Maybe you watch a silly movie. Talk a little bit about sex. And leave the rest to God. Maybe you convince your daughter to see a good Christian counselor and you leave the rest to God. (See the section titled "Finding a Counselor" at the end of this book for more information.) Maybe you ground your daughter for a month and ask her to write a paper supporting her choices, and then you leave the rest to God. Maybe you let your daughter see (and hear) your concern and sorrow, and then you leave the rest to God.

In other words, there is no right answer, no formula for leading our children to healthy intimate relationships. But there is this: we are more likely to be our daughters' allies if we are resting in an alliance with the Sign Maker. Only mothers with faith in a Sign Maker can read the signs. And here we are at the heart of the matter. Our daughters' struggles are signs not only about them but also about us. I love what author and psychologist Dan Allender writes in the preface to his book *How Children Raise Parents:* "May we all be amazed at how well God has written into the lives of our children *just what we are meant to know about him*" (emphasis added).[7]

JUST FOR THE TWO OF YOU

Watch *Bruce Almighty* together.

1. Tell your daughter what signs you see in her life. If you have condemned her behaviors rather than inviting her to relationship, apologize and ask for another chance.

2. Share with your daughter something you did that showed you your need for God.

3. Talk about the changes Bruce went through before he stopped using Grace and started caring for her.

4. Share with your daughter what you see when you look at her through God's eyes. If you have seen only her sin or mistakes, apologize and ask for another chance.

5. Talk about what Bruce thought would make him powerful. Why did being almighty get him in trouble?

6. Share with your daughter what you thought would bring you power (marriage, money, possessions, etc.) but didn't.

7. Come up with a definition of *authentic power*. Mine is "being able to give and receive love."

8. Share with your daughter about a time when you failed and then experienced God's forgiveness. Ask your daughter if she has had a similar experience.

Part III

Conquering Roadblocks
to Relationship

If you wish me to love you, you must begin by loving me. Imagine your soft white hand meets the lovely back of a porcupine. The charming animal is fully aware that the white hand will not do him any harm. He knows that he, poor wretch, is scarcely inviting enough to be made a pet of. Consider then whether you can give your heart to a porcupine. I am capable of anything. I will play a thousand silly tricks; I will make rude replies without the least provocation; I will reproach you with a defect which you do not possess; I will suspect you of an intention which you never had; I will turn my back on you; in short, I will make myself unbearable....Do then your best that you may enter my eyes, my ears, my veins, my whole being. You will, in that case, learn that nobody on earth loves more than I, because I love without being ashamed of the reason why I love. That reason is gratitude.

–GEORGE SAND, to her close friend the Countess d'Agoult,
in Michelle Lovric, *Woman to Woman: Letters to Mothers,
Sisters, Daughters and Friends*

Chapter 9

Abusive Dating Relationships

What we are actually teaching the young is an illusion of thoughtless freedom and purchasable safety, which encourages them to tamper prematurely, disrespectfully, and dangerously with a great power.... We presume to teach our young people that sex can be made "safe"—by the use, inevitably, of purchased drugs and devices. What a lie! Sex was never safe, and it is less safe now than it has ever been.

—WENDELL BERRY, *Sex, Economy, Freedom, and Community*

When I began to work with adolescent girls, I expected to hear angst over appearance, longings for friends or a boyfriend, and frustrations over curfews and homework. I did not anticipate hearing—from fifteen- and sixteen-year-old girls—about intimidation, manipulation, cruelty, isolation, and even sexual assault, all in the context of teenage dating relationships. There is no subject that shakes mothers to the core more than teen dating abuse.

We can't imagine a teenage boy pinching or twisting our daughter's arm to keep her in line.

We shudder at the thought of a boyfriend telling our daughter that she is dumb or a bitch or that no one else would ever go out with her.

We are confused when our once outgoing girl withdraws from friends and activities and engages in long, furtive, and emotional telephone calls with her boyfriend.

We wonder if our daughter's fiercely expressed contempt over her weight, her acne, or her clothes has something to do with her boyfriend.

We don't understand why anxiety and depression seem to have grown hand in hand with our daughter's developing romantic relationship.

And we don't dare entertain the thought that our daughter's boyfriend might be tearing off her pants even though she said no or might be giving her bruises in unseen places while he pressures her to have further sexual contact.

The sobering truth is that teen abuse is an epidemic. It is estimated that "every nine seconds a teenage girl is battered [physically, emotionally, or sexually] by someone with whom she is in a relationship."[1] According to the National Crime Victimization Survey, the highest rates of physical violence by an intimate partner are against women between the ages of sixteen and twenty-four. In 1999, 15.6 out of 1,000 teenage girls in this age group experienced intimate-partner violence, whereas the overall rate for women was 5.8 out of 1,000.[2] It has also been found that women who are physically abused by an intimate partner are often emotionally abused as well.[3]

Dr. Jill Murray, one of the nation's leading experts on teen dating abuse, uses the definition of dating abuse articulated by the University of Michigan Sexual Assault Prevention and Awareness Center: "The intentional use of abusive tactics and physical force in order to obtain and maintain power and control over an intimate partner."[4] For the purpose of this chapter, I want to broaden the definition of dating abuse to include the deliberate disregard of a girl's values, expressed desires, and personal well-being.

Abusive Tactics and Physical Force to Obtain and Maintain Power and Control
Specific behaviors include:
- angry outbursts that are not appropriate to the situation
- accusations that attack a girl's character
- name calling
- isolating a girl from family and friends
- violent behavior (hitting walls, throwing objects)
- dual personality (nice to others but different in private)
- abuse of alcohol or drugs
- demanding all of a girl's time and attention
- moodiness (rapidly changing moods)
- irrational jealousy or possessiveness

- lack of respect for the opinions, interests, ideas of others
- a tendency to blame others
- sexual coercion
- using sex as a measuring stick for commitment
- shaming or hurtful sexual behaviors

Deliberate Disregard of Values, Expressed Desires, and Personal Well-Being
Specific behaviors include:
- making a girl wait by the telephone
- smothering a girl and monopolizing her time
- expressing dislike or contempt for a girl's friends and family
- fostering a girl's insecurity by pointing out flaws or mistakes
- saying "I love you" to get something
- talking down about the relationship in front of peers
- continually requiring a girl to say no to sexual advances
- touching or kissing a girl even though she says no
- abusing drugs or alcohol
- showing little or no interest in a girl's activities or achievements

The statistics and the descriptions of teen dating abuse are hard to read. Even if we ourselves have been in an abusive relationship at one time or another, we find it hard to imagine that our little girls might find themselves drowning in the swirling sea of desperately destructive relationships. In this chapter we will consider how a teenage girl gets into an abusive relationship, why she stays, and what you can do to be her ally during this critical time of her life.

HOW DOES A NICE GIRL END UP IN A PLACE LIKE THIS?

The story about abusive relationships that I am going to highlight in this chapter involves a controlling relationship that eventually ended in date rape. Don't stop reading if you think this doesn't apply to you because your daughter has not been raped. The same dynamics exist in all abusive relationships—even those less dramatic ones that don't end in rape. And teenage girls must go through the same process to disentangle themselves from an abusive relationship. The dynamics that characterize all abusive relationships include:

- pressuring a girl for any type of sexual activity
- calling a girl demeaning names or constantly criticizing her
- exhibiting jealousy, possessiveness, or suspicion
- prohibiting a girl from spending time with family and friends
- abusing alcohol or drugs
- blaming a girl for going too far sexually

Now to Liz's story. Liz came to see me after she graduated from high school. She came on her own, with prompting from her mom, and she told me right from the start that she needed to talk about something.

"I think I was raped by my boyfriend," she said quietly.

When I first began hearing unthinkable disclosures like Liz's from bright, beautiful, articulate Christian girls, my mind was flooded with questions:

- What do you mean you *think* you were raped?
- How could you have let things get so out of hand?
- How could you pick such a creep for a boyfriend?
- Why haven't you called the police?
- Are you still with this jerk?
- How could your parents let you be in such a dangerous relationship?
- What did you do to end up in this situation?
- How does a smart, pretty Christian girl end up in a place like this?

Perhaps you have wanted to ask your daughter similar questions about her and her relationships. But I have since learned that smart, pretty Christian girls are not immune from losing their perspective in a romantic relationship. I also have learned that abusers sometimes come calling as nice, engaging Christian boys. And I know that *especially* smart, pretty Christian girls have a hard time acknowledging that they made a mistake (or a series of mistakes) that resulted in situations that they fear smart, caring Christian parents will never understand.

When Liz disclosed to me that she might have been date-raped, I knew that she was making a courageous step toward taking back her life, and I asked her to write out the "story" of her relationship. I have learned that adolescent girls gain much from going back and understanding the beginning and the middle of a relationship as well as the ending that brought them into counseling.

Liz came back to our next session with pages and pages of her story written in a red spiral notebook. She read to me about meeting this boy in her church youth group her junior year of high school. He was one year older and definitely the most sought-after boy in the youth group. For a year Liz flirted with him and daydreamed about the possibility of their getting together. When he graduated from high school, this boy stayed in town. He attended community college and volunteered in the youth group. When he asked Liz out on a date in the middle of her senior year, she thought, "Finally, my dreams are coming true!"

Liz told me that from the beginning things seemed great. "We could talk about anything and everything." She explained that both their emotional and physical connection was intense. "When things went too far physically," she said, "I'd pull away, and he would stop." When I asked her how often this push and pull occurred in their relationship, she said, "Almost every time we were together." Before I could say anything, she continued, "I know. I know. I should have seen something then. But to be honest with you, I was flattered by the fact that he wanted me so much."

Girls are raised in a culture that tells them love is out-of-control passion. Most teenage girls do not know that sexual desire is not the same thing as love. Smart girls end up in unthinkable places in a relationship because the teen world is more intense, dramatic, extreme, and less restrained than the rest of the world. Many adolescent girls think that an abusive dating relationship is normal. It seems to fit with the rest of the drama in their lives. They are even more prone to believe that what they are experiencing is all part of a normal, developing relationship if they are not talking to their mothers about the realities of their relationships.

Furthermore, high school is a pressure cooker for girls. They agonize over their appearance and about finding a place to belong. From their freshman year on, they are pressured to keep up with their grades and to plan ahead for college. Even the most popular, seemingly confident girls go through high school running from the ghosts of peer pressure, parental pressure, and the internal pressure to be "somebody." And then along comes a teenage boy who is funny, seems confident, and offers a place to belong. He flatters her by asking for all her time and attention. He begins to tell her who she is (even though he is as unsure and unsteady as she is), and she believes him. Even when the relationship is smothering, uncomfortable, or unsatisfying, it still seems a lot better than getting lost again in that sea of adolescence. The hook is the pleasure of security in an insecure world.

Probably no one told us what we understand as we mature: a prince doesn't just appear in your life—you create a whole person in yourself and then seek out another whole person with whom to share your life. A woman or man cannot be half a person, hook up with another half a person, and create a whole relationship.

—JILL MURRAY, *But I Love Him*

Finally, a girl may stay in an abusive relationship *because* of shameful or painful behaviors. She may feel obligated to stay in the relationship because getting out would be admitting to herself and others that she wasn't as desirable as she thought she was.

Liz told me about the night when things "got totally crazy" with her boyfriend. He told her that he was depressed about not attending a "real" college and that he didn't think he was good enough to be her boyfriend. When she tried to make him feel better, he told her that there was only one way he could "get through this."

Liz explained what happened next: "He kissed me so intensely, and we just kept kissing, and then when things went further, I didn't have the heart to stop him. He was already feeling so badly." Liz didn't know that this was the ultimate manipulation. Her boyfriend led her to believe that she could fix his unhappiness. That is an unbearable weight for a teenage girl. Before I could explain this dynamic to Liz, she told me about the "double whammy" this night had in her heart. "Because I had worked so hard to keep my virginity, once I lost it I believed I *had* to stay with this guy. I believed that I would have to marry him."

Unfortunately, Liz's story is not uncommon. She lost herself in an unhealthy relationship, and because she wasn't talking to anyone with a broader perspective, she believed that she was sentenced to a relationship that manipulated and violated her. Liz didn't end up in this relationship because she was stupid, shallow, or willing to settle for a creep. She ended up in this relationship because she was smart, had deeply felt values, and took seriously her interactions with her boyfriend. And she ended up in this relationship because she was alone in the confusing mix of hormones, manipulation, sex, and the longing for something wonderful.

JUST FOR THE TWO OF YOU

1. Talk with your daughter about abuse. It would be good to watch a movie about an abusive relationship. Talk about the movie and what you know about abuse, such as the following:
   - Abusive boyfriends are not always mean.
   - Abuse usually happens in private. Everyone else usually sees what looks like a good relationship.
   - Abuse is not an okay reaction to stress or life difficulties.
   - Abusers usually blame the other person for the abuse.
   - Alcohol and drugs often fuel abusive behavior.
   - Abusers want you to feel responsible for their well-being.

2. If you have ever been in an abusive relationship, consider telling your daughter about it and what you learned about yourself and relationships.

3. Ask your daughter if she feels like she can be honest with you about her relationships. If not, why not?

4. Talk about the differences between infatuation (that exciting, intense beginning of a relationship) and love. Tell her about your own experience with each.

5. Ask your daughter if she thinks you like her boyfriend. If not, why not?

6. Take the time to look for good qualities in her boyfriend and express them to her. She will be more likely to listen to you if she knows you respect some things about her choice of a boyfriend.

7. Be careful not to praise or like her boyfriend too much. Remember that abusive relationships sometimes continue because it is too hard for a girl to tell the truth about what is going on. You are your daughter's advocate, not her boyfriend's.

8. When your daughter has a boyfriend, this is the time to keep communication open, not start an interrogation. Tell her about your teenage romances. If you did not have teenage boyfriends, tell her what that was like for you.

9. In a good moment, ask your daughter how she would like you to talk to her about your concerns for her health. Don't criticize her boyfriend. You can't change him. Now is the time to talk about your concerns about who your daughter is in this relationship. You might say something like, "You seem to spend a lot of time reacting to your boyfriend's moods or his scheduling demands. Do you ever feel like your own emotions and your schedule aren't that important?"

10. Above everything else, let your daughter know that you will support her in—and out—of this relationship.

WHY DO THEY STAY?

Liz explained to me, with a great deal of shame, that her relationship did not end after she had sexual intercourse with her boyfriend. The relationship only intensified. She told me that as a result of enormous guilt, she finally told him that they couldn't have sex anymore. She said, "At first he seemed okay with it, but then he started saying little things about me and our physical relationship that made me feel so pressured." Most girls don't know that when they start down a path by having their first sexual experience with a boy, they may lose the ability to turn around.

I respected Liz for going to great lengths to bring her relationship back in harmony with her values. But this crisis of integrity left her anxious, restless, and guilty. Why would a girl stay in such a state? The answer to this question is complex, but the reason a girl stays in an abusive relationship is usually based in two types of conflict—unresolved internal conflict and unre-solved external conflict.

UNRESOLVED INTERNAL CONFLICT

A girl typically stays in an abusive dating relationship because she is not cer-tain it's abusive, and she's afraid of the void it will leave if she breaks up with her boyfriend. If she admits to herself that the relationship is hurtful or less than satisfying, she may fear that she'll be judged (especially by her parents) or that it means something is wrong with her. Liz told me that everyone loved her boyfriend. She feared that if she suggested that something might be wrong with him, everyone would point to her as the cause of what was wrong.

A girl may also become isolated from friends or family when she is caught up in an intense dating relationship. Consequently, no one really knows what is happening to her, and she doesn't know how to begin to talk to someone about her concerns. The Just for the Two of You sidebar on pages 181 and 182 suggests some conversation starters you might try with your daughter to help her talk about her concerns.

Some girls may want to discuss their concerns with someone but are afraid that a parent will make them break up with their boyfriend or restrict their freedoms. Girl after girl has told me that when she gets into a dating relationship, everything is secondary to maintaining the relationship. She becomes willing to let go of her interests and talents. She gives in to behav-iors that don't fit with her value system. The relationship becomes who she is, and she is afraid that if she gives up the relationship, she'll lose herself.

When Liz began to pull away from her boyfriend, she doubted herself. She feared being alone. But she didn't talk to anyone about what was going on with her or in the relationship. Her boyfriend resorted to manipulating her the way he had done before. He told her that he needed her, that he loved her, and that his life was dependent on her. Liz acknowledged that although something about his neediness felt "icky," it also felt like love.

During their last time together, he crossed her boundaries again in their physical relationship. Liz said no, but he kept going. She described to me a har-rowing hour of frantically trying to keep him from going further by kissing him. When he continued toward sexual intercourse, Liz pushed him off. He got on top of her and whispered, "It's too late. Stopping now would hurt me."

Liz was lost in the confusion of what was her responsibility and what was his. She let him finish and pushed him away again. While her boyfriend got dressed, he told her, "See, we were meant to be together."

Liz told me that she spent the rest of the night curled up in a ball, crying and wondering if this is what the rest of her life would be like. She was terrified that she had somehow made an unspoken agreement with her boyfriend to keep repeating this scenario forever.

"And then I wondered if what happened was rape. I mean I did say no, but I didn't make him stop. I am so confused," Liz said as she ended her story.

In a nationwide survey of high-school girls, approximately 9 percent reported that they had been hit, slapped, or physically hurt by their boyfriends during the past year.[5] Dr. Jill Murray, a therapist who specializes in abusive teen relationships, writes that many boys in date-rape situations say what Liz's boyfriend said—that they can't stop. Dr. Murray asks these boys, "If your mother or a priest walked into the room at that moment, would you be able to stop?"[6]

The difficulty in many date-rape situations is that the girl is responsible for some things. She is responsible for staying in the relationship. She is responsible for using drugs or alcohol. (Twenty-eight percent of teenage girls do more than they plan on doing sexually because they have been drinking alcohol or using drugs.[7]) She is responsible for putting herself in a position where she is vulnerable to unwanted sexual advances. But she is not responsible for the emotional needs of her boyfriend. She is not responsible for her boyfriend's use of alcohol or drugs. She is not responsible for a boy's unwillingness to stop.

Liz and I talked about her misplaced sense of responsibility with regard to staying in the relationship, taking care of her boyfriend, and being obligated to have sex because her boyfriend said that stopping would hurt him. We talked about the significant difference between "I can't" and "I won't." Liz did courageous work in acknowledging her responsibility in the relationship and her responsibility to get out.

"But why can't I shake this awful feeling that this is really the way relationships are supposed to be?" Liz asked.

Her heart-wrenching question opened the door for us to consider the unresolved external conflict in her life.

JUST FOR THE TWO OF YOU

1. Just because your daughter acts as if she knows all about sex, don't assume that she does. Talk with her about the physical realities during sex for both a boy and a girl. Talk through what her response might be if a boy says he can't or won't stop.

2. If possible, have your daughter's dad, older brother, or a man you both respect talk about what goes on in a boy's mind during physical contact or at the sight of a girl who is provocatively dressed. Although girls are not responsible to keep a boy's mind in the right place, they often don't understand how a boy's mind works. Talk with your daughter about why clothing matters and about what clothing is appropriate when. Discuss with your daughter the following quotation from Lauren Winner's book *Real Sex:* "There is, it seems to me, a certain power in modest dressing, an assertion that though my body is beautiful, I am more than a sex object designed for your passing entertainment. But the power of dressing is also the power of narrative. For our clothes tell stories, and it would be naive and irresponsible to think otherwise."[8]

3. Ask your daughter about the possibility of talking with her and her boyfriend together about sex. I have done this with my daughter and her boyfriends and with many of my clients and their boyfriends. Although everyone thinks it's going to be awkward and awful, these conversations have actually turned out well. There are awkward moments, but it gives you an opportunity to be your daughter's advocate and to let her boyfriend know what your expectations are. Memories of your face and your words may be pivotal for your daughter and her boyfriend during moments of decision.

4. If you suspect your daughter is in an abusive dating relationship, you can begin a conversation by saying, "I've noticed that you seemed stressed out/distracted/sad lately. Is there anything I can do to help?" Reassure your daughter that you are not going to insist, at this time, that she break up with her boyfriend.

5. Listen to your daughter talk about her relationship and reflect back what you are hearing. Don't attack or lecture. You can continue the conversation by saying things like, "When you tell me about all the pressure you feel in this relationship, I feel sad for you because I know you have a lot of other stresses in your life."

6. Affirm her feelings, tell her how her mix of emotions makes you feel, and reaffirm your compassion for her. Don't put your daughter in the position of having to defend herself or her boyfriend. If you do, she may join her boyfriend to fight against you.

7. Talk with your daughter about rape and sexual assault. Define it. Watch movies about it. Let her know that if she ever experiences any kind of sexual assault, you won't judge or punish her. You simply want to be there to offer support.

8. Find stories about powerful women—women who are faithful in difficult situations, women who channel their loneliness into spending themselves in ministry to others, women who have been brokenhearted and yet continue to pour out their love to others—and share them with your daughter. Notice when your daughter is strong and is making good decisions, and applaud her for this. For example, my daughter had a boyfriend I really liked. He was active in his faith and had a good reputation in our community. But shortly after they started dating, he became very needy and clingy and started calling my daughter many times a day to tell her that he loved her. She immediately told me that he was giving her "the creeps," and she backed off from the relationship. Even though I liked this boy, I applauded my daughter for her intuition and for following through with what her inner voice told her. Our daughters internalize what we tell them (even if they act like they shrug it off). We don't want to send the message that girls are victims of boys. We want to let them know that they can take positive action in their own lives.

UNRESOLVED EXTERNAL CONFLICT

This section may be hard for you to read if your relationships are characterized by emotional, physical, or sexual abuse. The single greatest indicator of whether a girl is vulnerable to an abusive relationship is the presence of abuse in her family. Liz explained to me that her parents fought a lot. When I asked about the conflict at home, Liz became uneasy and said, "I know everyone's parents fight. Mine yell, and sometimes my dad throws things. I just learned to go in my room and turn the music up loud."

"That must be pretty scary when your dad seems so out of control," I said to Liz, wanting to keep the conversation flowing for her to tell someone the truth about what was going on in her home.

"I guess it's scary, but that's not what I hate the most," she said fiercely.

"What's worse than your dad throwing things?" I asked.

"It's the way he doesn't respect my mom. He calls her stupid, and I heard him say that no one else would ever love her, that she was lucky to have him. Sometimes after dinner he says that all of his friends' wives cook better than my mom. Once he was yelling at her and said that she wasn't even pretty anymore, that she'd gotten fat! I ran into their bedroom and yelled at him. I said, 'Stop talking to her like that!' And you know what? He did. He just shut up. Why doesn't my mom tell him to stop?" Tears were running town Liz's face as she described the sick dynamics of her parents' relationship and her belief that she was somehow responsible for healing it.

Liz learned more from her parents than how to drown out anger or protect her mother. She learned how male-female relationships work. She learned that anger and tension are normal in relationships. She wondered why her mother couldn't stop her dad from throwing things or hurling demeaning insults. She learned that it is okay for one partner to violate another.

According to a University of Maryland study, hearing verbal aggression between parents is more traumatic to children than observing physical violence.[9] Perhaps this is because the subtleties of verbal abuse become woven into a child's heart and convince her that tension, intimidation, and the crossing of boundaries are normal in relationships. If our model of parenting is "Do as I say, not as I do," we are kidding ourselves if we think that our daughters will avoid the same traps we have in our own marriages.

Now is the time to reexamine your marriage relationship. If you answer yes to one of the questions in the following Just for You section, pray about getting marriage or individual counseling. (See the section titled "Finding a Counselor" in the back of this book.) If you are asking your daughter, "Why are you staying in this unhealthy relationship? You deserve better!" your words will fall flat if she is wondering the same thing about you.

JUST FOR YOU

The following questions can help you evaluate the dynamics in your own family:[10]

- Has your daughter witnessed you being called "stupid," "bitch," or other derogatory names in your home?
- Are males superior to females in your home? Do boys receive preferential treatment? Ask your daughter what she thinks.
- Are women the butt of jokes at home?
- Does anyone in your home use vulgar words to describe women's body parts?
- Is sexual innuendo a regular part of conversation?
- Has your spouse ever hit, pushed, slapped, grabbed, or restricted you with physical force?
- Has your spouse ever exploded in anger and left?
- Does your daughter often see you crying over difficulties in your marriage?
- Does your spouse always have the last word?
- Does your husband use the church or the Bible to justify using power and control in your relationship?
- Does your spouse "allow" or encourage you to develop your own life, or does he see your role solely as taking care of the needs of others?

Liz did a lot of hard work in counseling. She came to understand what happened in her relationship. She identified what was her responsibility and what was her boyfriend's. We talked about the legal definition of rape and the possibility of pressing charges against her boyfriend. Liz, who never disclosed the name of her boyfriend to me, decided that the trauma of pressing charges would drain too much from her. She broke away from her boyfriend completely. She took with her some pain and heartache, but she also took the greatest gift we can receive from an abusive relationship: *she learned from it.* Liz also shared with her mom about how the fighting at home impacted her. Her mother is now in counseling and confronting the unhealthy aspects of her marriage. She is becoming her daughter's hero.

Chapter 10

Addictive Teenage Relationships

My problem was that, because I entered relationships prepared to ask for so little, I found people who, for reasons having nothing to do with me, had little to give.

—STERLING THOMPSON, *Sacred Hearts*

O nce a month Marcia spends at least half of her weekend in the emergency room. There's nothing wrong with her; it's her boyfriend who is sick. Marcia has dated this boy for almost all of high school. Her boyfriend struggles with depression and medicates it with heavy drug and alcohol use. He ends up in the emergency room at least once a month from unintentional overdose or attempted suicide. Marcia and her boyfriend started having sex when she was fifteen. "I can't break up with him," she explained to me. "He needs me."

Leah spends at least two hours every night on the Internet. She admits that she is addicted to spending time on *MySpace.com*, a Web site for high-school students across the country who want to connect with other kids online. Teenagers can post their pictures and their profiles on the site, send messages to friends, or meet new people. As a joke, Leah and her friends posted some snapshots of themselves on the site that were modeled after pornography poses they had found on the Internet. They were not nude poses—at first. Leah was overwhelmed with the number of new male friends who wanted to be in an Internet relationship with her. So she started taking more risks with the camera. She admits that most of the conversations with her new friends were completely sexual in content. "I like all the attention," she told me when her parents brought her in for counseling after finding some of her pictures. "I feel grown up and powerful. These relationships are so much more real than the relationships I have with the immature boys at school."

Currently, more than 60 percent of all visits and commerce on the Internet involve a sexual purpose.

—Alvin Cooper, "Online Sexual Compulsivity: Getting Tangled in the Net," cited in Jennifer Schneider and Robert Weiss, *Cybersex Exposed*

Kayla and her boyfriend have sex every weekend. "Sometimes we do it at one of our houses or in the car. Once we got enough money to go to a motel. I don't really want to have sex so often, but my boyfriend really needs it." Kayla came to see me for counseling because her parents were concerned about her dropping grades and withdrawal from family life. "I feel like my boyfriend is more my family than my family," Kayla explained.

All three of the girls in these vignettes are in addictive relationships. Marcia and Kayla would tell you that they are in love. But they are mistaking being needed and wanted (especially for sex) for love. All three girls would tell you that they are in control when really they are exchanging their *selves*—body, soul, and spirit—for a relationship, or a pseudo-relationship. All three girls believe that their relationships or behaviors are making things better in their lives, but eventually these relationships and behaviors will make everything worse and may destroy them completely.

The Tale of the Skylark

Whenever I hear of a teenage girl who is losing herself in a sexual relationship, I think of the tale of the skylark.[1] The story is about a white skylark that flew high in the sky. One day as she flew closer to earth, she heard a merchant offer, "Worms! Worms for feathers!"

The skylark ate worms to live and felt her hunger grow when she saw the merchant's worms. These worms looked fatter and more wonderful than any worms she had seen before. She approached the merchant. "Two worms for one feather," he offered. "Only one feather for two worms!"

The skylark couldn't resist. After all, she had so many feathers. She plucked out a feather and gladly exchanged it for the fattest worms. Never before had she experienced such pleasurable eating. She ate the worms and returned to flight.

The skylark began to come to the merchant every day. The merchant always had fat, delicious worms. But one day after eating her two worms, the skylark tried to take flight and fell to the ground. She was unable to fly! She had lost all her feathers. It was then that she acknowledged to herself that for several days, almost imperceptibly, it had been getting harder and harder to fly. But she had told herself that it was worth it for the worms. She could always stop. But now she was trapped on the ground.

Each time a girl tells herself that losing herself to a boy or to an activity is worth the status of having a boyfriend, the attention from others, or the pleasurable sense of being wanted, she—almost imperceptibly—loses her freedom to choose. She reaches a point when she is trapped, feeling a sense of powerlessness not only to live in the relationship but also to live without it. Addictive relationships become increasingly difficult to change—so much so that girls find themselves doing things again and again that they don't really want to do and paying an extremely high personal price. The relationship or behaviors continue in spite of the evidence of self-destruction—sliding grades, loss of friends, withdrawal from family, and abandonment of personal goals and interests.

I love the story of the skylark because it poignantly reminds us that we are not meant to spend our lives exchanging ourselves for momentary pleasure and gratification. We are meant to fly.

In this chapter we will define addictive teenage relationships, decode what they reveal about the girls involved in these relationships, and discover how you can become your daughter's ally in helping her recover from an addictive relationship or behavior.

Unlike the skylark, who cannot reattach her feathers, teenage girls can recover from addictive relationships and behaviors and emerge wiser and more certain about who God created them to be.

CHARACTERISTICS OF ADDICTIVE RELATIONSHIPS

Teenage addictive relationships or behaviors have four characteristics:
1. They are habitual.
2. They are compulsive.
3. They are secretive.
4. They are isolating.

An adolescent girl seldom leaps into an addictive relationship or behavior. Instead, she makes choices that she initially believes are filling her up with love, attention, power, and pleasure, but in reality she is gradually exchanging her self for the relationships or behavior.

-----

*Affairs of the heart take root when we discover a relationship
that initially promises to be safe, satisfying, predictable, and
within our control. Affairs of the heart grow as we relinquish
not only our longings but also our will to these negative
relationships. We become willing to sacrifice time, judgment,
healthy relationships, even our spiritual life to the overtly destructive
or subtly deadening relationship substitute. Affairs of the heart
flourish as we surrender our God-given desires to people,
behaviors, or things that eventually rule our lives.*

—SHARON HERSH, *Bravehearts*

UNHEALTHY HABITS

Addictive relationships develop when repeated behavior becomes associated with certain "benefits" that it delivers. When Marcia began to associate feeling needed and important—even crucial—with her boyfriend's sick cries for help, she was hooked. She exchanged her God-created hunger for love and authentic power for a sick dependency. She believed that she couldn't leave her boyfriend because he couldn't live without her. When we talked about the beginning of their codependent relationship, Marcia explained that it was really cemented for her after she and her boyfriend had sex. "I just knew that no one was as special to him as I was," she said. "I feel like I'm keeping him alive."

With each trip to the emergency room and each sexual encounter, Marcia became more enmeshed in the relationship. She actually craved the sense of being needed and wanted. She depended on her boyfriend (and his sickness) to feel good about herself. The unhealthy mix of depression, neediness, and sexual intimacy provided Marcia with the powerful benefit of being needed, special, and intimately connected to her boyfriend. She only had to give up her time, interests, freedom, and autonomy. She became more committed to not losing her boyfriend than she was to gaining anything else.

JUST FOR THE TWO OF YOU

The following questions will help you and/or your daughter evaluate any unhealthy habits and determine whether you might be in an addictive relationship.

1. Are there repeated patterns in your relationships and/or activities that take all your time and energy?
2. Have you given up other interests, relationships, or activities for this relationship or behavior?
3. Have friends or family members complained that they don't ever get to spend time with you anymore?
4. Have friends or family members suggested that you are being manipulated?
5. Could you be mistaking sex and intensity for love?
6. Do you have sex with your boyfriend even though you don't want to?
7. Have you missed important family functions or personal activities because of this relationship or behavior?
8. In a typical week, how much time, planning, energy, and worry do you spend on this relationship or activity?

COMPULSIVE BEHAVIOR

Compulsive behavior is fueled by feeling that we have no choice. Kayla revealed the compulsive nature of her relationship with her boyfriend when she said that she didn't want to have sex so often, but she did it anyway. The powerful combination of pleasure and passion made Kayla willing to exchange her true wishes and values for the relationship.

Of all the biological drives, the sexual drive is linked most strongly to pleasure. For Kayla, repeated sexual activity and the resulting expressions of love and commitment from her boyfriend convinced her that without the sexual activity, all pleasure—including the verbal expressions of love and commitment—would be drained from the relationship. Although Kayla could say no, the experience of pleasure and of feelings she thought were love became powerful, behavior-controlling incentives to continue in an un-

JUST FOR THE TWO OF YOU

The following questions will help you and/or your daughter evaluate any compulsive behavior and determine whether you might be in an addictive relationship:

1. Do you sometimes feel uneasy in your relationship or behavior and yet feel desperate at the thought of being out of the relationship or stopping the behavior?
2. Do you fear that your relationship would end or wither away without the sexual behavior?
3. Have you ever promised yourself or others that you would leave the relationship or behavior but have been unable to do so?
4. Do you repeat painful behaviors even though you've promised yourself you wouldn't?
5. Is your whole identity wrapped up in this relationship or activity?
6. Do you feel terrified of being alone?
7. Do you have to do things that you don't want to do in order to keep the relationship?
8. Do you have to have sex to keep the relationship?
9. Do you break off the relationship only to go back to it?
10. Have family members or friends ever told you that this relationship is not good for you?

healthy relationship. Kayla concluded that she would rather say no to the part of herself that didn't want to have sex than lose the rewards associated with the relationship.

Addiction occurs when we regularly "ingest" an activity that closely mimics those things we were made for. Kayla didn't only believe that her boyfriend needed her (as long as she fulfilled his needs), she also feared that without him she would be unloved and unnecessary.

KEEPING SECRETS

Addictive relationships always require that we keep secrets. Somewhere deep inside, a girl may be aware that she is involved in a scary or unhealthy relationship or behavior, but she believes that no one else will understand, so she has to keep it—or things about it—secret. On one hand, she fears that if she acknowledges what is really going on, she'll have to give up the relationship. On the other hand, she wants to hold on to the relationship or behavior because of the rewards it delivers. She lives, increasingly, in a private world alienated from her own true desires and from other people because she can't divulge her secrets.

Constantly…chasing those who are emotionally unavailable leaves the romance addict again longing for another intense "love" experience. Maybe next time, the "right one" will come along.

—JENNIFER SCHNEIDER AND ROBERT WEISS, *Cybersex Exposed*

Leah didn't even talk to her girlfriends about the increasingly scandalous pictures she had posted on the Internet. She never shared the messages she sent and received from the *MySpace.com* Web site. She was ashamed of some of the things she had written and that boys had written to her, but she also secretly cherished them. She fantasized about boys who wanted her and would fall in love with her. She was willing to exchange herself for fantasy in her relationships. Being on *MySpace.com* became the highlight of Leah's day. She spent school hours obsessing about the boys she communicated with. She gave up time with family and friends to be on the computer. She lived increasingly in her own world. When her parents found her pictures and forbid Leah to be on the computer, she sank into a deep depression and told me that she didn't have a reason to live anymore.

JUST FOR THE TWO OF YOU

The following questions will help you and/or your daughter evaluate any secretive behavior and determine whether you are in an addictive relationship.

1. Is this relationship or activity your primary source of companionship?
2. Do you use this relationship or behavior exclusively for comfort, excitement, escape, approval, and self-esteem?
3. How much time do you spend thinking about this relationship or activity?
4. Do you feel that you have to hide your relationship or behavior from others? If so, why?
5. If the Internet is a major component in this relationship, do you think your e-mail or chat-room messages are private and that no one else can read them? If so, what leads you to believe this?
6. Do you feel that family and friends don't understand your relationship or behavior? If so, why?
7. Do you fantasize about this relationship going further?
8. If you have an Internet relationship, how much of your online communication is sexual in nature?
9. Does this relationship or behavior take place in private? If so, why?

CHOOSING TO ISOLATE

Addictive relationships gradually isolate us from friends, family members, and outside interests and activities. And because an addictive relationship requires a tremendous amount of energy, time, thought, and planning, there is little energy or time left for anything else. All three girls introduced in this chapter experienced declining grades, withdrawal from other interests and activities, and isolation from family and friends. They all reached a point where, if forced to choose between the relationship or behavior and anything else, they would have chosen the relationship or behavior.

Obsession is on the other side of passion.... But if we cross the codependency line, we find ourselves being only who other people want us to be and forgetting who we are.

—MELODY BEATTIE, *Playing It by Heart*

I tell girls that addictive relationships become like painting with only one color. Girls become willing to exchange all the colors in their lives for that one color. Their lives shrink, their self-image becomes dependent on the relationship or behavior, and their future becomes unimaginable without it.

JUST FOR THE TWO OF YOU

The following questions will help you and/or your daughter evaluate any isolating behavior and determine whether you are in an addictive relationship.

1. Have you lost a lot of close relationships since you've been involved in this relationship or activity?

2. How often do you feel that you have to choose between this relationship or behavior and other relationships or activities?

3. If you choose other relationships, do you fear that you will lose this relationship?

4. Have family and friends complained that they don't see you anymore?

5. Have you lost interest in hobbies or goals since you began this relationship or activity?

6. Do you feel that your future is dependent on this relationship or activity? If so, why?

7. When you are not with this person or involved in this activity, do you still spend most of your time thinking about the relationship or activity?

8. Have your grades at school or your job performance declined since you began the relationship or activity?

DECODING ADDICTIVE RELATIONSHIPS

If you have ever observed your daughter's relationships and sighed, "How did such a smart, beautiful, and even spiritual girl get into a mess like this?" you need to understand the complexity of addictive relationships. Addictive relationships arise from our attempts to satisfy our God-given desires while relieving the distress of disappointment, loneliness, and powerlessness that are inevitable in life.

Marcia grew up in a home filled with uncertainty and loneliness. Her father was an alcoholic, and Marcia lived with a growing awareness that she could not make him stop drinking. She faced the painful reality that her father often wanted alcohol more than he wanted a relationship with her. She longed to be wanted and to be able to make an impact—both God-given hungers. In her relationship with her boyfriend, she believed that she found what she was longing for. He told her that he wanted her and needed her to make his life okay. Initially Marcia believed that her boyfriend was not only satisfying her hunger for relationship, but that he was also relieving the distress from her family life. Eventually Marcia realized that pain and disappointment were part of this relationship, too, but she felt compelled to overlook those realities to keep from feeling completely powerless and unloved. She didn't realize it, but she was compounding the impact of her father's sins by choosing a sick, manipulative boyfriend.

As we discussed earlier, Leah was involved in secretive activities on the Internet. But she had another secret. When she was eight years old, she was sexually abused by an older boy in her neighborhood. Leah tried to tell her mother what happened, but her mom shooed her away and told Leah to just stay away from the older kids. Leah felt conflicted about her shameful experiences with the neighbor boy. She knew that what he had done to her was bad, but she liked the good feelings of attention and praise that she had experienced, especially from an older boy. So later, when she discovered that she got attention and praise on the Internet from doing something sexually bad, she began to believe that this combination was necessary to get what she really wanted. Leah decided that it was worth being bad to feel good.

Kayla's parents were divorced. She didn't have a relationship with her dad. Her more introverted personality made her feel as if she didn't really belong to any group at school or church. When she started dating her boyfriend, she thought that all the feelings of belonging and being loved that she was experiencing were too good to be true. These feelings flooded her mind and heart after she and her boyfriend had sex. She believed almost immediately that sex was the hook to keep the feelings of love and belonging flowing. She was scared to death that if she stopped having sex with her boyfriend, she would return to that awful state of emptiness and loneliness.

JUST FOR YOU

Finish these sentences:

When life is unsettling, I cling to _____.

When I am upset, I crave _____.

When I am overwhelmed, I grasp for _____.

When I am alone, I hold on to _____.

When I am angry, I want _____.

When I celebrate, I _____.

When I am disappointed, I try to _____.

When I feel unloved, I seek _____.

When I want to feel that I belong, I _____.

When I need comfort, I soothe myself by _____.

1. What do your responses to these statements reveal about any addictive relationships or behaviors in your life?

2. What insights do your responses give you into your daughter's choices?

3. List the painful family realities that might make your daughter seek relief outside your family.

4. Think about your daughter's social realities: Did she try out for a team but not make it? Has she ever had a boyfriend? Does she have siblings who make friends more easily? How might these realities make her more vulnerable for developing an addictive relationship?

5. Has your daughter experienced trauma or abuse? How might these experiences affect her relationship choices?

Girls who stay in addictive relationships or behaviors are really trapped. They've been given a taste of what they were made for, but then they discover that they have to give up themselves in order to keep getting a taste. They fear that if they give up the relationship or activity, they will starve. This combination of fleeting satisfaction and desperation to not feel relationship hunger keeps them coming back for more—exchanging all their feathers for a few worms that only temporarily sate their hunger.

In *Stumbling Toward Faith*, Renee Altson describes this tragedy poignantly:

> I spent my life trying to fill that vacuum. I was the perfect example
> of everything the point was meant to illustrate—busyness, sex, rela-
> tionships, addictions—I dumped it all in and waited to feel whole.
> Wholeness never came. I was weak with the longing, the desperateness
> of being unfulfilled. I felt as if the hole would devour me from the
> inside, that it would swallow my very self.[2]

LIVING IN RECOVERY

As is so often the case with adolescents, the solution is found in the problem. Helping our daughters recover from addictive relationships requires acknowledging and affirming their God-given desires and helping them learn to live in the midst of disappointment, hurt, joy, satisfaction, and dissatisfaction. The process is complicated and unique to each girl. However, four actions are necessary in the recovery process for every girl who is in an addictive relationship:

1. S—separating from the relationship or activity
2. A—acknowledging and affirming core needs
3. F—finding a focus that is life giving
4. E—exercising vigilance to continue evaluating relationship choices

Mothers can become their daughters' allies in keeping them SAFE from addictive relationships by joining them in these four actions.

Much additional work needs to be done in recovery, including the work of admitting the realities of addiction, acknowledging how we've harmed ourselves and others, and seeking forgiveness and strength from God. The focus of this chapter is not on those specific aspects of recovery but on forging an alliance with your daughter that will enable her to do the work of recovery. (See the resources section in the back of the book for additional resources on recovering from addictive relationships and behaviors.)

SEPARATING FROM THE ADDICTIVE RELATIONSHIP OR ACTIVITY

Just as an alcoholic cannot experience recovery without abstaining from all alcohol, a girl who is trapped in an addictive relationship or activity needs to completely separate herself from the relationship or activity. She must come to a point of surrender, acknowledging that the relationship and the problems it is creating in her life are too big for her to handle.

If your daughter is unable or unwilling to separate herself from a relationship or activity because the sense that she is in control is deeply ingrained, it may be necessary for you to initiate the separation. However, if addiction has a stronghold in your own life, you will be ineffective in helping your daughter separate from addictive relationships and activities. Before trying to help your daughter, you need to evaluate whether you are in an addictive relationship with a person, substance, or activity. If you are, get help to begin your own recovery first. Your daughter will have a better chance at believing that her own life is worth saving if she sees you working hard to save your own. (See the resources section at the back of this book for resources on addictive or abusive relationships.)

I worked with Marcia, Leah, Kayla, and their parents for many months. All three girls needed to separate physically from their relationships or activities before they could recognize and acknowledge the destructiveness of these relationships and behaviors. Kayla's parents asked her to take a break from her relationship. She refused, and her behavior quickly escalated. She would leave home for several days to stay with her boyfriend, without telling her parents where she was. Because Kayla was only sixteen and her boyfriend was nineteen, her parents feared that Kayla might leave home permanently. So they made the agonizing decision to send Kayla to an inpatient treatment program for those who struggle with relationship addictions. Kayla spent two months in treatment, and it took the entire first month for her to surrender to the truth that she was exchanging her self for a destructive relationship.

Later in the chapter I will tell you more about Marcia's and Leah's struggles to separate.

ACKNOWLEDGING AND AFFIRMING CORE NEEDS

As you begin to confront your daughter with her choices and the consequences, she will experience shame and contempt. Beware. The contempt she is feeling might be unleashed at you. You and your daughter may need professional help to sort through all the blame and intense emotions. (For more information, see the section titled "Finding a Counselor" at the end of this book.)

Following are three principles for acknowledging and affirming your daughter's core needs. She will be more open to saving her life if she has some reason to believe it's a life worth saving. First, we will look at what it means to become a "detective for dignity." Then we'll explore how your own story can help your daughter uncover her story. And, finally, we'll discover how your daughter's story as well as your own story can lead to the larger story of the Lover of our souls, who never abuses, abandons, or fails us.

1. Become a detective for dignity. Remember that at the root of your daughter's relationship or behavior addiction is a longing to give and receive love. God created us with a desire to love and be loved. We humans are experts at "looking for love in all the wrong places." Your job is to look for your daughter's holy longing. In my book *Bravehearts,* I write that this longing whispers, "Ask me, notice me, hear me, know me, understand me, believe me, enjoy me, stay with me, care for me…and receive all of these from me as well."[3]

Kayla's mom did a lot of work to learn about sexual abuse and its effects on children. She acknowledged that she had not been there for her daughter and had left her to deal with her hurts and longings all on her own. To show Kayla that she was making the effort to change first, she made Kayla a wonderful gift: a scrapbook of Kayla's life. Kayla's mom included a picture in the scrapbook of Kayla swinging, shouting out, "Watch me!" She also included a caption next to a picture of Kayla handing out Christmas presents at a local charity: "You have always had so much love to give." The scrapbook reminded Kayla (and her mom) of who Kayla is—a girl full of passion to love and be loved. Kayla's mom decided to look through the eyes of love for Kayla's gifts, talents, and even eccentricities, believing the scripture that says:

> Don't allow love to turn into lust, setting off a downhill slide into sexual promiscuity, [and] filthy practices.... You groped your way through that murk once, but no longer. You're out in the open now. The bright light of Christ makes your way plain.... It's a scandal when people waste their lives on things they must do in the darkness where no one will see. Rip the covers off those frauds and see how attractive they look in the light of Christ.[4]

2. Make your story available for the sake of your daughter. Now is the time to share with your daughter your own experiences of looking for love in the wrong places and what these experiences taught you about yourself and relationships. This is the time for transparency. Your daughter will be more open to forming an alliance with you if she knows that you understand the mix of need, disappointment, satisfaction, and joy that comes in relationships. She will look to you for hope as you share wisdom from your story that is rooted in your growing knowledge of God and His heart for you. Your daughter will be relieved to discover that she is connected to you not just by flesh and blood but by sweat and tears and the holy longing to love and be loved.

3. Let your daughter's story and your story lead you to the Greatest Story ever told. As you share your story and enter into your daughter's story, you are in the best position to lead her to the only unfailing Lover of her soul—Jesus. What a journey the two of you can share in acknowledging and affirming your hearts' longings, grieving over the painful realities of relationships, and resting in the One who never fails to love us. In fact, our holy longing to love and be loved is only a reflection of His longing that whispers, "Ask me, notice me, listen to me, enjoy me, think about me, love me, stay with me, and receive all of these from me as well."

One of my favorite books is *Telling Secrets* by Frederick Buechner. He writes of his own relationship addictions and how he began to recover (in part, after learning of his daughter's addiction):

It is important to tell at least from time to time the secret of who we truly and fully are—even if we tell it only to ourselves—because otherwise we run the risk of losing track of who we truly and fully are and little by little come to accept instead the highly edited version which we put forth in the hope that the world will find it more acceptable than the real thing. It is important to tell our secrets too because it makes it easier that way to see where we have been in our lives and where we are going. It also makes it easier for other people to tell us a secret or two of their own, and exchanges like that have a lot to do with what being a family is all about. Finally, I suspect that it is by entering that deep place inside us where our secrets are kept that we come perhaps closer than we do anywhere else to the One who, whether we realize it or not, is of all our secrets the most telling and the most precious we have to tell.[5]

FINDING A FOCUS THAT IS LIFE GIVING

Needing to replace an unhealthy habit with something healthy may be a purely behavioral tenet of addiction recovery, but it is a good practice. When our daughters have begun to define themselves by their addictive relationships, they will feel stripped and at a loss when that relationship is no longer a part of their lives. They may feel angry or resistant to moving forward. It is our job as mothers to help them find a focus that is life giving.

Marcia's mom took note of Marcia's longing to be important in people's lives and to care for them. Her mom took an enormous leap of faith and volunteered herself and her daughter to participate in a mission to the tsunami-ravaged country of Indonesia, where they worked for three months with children who had been orphaned by the disaster. (Marcia's mom is a dentist and was able to go to Indonesia with a health-care organization.) Marcia was resistant to leaving her boyfriend, but she was also intrigued by her mom's "extreme" plan. Her mom even made arrangements with Marcia's school to give her credit for the time they were gone. It didn't take long for Marcia's focus to shift. In a short e-mail, her mom gave me a few details about their mission and ended with these words: "I have my daughter back, but more important, she is finding herself again!"

Leah's parents took the courageous move of removing the computer from their home so that Leah could not access the Internet. They took this drastic step because they recognized that separating Leah from this activity was essential to her recovery. And they determined that if they needed to access a computer, they could do so at work or at a library. Leah's mom told me that at one time Leah had loved art. So Leah's parents decided to change the computer room into an art room and replace the computer with paints and other art supplies. When Leah came home, her mom calmly walked her into their former computer room. As soon as Leah discovered that the computer was gone, she was furious. Leah's mom told her angry daughter that she could paint or decorate every inch of the computer room however she wanted to. At first Leah sulked in her bedroom. Then after several days she began to paint angry messages on the walls in the art room. But eventually she began to create a work of art in the room that reflected her grief, confusion, acceptance, and hope for something more.

Helping your daughter find a life-giving focus will gradually—sometimes imperceptibly—give her hope that there's something worth saving her life *for*. She may even remember that she was meant to fly!

EXERCISING VIGILANCE TO CONTINUE EVALUATING
RELATIONSHIP CHOICES

Once a girl has been involved in an addictive relationship or behavior, she is vulnerable to falling back into an addiction, even after recovery. Addiction literally carves a permanent pathway in the brain. While we are immersed in an addiction, we continue to carve deeper ruts in the path. In recovery, the path becomes less deeply rutted, but it remains, leaving us vulnerable to addiction.

Your daughter may express resentment that she has to continually be aware of her vulnerability to an addictive relationship or behavior, and she might become angry with you when you question her choices. It is important for both of you to acknowledge that part of recovery is surrendering to a *life* of recovery.

I am a recovering alcoholic. In my early days of recovery, I wondered why anyone would participate in Alcoholics Anonymous and continue to remind themselves of their shameful and destructive past choices. Since then, I have learned that just as addiction carves a path in the brain, recovery carves a path as well. Every time I acknowledge my addiction and my need for vigilance, I am carving a path of life. I am also acknowledging that I need others in my life and, most of all, that I need God. My weakness makes me depend on His strength. My limitations make room for His power. My emptiness reminds me that I need Him to fill me with His love and acceptance. The apostle Paul expressed his own vigilance this way:

> Three times I pleaded with the Lord to take it [his thorn in the flesh] away from me. But he said to me, "My grace is sufficient for you, for my power is made perfect in weakness." Therefore I will boast all the more gladly about my weaknesses, so that Christ's power may rest on me.[6]

INTO THE LIGHT

This chapter has really been a crash course on addictive relationships. I hope it gave you some idea of where addictive relationships and behaviors come from, how to recognize them, and how you can form an alliance with your daughter to help her recover from them. If you need additional information, counsel, or resources, you can find helpful information in the back of this book. Let me end this chapter by encouraging you that what first looks like a dark and scary place can become a place of light and love as you determine to parent with both eyes open, with a heart ferociously committed to your daughter, and with a deep dependence on God and His abiding love for you and your daughter. Consider the hopeful words of a song titled "Into the Light," part of a wonderful project about conquering sexual addiction:

> The walls are crashing down
> My illusion has been shattered
> Those thoughts that held me captive in my skin
> I've let the secrets out
> I've felt the demons scatter
> Maybe now the healing can begin

Into the light
Into the place where nothing's hidden
Into the light
Into the hope that I'm forgiven
Climbing from the shadows toward the way
That leads to life
Out of the shame
Out of the chains
Into the light

There's going to be a cost
Habits that need breaking
I know the path I'm on will change my life
Oh God, I need you so much
Without you I won't make it
Lord, take the veil of darkness from my eyes

The unrelenting guilt that I've belonged to
Is finally letting go from deep within
Through the brokenness and tears
I've found it's love I've feared
Yet love can take my heart from where it's been[7]

Questions Regarding Sexual Orientation

But even if we can locate the common denominator in some consistent incli-
nation toward sexual relations with people of the same sex, we are talking
about a mystery.... We are talking about images of God.

—LEWIS SMEDES, *Sex for Christians*

My doorbell rang, signifying the arrival of a new client. I opened the door to an older adolescent girl and her mother. I knew from an earlier telephone call that Debbie was seventeen. Her mother appeared to be guiding her into the room. At first I wondered if Debbie was disabled—perhaps visually impaired. She didn't look at me when I greeted her and her mother. She didn't say anything. I escorted Debbie and her mom into my office, and they took a seat on my couch. I gave my usual introductory remarks, and Debbie continued to look away from me.

"Debbie thinks she's gay." Her mom spoke the words quickly, as if she needed to get them out before she lost them. Tears began to course down Debbie's mom's face. "We don't know what to say or do. Debbie is so depressed. She won't talk. She just sits in her room. We're so worried about her. We just want her to be happy."

I looked at Debbie, understanding more fully her withdrawn demeanor. I tried to ask a few surface questions: "Where do you go to school?" "What year are you in at school?"

Debbie was quiet, so her mom filled in the answers. I talked with Debbie's mom for a few minutes and then turned to Debbie again, "Do you have any questions for me?"

"No," Debbie mumbled.

I was feeling a bit stuck. I wanted to hear from Debbie, but I could not seem to find the key to unlock her fiercely protected world. Most clients I see are initially guarded, but Debbie was shut down.

"What about hell?" Debbie surprised me by suddenly blurting out the question.

"I'm not sure what you're asking?" I said gently, wanting to keep the conversation going.

"The last counselor I went to told me I was going to hell if I was gay and that everyone in the church would hate me." Debbie looked me straight in the eyes for several seconds and then asked one parting question before she withdrew again into her private world, "Do you think gay people are going to hell?"

I started to cry. Tears flowed down my face as I looked at Debbie, hoping that she would look at me again. Finally, almost imperceptibly, she quickly glanced into my eyes. My tears were the best answer I had to Debbie's heartbreaking question.

Debbie's question told me she was hurting, confused, and afraid. The words Debbie's mom spoke also told me she was hurting, confused, and afraid. I knew that Debbie was a deeply wounded girl, but she was not the one who was blind—her previous counselor was. I prayed that God would give me wisdom for this mother and daughter and that He would allow me the privilege of ministering His love to two hurting people.

Perhaps no other issue today mobilizes and immobilizes the Christian community like homosexuality. God has called me not to speak to the issue of homosexuality but to minister to people—image bearers—in the midst of their real lives and real struggles. This chapter will not focus on making a case for or against homosexuality. There are more than enough books on the subject. Instead, this chapter will focus on helping you become your daughter's ally when she asks questions about her sexual identity or has experiences that challenge her identity.

Of one thing I am certain: what we long for most regarding our daughters' sexual identity is an attainment of the heart that will lead them to live lives of love for God, others, and themselves. This heart change does not come through law, rules, condemnation, or attempts to control. Our daughters (and we mothers) need something more powerful. We need the love of God as demonstrated at the Cross. I am called not to issues or debates about laws but to Jesus Christ, the crucified One. The apostle Paul put it his way:

> So spacious is he, so roomy, that everything of God finds its proper place in him without crowding. Not only that, but all the broken and dislocated pieces of the universe—people and things, animals and atoms—get properly fixed and fit together in vibrant harmonies, all because of his death, his blood that poured down from the Cross.[1]

If your daughter is questioning her sexual orientation, I know that you are like Debbie's mom—hurting, confused, and afraid. Actually, Debbie's mom was unusual because she was not trying to control her daughter or to find an ally in condemning her. If you respond to your daughter's questions and behaviors with condemnation or disgust, you put her in a box. She will, in turn, respond to you with anger and defensiveness, putting you in a box. You will be walled off from each other at a time when your daughter is most in need of an ally.

WHAT DOES IT MEAN TO BE YOUR DAUGHTER'S ALLY IN THE MIDST OF QUESTIONS ABOUT SEXUAL ORIENTATION?

It is easy to be your daughter's ally when all is well. When your daughter is well liked, outgoing, doing well in school, and an active participant in her faith, it is easy to come alongside her and cheer her on her way. But what if your daughter is withdrawn, depressed, and engaging in behaviors that provoke anger and fear in others? *That's the time she really needs an ally.* If you withdraw, she may form unhealthy alliances or aimlessly wander alone. This chapter will give you some insight and ideas that can help you form an alliance with your daughter as she grapples with her sexual identity. You will have an opportunity to look honestly at your family dynamics and examine how they may have contributed to your daughter's struggle and how you can use them to form a life-giving alliance with her. We will also look into the world of female friendships and consider how it has impacted your daughter.

Finally, we will examine how you can form an alliance with your daughter in the midst of her questions and struggles about sexual orientation.

The goal of this alliance is not to control your daughter so that she will be who you want or need her to be. Instead, your goal is to love your daughter in a way that gives her a taste of God's love and sends her into His arms. And then you must leave the rest up to Him. Let the following principles guide you in demonstrating love to your daughter:

- Do nothing because you are offended.
- Do everything because you yourself have offended the God of glory, and He has forgiven you so that you might live in forgiveness toward others.
- Do nothing out of fear.
- Do everything by faith.
- Do nothing from hatred, anger, or disgust.
- Do everything from love. ("Not that we loved God, but that he loved us and sent his Son as an atoning sacrifice for our sins."[2])

How can we live in such a Christlike way toward our dear daughters? By doing nothing in our own strength and doing everything by the Spirit of God.

Do you think I am oversimplifying things here and ignoring all of the scary choices your daughter is making and their consequences? Although it's true that I am simplifying things, I am by no means saying that addressing the issue of sexual orientation is simple. If you depend on the Holy Spirit to lead you in loving your daughter, you *will* be the mother God intends you to be. Will your daughter conform to your agenda and consequently be safe from all the dangers that lurk around her? Perhaps, but that's God's job. And maybe you'll discover that He really can be trusted. Just ask Debbie's mom.

JUST FOR YOU

Now would be a good time for you to be honest about your feelings toward your struggling daughter. Denying or trying to hold these feelings in will only paralyze you from becoming her ally.

1. What offends you about your daughter's behavior or her questions about her sexual orientation?

2. What are you afraid of for her? for yourself?

3. What disgusts you about your daughter's questions or behavior?

4. What confuses you?

5. Take a few minutes to fully process the answers to these questions. Offer all your feelings to God, asking for His healing and leading. Meditate on Ephesians 5:8, 10: "You groped your way through that murk once, but no longer. You're out in the open now. The bright light of Christ makes your way plain. So no more stumbling around.... Figure out what will please Christ, and then do it."

6. Recall all of the positive things you know about your daughter—her character qualities, personality traits, gifts, and abilities. Ask God to keep these at the forefront of your heart and mind as you work to form an alliance with her.

FAMILY DYNAMICS

Thankfully, Debbie and her mom's story did not end that day in my office. Debbie decided to come back and give me a chance to be her counselor. I still marvel at Debbie's courage and willingness to try again. Although she remained tough and withdrawn for a few more sessions, I knew that Debbie had a tender and resilient heart, mostly because she offered grace to me in spite of how the counseling profession had already wounded her.

When Debbie began to open up to me, I asked her about her family. She told me that her mom was "way involved" and would "do anything for me." I could hear a "but" in her voice, but I wasn't sure how to ask about it. When I asked Debbie about her dad, she visibly shuddered. I asked about her visceral response to my question about her father. "I don't know. I just don't like him," she said. Debbie spoke with a finality that I knew had shut the door on that conversation. So I decided to ask Debbie's mom to come in alone.

I described Debbie's comments about her father to her mom and asked if she knew what was behind Debbie's response. Debbie's mom thought about my question for a long time and finally answered. "We've had some hard times in our marriage. My husband has had two affairs during our twenty-year marriage. I thought I did a good job of keeping this from the children, but I'm sure they know something is going on. There is a lot of tension between us, and...well...sometimes my husband can be a difficult man."

"What do you mean?" I asked.

"Debbie told me once that she thinks he is mean to me. I don't know if he's mean—he's just opinionated and likes to argue his point of view. He and Debbie get into some pretty heated arguments." I noticed that Debbie's mom had pulled into herself and was becoming visibly smaller.

"Is he abusive toward Debbie?" I asked.

Debbie's mom thought again for a few minutes. "No, not really. I almost think he enjoys their conversations. I think Debbie might be his favorite. Our other daughter keeps more to herself."

Just for You

1. Is your daughter's father sexually abusive or engaged in sexual immorality?
2. Is his behavior inappropriate or does he demean women?
3. Is pornography used in your home?
4. Do your daughter and her dad engage in a lot of verbal conflicts?
5. If your daughter has a male sibling, is he treated differently than his sister? If so, who gives him preferential treatment? (If a boy is treated preferentially by either parent, it perpetuates a girl's confusion about her feelings toward the opposite sex and the desirability of her own gender.)
6. Have you confronted your husband's inappropriate sexual behavior? If not, why?
7. Have you allowed him to disrespect you in front of your daughter?
8. Do you leave your daughter to fight it out with her dad?
9. Does she see you model healthy ways to engage in conflict?

    I realize that answering these questions can be difficult and may leave you feeling guilty. But guilt can be a blessing by revealing the places where we need to change. I hope and pray that you don't stay trapped in the quicksand of guilt but allow it to lead you toward change.

Debbie's mom described the type of home where girls often grow into a conflicted state with regard to their own sexuality. In some ways, Debbie's father was a predator. He was demeaning of his wife and preyed upon other women. Although it was never talked about, there was an air of immorality in the home. Debbie responded with an appropriate shudder to what she sensed of her father's dangerous sexuality, based in his need for power. Although she engaged with her father intellectually when he was in the mood for a debate, she shuddered at the thought of his dark sexual "scent" and his abuse of her mother. I now understood the "but" in Debbie's voice when she talked about her mother. Although Debbie's mom hovered close to Debbie, she did not stand up for herself. She did not give Debbie a model to respect in response to her dad's difficult and demeaning behaviors.

I asked Debbie's mom, "Why have you stayed with your husband? Has he repented and changed his ways?"

With great shame she answered, "Not really. I always worry about when he'll have another 'fling.' I guess I haven't left because I'm afraid to be on my own. I'm also afraid of my husband. Debbie stands up to him more than I do."

Gently I said to Debbie's mom, "You may have sacrificed your daughter on the altar of your own fear."

Debbie's mom dissolved into tears, but it did not take her long to collect herself. Her next question revealed to me where Debbie had gotten her resilient heart. "Is it too late?" she asked.

I began to work with Debbie and her mom to acknowledge the truth about what was going on in their family. As Debbie watched her mom tell the truth about her marriage, confess her failures, and begin to stand up to Debbie's dad, Debbie found new respect for her mother. This did not happen quickly. I have worked with many moms in similar situations who have not been willing to do the work themselves first. They just want their daughters to change. Debbie's mom accepted that her daughter would not be able to look at herself clearly while her home was filled with so many dark shadows.

In a home where the dad is surrounded by a cloud of sexual darkness and the mom is silent or superficial in addressing that darkness, a girl is vulnerable to feeling a shudder toward her dad (as Debbie did) and disrespect for her mom. She may be like Debbie and engage with her dad in verbal sparring while she hides her feelings for her mom, not wanting to hurt her further. The result is a lot of conflicted feelings about gender. The masculine is dark, dangerous, and a source of conflict. The feminine is small, pitiful, and helpless. Neither is respected. I wondered if Debbie's questions and experiences with regard to her sexual orientation had something to do with an environment that produced in her a shudder at the thought of men, a disrespect for the male-female relationship, and a longing for a powerful woman as a role model.

Just for the Two of You

1. Consider acknowledging the inappropriate sexual climate in your home. You can be certain that your daughter knows something is going on in your marriage. Ask her what she suspects or wonders about. You don't need to tell her all the details, but you can acknowledge that things have not been as they should be. A determination to keep all sexual matters out of conversations may lead children to believe that sex is the most important reality in life. An undiscussed, dark sexual climate can become subtly suggestive and seductive.

2. Confess your own failure to provide a healthy home environment for your daughter and to stand against the dark, abusive forces in your home. Children have a need to forgive their parents. Your heartfelt confession undergirded by actions to get help and make changes will be some of the most powerful "glue" in forming an alliance with your daughter.

3. Be willing to get help. If you begin to change, speak up for yourself, and engage in conversation with your husband, your marriage will be shaken to its foundations. You may need individual or marriage counseling. This will model to your children that when you are in the midst of struggles, asking for help is a good thing.

FEMALE FRIENDSHIPS

When Debbie realized that her mother was serious about making changes at home, Debbie was able to start looking at herself with more compassion and clarity. She quickly acknowledged that she had escaped from the tension and distasteful realities at home by turning to friendships. "I've never had a lot of friends," Debbie explained to me, "but I've always had one or two really good friends."

I asked Debbie to tell me about her close friends. She was quiet for a long time, and then the tears started. Soon she was gulping back sobs, unable to speak. I knew that we had come to an area of great passion and pain for Debbie.

When she finally was able to talk, she began her story by talking about soccer. Debbie had once been an avid soccer player, making the all-state team as a freshman. Because she was a freshman, many of the older girls regarded her with suspicion, which made Debbie feel a bit out of place. Then a sophomore player on the team befriended her, and before long they became inseparable. They hung out together after practice, talked on the phone, and spent practically every weekend together. Debbie's new friend was confident, outgoing, and a compassionate confidante for Debbie in talking about all of the tension she felt at home.

Perhaps you've been in Debbie's shoes. You know what it's like to be an outsider, to feel awkward, to long for a friend. I don't know a girl who does not dream of a "kindred spirit" who will ease her loneliness and make it a little more "okay" to be in this world. Often in female relationships a tender and deep intimacy grows. For Debbie, this growing friendship was like a cup of cold water in a parched desert.

"Debbie," I encouraged, "you were made for close, mutual relationships. Your heart responded as it should have!"

Debbie bit her lip and looked away. "You don't know what happened..."

I didn't know for sure, but I suspected. Many female homosexual relationships begin as close, nonsexual friendships that meet legitimate needs, but then casual touching gradually becomes sexual. Debbie deeply desired to join someone. We all do. God wired this longing into our cells at a biological level. Debbie was especially hungry for this connection because it had been missing all her life.

Debbie courageously told me about the first encounter with her friend that included sexual touch. She said to me, "I never even thought about sex when I was with her at first, but when she started touching me, I liked it. It felt good."

"Of course it did." I surprised Debbie with my response. "You were starving for touch, kindness, strength, and intimacy. Your friend's touch was as nourishing to you as food."

I have heard many similar stories from girls and women who have experienced profound emptiness in their relational life. Physical touch opens the relationship to new levels of intimacy that feels nourishing. Over a period of time, physical contact will grow into lengthy embraces, kisses, and more touch. Many girls who experience such relationships have no one they can talk to about what is happening. As a result, they leave one kind of loneliness for another. Their sexual life becomes a journey into anxiety and loneliness. Anxiety because they do not know what is happening to them or what it means, and yet they don't want to lose the first thing that has really felt like relational life to them. Loneliness because they have to struggle with their sexual identity alone, believing at best that people will not understand or, at worst, that people will banish them from relationship or condemn them to hell.

Debbie's friendship with her soccer teammate ended as many of these teenage relationships do. Because the girls could not talk with anyone about what was going on, they continued to cross boundaries in their physical relationship, which produced a lot of guilt and shame for both of them. Eventually there was an abrupt falling out between them. They went their separate ways and never talked about their relationship again. No wonder Debbie was depressed!

The Just for the Two of You section that follows will help you become your daughter's ally by opening the door for meaningful conversations with her regarding her relationships. It is important that you show her you care about her and her relationships. It would also be a wonderfully generous gesture on your part to take the time to get to know her friend or friends. Take them to lunch or shopping. I know that might be painful, but it's always better to love than to be offended.

After you have taken the time to get to know your daughter and her friends, you will be ready to gently lead the conversation toward two important goals: affirming her need for intimate relationships and talking openly about her sexual relationship with her friend.

JUST FOR THE TWO OF YOU

If your daughter is struggling with her sexual identity, one of the greatest gifts you can give her is to enter into her relational life. Following are a few questions that might help open the door to meaningful conversations with your daughter. Before you ask her these questions, your daughter will need to sense that you are not on a witch hunt, but that you are truly curious and compassionate.

1. Who is your closest friend?
2. Tell me the story of your friendship.
3. What attracted you to your friend? What attracted her to you?
4. What do you have in common?
5. What is she really good at?
6. Tell me about her family.
7. What do you talk about together?
8. If she moved away, how would you feel?
9. Is there anything about her that annoys you?
10. What are your favorite things to do together?

AFFIRMING THE NEED FOR INTIMATE RELATIONSHIPS

You will best be able to affirm your daughter's need for intimacy if you are in touch with your own longing to know and be known by another person, to be enjoyed, to be touched, to be loved. If you have deadened your own desires, you will not be able to effectively address your daughter's desires. If you are struggling with your own need for relationships, I suggest you read my book *Bravehearts,* which affirms our longings and discusses how to live with them in a sometimes difficult and disappointing world.

When Debbie began to understand that intimacy was what she was made for and that rather than signifying that something was wrong with her, her longing for intimacy signified that something was more profoundly right than she had ever imagined, she began to relax. She began to understand that many of her feelings in her friendship with her teammate were natural and good. But affirming Debbie's longing for relationship was not enough to give her clarity about her own heart and sense of self. We needed to talk about the sexual nature of their relationship.

Talking Openly About the Sexual Relationship

"Do you think I'm gay?" Debbie asked after a conversation about our natural longings for intimate relationships.

I never answer that question for a client. I do not avoid the issue, but I do try to approach it with humility, compassion, and sober judgment, just as I would when talking with a teenager about a heterosexual relationship. Teenagers who are engaged in a homosexual relationship will regard our unwillingness to take a look at what is actually happening as an indication that we are afraid of them and their experiences, just as any teenager engaged in a sexual relationship would.

So instead of answering Debbie's question, I asked her to tell me about the sexual activity.

When she finished telling me about the sexual intimacy with her friend, she said, "So, now do you think I'm going to hell?"

We…must show compassion because we are not talking about strange, subhuman, monotonously stereotyped creatures; we are talking about persons who are as different from one another as heterosexual people are.

—Lewis Smedes, *Sex for Christians*

My heart winced again at the harm the previous counselor had done, and I was reminded that once words are spoken, they cannot be taken back. If you cannot speak to your daughter with compassion, do not say anything, or simply say, "I don't know what to say, but I am glad we are talking about this."

I told Debbie, "I don't think you are going to hell because of sexual intimacy with a girl any more than a girl is going to hell because she had sex with her boyfriend. I do think that both behaviors are destructive to relationship and to your own soul."

Debbie and I spent several sessions talking about the material in the previous chapters of this book. We talked about the biology, psychology, and
spirituality of sex. If your daughter struggles with her sexual identity, you
don't need to change your language when talking with her about sex. The
message is the same. I think Debbie really got that, but her question still lin-
gered: "Do you think I'm gay?"

FORMING AN ALLIANCE WITH
YOUR DAUGHTER

What if your daughter still wonders about her sexual orientation even after
you have courageously addressed the dynamics of your family and explored
the nature and development of your daughter's friendships? You cannot lock
her in her bedroom until she becomes who you want her to be any more than
you could if your daughter wanted to engage in heterosexual relationships.
Eventually, she will have to make her own choices. You can offer her three
things that will help her form an alliance with you that she desperately needs
as she makes decisions about her sexual relationships.

SELF-KNOWLEDGE

Continue to engage with your daughter as she interacts with your family
and with others. Ask her to assess her feelings about men and women, to
acknowledge her internal emptiness, and to recognize her need to fill that
emptiness with something. Teenagers are not fully developed in any area,
including their sexual development. If you can keep communication open,
your daughter's sexual orientation will most likely grow in healthy ways. But
if you get into a power struggle with your daughter over this issue, she may
stay stuck at her current level of development just to "win." Once again, you
will be most powerful in talking with your daughter about these things if you
are honest about your own life.

An important part of self-knowledge for you and your daughter is to recognize your own responsibility for what you do with the inner emptiness and
loneliness that propel you into relationships. We are responsible for making
righteous choices no matter how hungry, hurt, or lonely we may be.

JUST FOR YOU

The following questions will help you uncover your own understanding of masculinity and femininity and think about what you may or may not have been conveying to your daughter.

1. What do you believe it means to be uniquely female?
2. What do you love about being a woman? What do you hate?
3. What do you believe it means to be uniquely male?
4. What do you appreciate most about masculinity? What do you hate about it?
5. Describe a time when you felt emotionally empty.
6. When you feel that emptiness, what do you do to fill it? A few options are:
   • eat
   • get busy
   • call a girlfriend
   • demand something from your husband
   • pray
   • create something

SELF-DISCIPLINE

Even if your daughter remains firm in her belief that she is homosexual, she is still responsible to live a righteous life. Just as it would be for any adolescent girl, she is responsible to keep herself away from situations and people that might entice her toward sexual sin. Just as with any teenage girl, she needs to develop the other areas of her life with passion and creativity. She needs to develop relationships with members of both sexes that are characterized by honor and respect.

Christian ethicist and professor of theology Lewis Smedes writes,

Sin infiltrates our sexuality to prevent its development into a truly humane component of our life together. The basic fault that has crept into our sexuality is the failure of the mysterious power of biological sex to lead us into a life of love.[3]

Talking openly with your daughter about her sexual behavior, without condemnation, will allow you to help her understand her sexuality as a means of leading a life of love. Sexual sin for any adolescent can prevent healthy, life-giving sexual development. That's why sex *is* a big deal!

HOPE

What hope can you offer your daughter if she questions her sexual orientation? Certainly, if you are active in an evangelical church, she may fear being rejected by everyone, just as Debbie's counselor warned. Reassure your daughter that you will want a close relationship with her no matter what. Offer to provide counseling for your daughter if she wants to talk to someone besides you.

The greatest hope you can give your daughter is to point her to Jesus. When you are filled with longing for your children as well as emptiness and angst over their choices, where do you turn? If you try to control, you will end up emptier still.

Almost unbelievably, God doesn't seem all that concerned with protecting us from our bad choices. I mean, why did He make us with sex organs in the first place, considering all that can go wrong? It's almost as if He wants us to have choices.

God desires love, and love is a choice that can't be forced. It's a choice that must be made in freedom. I know that you want your daughter to be safe, but you must have a vision for her that involves more than safety.

Last fall my daughter's roof collapsed due to one rainstorm after another in our area. When we started to arrange for repairs, I discovered that our county has a lot of safety rules and regulations that we had to comply with. I know these laws and regulations were designed to keep us safe and yet I have no abiding love for our county.

Your daughter will not find healing or health in laws and regulations—and neither will you. Hope is not found in the law; it is found in love—ultimately, God's love. Your responsibility is to love your daughter in a way that makes her hungry for God's love. Do you *know*—heart and soul—the One who whispers, "No more shame, no more hiding, no more condemnation"? If you do, then you can offer, with a heart of gratitude for what God has given you, that same kind of love to your daughter.

Perhaps you have read this chapter hoping to find a five-step plan for keeping your daughter from being gay or sexually active. But that is not my message, nor do I believe that it is the spirit of the gospel. My hope is that this chapter has helped you better understand your daughter and has given you direction for creating a life-giving relationship with her in the midst of her struggles.

No matter what our daughters are struggling with, and no matter how confusing or scary those struggles may be, we as mothers are left with one thing. Perhaps the only thing: love.

Don't tolerate people who try to run your life, ordering
you to bow and scrape.... They're completely out of touch with
the source of life, Christ, who puts us together in one piece,
whose very breath and blood flow through us.... We can
grow up healthy in God only as he nourishes us.

—COLOSSIANS 2:18, 19

The great Russian novelist Fyodor Dostoevsky told a story about Jesus during the Spanish Inquisition. The Grand Inquisitor attacked Christ, saying, "Why have you given us so much freedom? You give us choices that condemn us. You've made things more difficult for us! I shall have you burned tomorrow!"

The Grand Inquisitor waited for Christ to answer, but Christ was silent for a long time. The Inquisitor longed for him to say something, but Christ only looked intently at the man.

Finally, Christ went over to the old man and kissed him gently on his old rugged lips.

That was His final answer.

The old Inquisitor was startled and released the prisoner, saying, "Do not come back again."

Dostoevsky wrote of the old man, "The kiss glowed in his heart."[4]

May our love for our daughters do the same.[5]

The Healing Story

All Jesus did that day was tell stories—a long storytelling afternoon. His storytelling fulfilled the prophecy: "I will open my mouth and tell stories; I will bring out into the open things hidden since the world's first day."

—MATTHEW 13:34–35

Have you ever wished that Jesus would just show up? I mean, show up in the flesh. If He walked into your kitchen, sat down at the table, and waited for you to speak, what would you say? Perhaps you would blurt out or stammer a question provoked by the material in this book:

- How can I help my daughter appreciate the importance of sexual purity?
- Why did You make teenagers with sex drives?
- How can my daughter heal from the sexual experiences she's already had?
- Will my daughter ever trust herself, men…or You again?
- Can You help her not to feel stained and dirty because she has a sexually transmitted disease?
- Will You punish the one who sexually abused my daughter?
- How can I help my daughter with questions about sex when I myself am hurt, angry, and confused?

If Jesus really showed up, sat down at your kitchen table, and responded to your heartfelt questions, I have a feeling that you would hang on every word. I also have a feeling that He would answer your questions by telling a story. I, of course, am not wise enough to know the exact story He would tell, but I have an idea. I think He would tell a story of a woman who had experienced sexual woundedness and had responded in human, sinful ways. I think He would tell a story of romance and describe a love that sweeps her off her feet. I know He would tell His story—the healing story.

When Jesus did show up in the flesh,

> The disciples came up and asked, "Why do you tell stories?"
>
> He replied, "…Whenever someone has a ready heart for this, the insights and understanding flow freely.… That's why I tell stories: to create readiness, to nudge the people toward receptive insight."[1]

The story I have imagined that Jesus might tell is a story He has already told in the gospel of John. I have imagined further details of this story, based on the little I know of Bible history and the little more I know of female human nature and experience. I do believe that we experience God's Word most powerfully when we put ourselves in His stories and allow Him to enter our stories.

I pray that this woman's story will become your story and your daughter's story, as it has become mine. Then all the questions and details about sex and sexual boundaries, about abuse and sexual brokenness, about human folly and sexual sin, about real teenage girls caught in the real-life struggles and temptations of a world way out of control will fade away into the substance of the One who is more real than any experience, longing, sin, or question we may have.

To set the scene, imagine a woman in a wedding dress. You can give the dress any qualities you like. Perhaps you imagine a dress you've seen in a bride magazine or a dress a celebrity wore. Perhaps you imagine your own wedding dress. There is one distinguishing quality about this dress: it is tattered and torn—worn by wear, smudged with dust and dirt from travel. The condition of this dress makes sense when you know the bride's story. Everyone who knows her or knows of her calls her…*the runaway bride.* Let's listen to her story:[2]

"You're probably wondering about my attire. It's a wedding dress. It's really the only nice dress I have. I've worn it a lot. I've had five weddings— well, really six, but I'm getting ahead of myself.

"They called me the runaway bride in my town in Samaria, my town called Sychar. Everyone knew I'd been married five times. People laughed at me when they saw me in my wedding dress. 'Already dressed for the next wedding?' they'd laugh.

"I wore the dress whenever I had to go out in my town, because it was the only dress I had. I had lost everything—possessions, reputation, family. Oh, I was with another man, but we were not married. He wanted me... well...he wanted me for one thing. And I gave it to him in exchange for a roof over my head, a place to hide from the taunts of everyone. 'Runaway bride. When are you going to run away? Better run away before everyone runs away from you!'

"They thought they knew me. But they didn't.

"I was born in Sychar. I had one sister, and I loved my mama and feared my papa. As kids, we spent all our time playing with the other girls. I especially loved to play dress-up. My favorite part of our play was being the bride. I would wear my mama's wedding dress, and we would dance to wedding songs. My favorite place to play was at the well that bordered our farm. The well was on a plot of ground that Jacob had given to his son Joseph. Jacob's well was where all the women, including my mama, would go during the cool of the day to get water for their families. We girls would play 'wedding' around the well. We would sing and dance and dream of the day we would be brides.

"Sometimes at night after a day of playing 'wedding,' I would start to wonder and worry, 'What if no one wants me to be his bride?' I'd come to my mama crying, 'What if no one wants me. What if I wait and wait and no one asks me?'

"My mama would say, 'Sweetheart, that's how God feels sometimes. He waits, and no one asks Him.'

"You see, even though we were Samaritans, we had heard of the God of Israel from our neighbors. My mama and papa believed, and every night Mama would tell us stories she'd heard from her friends. My favorite stories were about the God-man. What a man! That's the kind of man I wanted to marry. He was strong. It was the God-man who wrestled with Jacob, the man who owned the land with the well where we'd play the wedding game. The God-man wrestled with Jacob and gave him a new name. I dreamed of the day that I would meet a man who would give me a new name. My mama said she thought the God-man would give us a new name too. I wondered if He would wrestle with me and what He would name me.

"The God-man was not only strong; He was kind. He was always appearing to people who were afraid and tired, saying, 'Fear not.' I hadn't been afraid very often, but I imagined getting married would be kind of scary—leaving my mama and papa. The stories of the God-man gave me hope that I would marry a man who wouldn't laugh at me for being afraid.

"Well, every night Mama would tell me stories, kiss me good night, and help me pray. Every night. Even the last night. I was ten years old.

"I awoke to sounds of someone screaming. It was the sound of my mama being raped and murdered by a Roman centurion. The soldiers had already cut my papa's throat and had tied up my sister as a hostage. We all knew what they did to the girls they captured. I could smell smoke and knew that they were burning our village. Probably everyone was dead. I took one last look at my family and snuck out through a back window. I escaped and hid in the burned-out buildings around our town. While everyone else who was left alive rebuilt, I hid. I'm not sure why I didn't ask for help. Maybe I was in shock. All I knew was that my nice, comfortable world had been shattered, and I didn't trust anyone.

"I was so thirsty, I drank from a ditch. I would fall asleep every night crying.

"I hid, and no one looked for me. I'm sure that some people saw me wandering around the burned-out buildings, looking for food and water, but no one wanted me. No one asked me to come with them. No one cared, I thought.

"A day came when I stopped crying. I knew that crying wasn't going to bring my mama and papa back. Crying wasn't going to save my sister. Crying wasn't going to help me. I stopped crying and didn't cry again for almost forty years.

"I found that the best time to find food was at night when everyone was sleeping, and the best time to get fresh water was at noon. All of the women left in town would get their water during the cool of the morning. I went to the well at noon when others would be in the shade of their homes. I didn't mind the heat. I didn't mind being alone. It was better than trusting people only to have them hurt me, or worse. Loneliness became my hiding place. I loved it and I hated it. My heart was filled with hatred for everyone. My hurt and hate kept me company and gave me direction. There wasn't room in my heart for anything or anyone else, I thought.

"One day, almost three years after mama and papa were murdered and my sister was kidnapped, I went to the well at noon as usual. I was so thirsty and knew that everyone else would be in the shade of their own homes. No one would notice me or hurt me or want me.

"That's where I met my first husband. I was only thirteen years old. He was much older. He told me that he would be my husband, and I would be lucky to have him. He gave me a wedding dress, the one I am wearing today. He told me that it belonged to his first wife. He said, 'Put it on. Make yourself look like a bride.'

"For a moment I remembered those days of playing dress-up around the well. This was nothing like the wedding dress—or groom—I'd imagined. At first I screamed when he touched me so roughly, but the screaming reminded me of my mother. I hated his touch. I hated my body for sometimes responding to his touch. I learned to hide in my deep, dark loneliness while I was with him. I remembered my mama talking about sex as if it was something special. She called it sacred. She had no idea.

"Time passed, and I barely noticed. I went through the motions of living. My first husband died, and my only thought was that I might stay in his house by myself, safe at last. But another man—and his brothers—came and told me I would be his wife. He shared me with his brothers as if I was a possession to be passed around. The sheep were treated better than I was. I cursed being a woman for the pain and shame it brought me, and I hated men for all they wanted and did with their wanting. My hatred locked in a loneliness that kept me from both men and women. It was a place where I thought no one could touch me.

"I would hide my hatred for my husband and all men in that deep, dark place in my heart. 'I'm a victim,' I'd say. Victims can justify anything. And so in the middle of one dark night, I found a sharp ax and I killed my husband. I ran into the town screaming that he had been murdered in the night. Everyone shook their heads and wondered about me, I could tell. I didn't care. I thought I was safe.

"I didn't think about my husband's brothers. I became a wife to the next brother in line. It was more of the same. Loveless loneliness.

"To stay a victim, you must never forgive or believe you're forgiven. You must keep hatred alive. That wasn't hard. How could I forgive people for all they had done to me? And now how could I be forgiven—a murderer? There was no place for me to go but deeper into my own dark loneliness. And so I continued filling the darkness with more darkness.

"This husband and his remaining brothers decided to move deeper into Samaria, farther away from the border. The night before we were to move, I ran away and hid. I was good at hiding. I had been doing it since I was ten years old. I hid for a week. It was just like after my mama and papa died. I drank from a ditch because I was so thirsty. I couldn't go to the well. I couldn't go back to my husband and his family.

"Near the end of the week, I saw another family moving into our old house. I approached the house and asked if they needed a servant. The older man took pity on me and said I could be his wife. He already had three other wives. I stayed with him, but I didn't love him. I used him. I didn't love anyone. I didn't even love me. I hid in the darkness of my own anger, vengeance, pain, and loneliness—in my wounded me.

"When this fourth husband died, the family moved away. They didn't want me. They said I was only a taker. It wasn't long before word got out about me—that I couldn't keep a husband, that I ran away, that everyone ran away from me. Another man came to my door—my fifth husband.

"There are no words to describe what he did to me—and I to him. I knew men, evil men who knew how to rape, and so I learned how to hide, and even rape, to balance the power and protect my heart.

"And then one morning he was gone. I was so undesirable that even the most undesirable man didn't want me.

"Except for one—the man who came next, the man I did not marry. He was a tax collector. We lived like two lepers in our community—untouchables hiding in the darkness. Then one day the light shone into my darkness. I hated the light, but that day I couldn't run. I didn't want to.

"I awoke that morning to find we had no water in the house. The tax collector and I were both thirsty, and it was my job to get water. I waited until

I could wait no longer. I was so thirsty. I walked to the well—Jacob's well—at noon, hoping that everyone else would be in the shade of their homes during the heat of the day.

"I was just starting to draw water when a man approached the well. I could tell he was a Jew. I thought he would take one look at me and quickly leave—a Samaritan in her shame-smeared wedding dress.

"'Will you get me a drink?' he asked.

"I didn't have time for this. He didn't even have his own water jar. 'You are a Jew and I am a Samaritan woman. How can you ask me for a drink?'

"I cannot describe to you his face when he looked at me. No man has ever looked at me with such longing, but it wasn't like the longing of other men. He said, 'If you knew the gift of God and who it is that asks you for a drink, you would have asked him and he would have given you living water.'

"At first I thought he might be a bit heat sick, 'Sir,' I said, 'you have nothing to draw with and the well is deep. Where can you get this living water? Are you greater than our father Jacob, who gave us this well and drank from it himself?'

"He looked at me again. And the look undid me. He didn't need to say anything. He knew me. He saw past my anger and into the darkness of my loneliness, into my marriages, into myself. He knew me. He would not take from me.

"He answered, 'Everyone who drinks this water will be thirsty again, but whoever drinks the water I give him will never thirst. Indeed, the water I give him will become in him a spring of water welling up to eternal life.'

"I almost jumped on him. 'Sir, give me this water so that I won't get thirsty and have to keep coming here to draw water.'

"My heart stopped at his next words: 'Go, call your husband and come back.'

"Did he know? Was he mocking me like everyone else? *Runaway bride? Run away before everyone runs away from you.*'

"'I have no husband,' I replied.

"He looked at me again. It was as if he was the deepest ocean, undiminished by me. He gazed at me. I wanted to run, but I was so thirsty. I wanted to hide, but I was utterly naked as I stood there in my tattered wedding dress.

"'You are right when you say you have no husband,' he said. 'The fact is, you have had five husbands, and the man you now have is not your husband. What you have just said is quite true.'

"'Sir,' I said, 'I can see that you are a prophet.' I *could* see. I can't explain it. At this point I had nothing to give this man but my kingdom of loss and loneliness. I didn't know what this water was that he offered me. But I knew that he was good and that he was light and life and that I loved him.

"He talked about salvation and truth, and I didn't understand it all, but I knew that somehow he was both salvation and truth, and I was tired of being condemned and living a lie. I remembered the stories my mama had told me, and I said to him, 'I know that Messiah is coming. When he comes, he will explain everything to us.'

"His eyes locked on me as if I were a treasure he had just found buried in a field or a beautiful bride waiting for her bridegroom. He gave me a new name. He looked at me like a groom might look at a cherished bride. I was no longer a runaway, a hideaway, a throwaway. With that look, he declared, 'I who speak to you am he.'

"I started to hear music that sounded like a wedding song. I couldn't understand every note, but I was beginning to hear music.

"The music...

"That Jesus is God in the flesh—the Lord—and I was made for Him.

"That He cries, 'Bone of My bones and flesh of My flesh'[3] when he sees me.

"That He longs to enter me and fill me and give me His life, Himself, the Word, the Seed that bears fruit.

"That He completes me and that in some way I complete Him.

"That when I hid and ran away and murdered and did things that cannot be talked about in the light of day, He did not leave me or forsake me;[4] for what God has joined together, no man can tear asunder.[5]

"That He was bound to me from the foundation of the world in an eternal covenant.

"Well, just as I was hearing the music, some other men—some disciples of His—came to the well and saw me talking to Jesus. I braced myself, but no one said, 'What do you want?' or 'Why are You talking to her?' It was as if they could tell I belonged there, that I belonged with Him.

"Hope and love welled up within me. I wanted to run into the streets of my town and knock on the doors of all those people I had hid from for years. I wanted them to see me. I didn't even pick up my water jar.

"I ran into town shouting, 'Come, see a man who told me everything I ever did!' I wasn't hiding in darkness and shame anymore. He was my declaration of independence, and in those moments at the well, I declared my dependence on Him. I surrendered my difference—my different ethnicity, my different gender, my different experience of being a woman with five husbands and living with still another man. I surrendered my naked shame. I invited Him to fill my emptiness with living water. It was as if He became my groom and I was His bride. No longer the runaway bride—His love set me free to acknowledge that deep within me is a desire, a longing, a passion built into my very depths so that I could know Him and believe in His love. He found me, and it's as if everything I have ever thirsted for is there in Him.

"There I was at the well in my old wedding dress—the laughingstock of my town—and He came to take me as His bride, even though I was hiding, even though I had been raped time and time again, even though I had played the harlot and surrendered to other men.

"And when He looked at me the way a groom would, I knew He didn't despise my shame. He wanted to cover it with Himself. He didn't laugh at my thirst. He wanted to fill my empty craving with Himself. He came with healing, strength, love, and tender compassion.

"I knew at the well that the very craving I've felt in my flesh to be bound in communion with another person, to rest in another, to be complete in another, to reach ecstasy with another is all about Him.

"I tell this story because it is my story. It is your story. It is our story. You know all those townspeople who mocked me and looked down on me? Well, it must have been their story too, because after I ran into the town talking about this man who had swept me off my feet, they ran after Him. They believed and begged Him to stay in our town. He could stay only two days, but when He left, people said to me with respect and friendship in their voices, 'We no longer believe just because of what you said; now we have heard for ourselves, and we know that this man really is the Savior of the world.'

"This is what I know for sure. He romanced me at the well as I stood there in my tattered wedding dress. He started romancing me with my mother's stories and when as a child I played wedding dress-up with the other girls. Even in the dark loneliness, in all my hiding and running away, He found me. While I was being abused and abusing others—and even while I was murdering—He was looking for me, waiting for me to ask Him in.

"I know now that the key to my healing—my sexual healing, all healing—is to surrender my shame to the Lover of my soul."[6]

Whatever your daughter's struggles, I leave you with this promise: "But I, when I am lifted up from the earth, will draw all [people] to myself."[7]

Jesus Himself is the answer to all our questions about love and longing, sex and sexuality, abuse and abandonment, hope and healing. This is the Great Romance. As mothers we are responsible for accepting His love and loving Him in a way that makes our daughters long for just such a relationship with Him. That is the greatest gift we can give them.

FINDING A COUNSELOR

As you walk hand in hand with your daughter through all of her questions and struggles regarding sex and sexuality, both of you may need to talk with a counselor. The best counseling will not replace your relationship with your daughter but will enhance it by providing insight and guidance to strengthen your alliance. Listed below are some tips for finding the best counselor and some suggestions when insurance or income is not available to cover the costs of counseling.

- The best referrals come from those who have been through a similar struggle. If you don't know of anyone whose daughter has struggled with issues regarding sex, contact youth pastors and/or school counselors and ask them if they can help you locate other parents who have sought counseling and help for their daughters.
- Contact your local alternative pregnancy center. Share with them your concerns about your daughter and ask if they provide counseling on sex or if they can recommend a counselor.
- Contact your health-insurance carrier for a list of providers and information about how many therapy sessions they will pay for (both individual and family) and how much they will pay.
- Interview at least three therapists (with your daughter) before choosing a counselor. It is important that your daughter feel that she is part of the process of choosing who will help her.
- Choose a therapist whose work focuses primarily on adolescents.
- When you interview the counselor, explain that you want to be involved in your daughter's work in this area, and ask the therapist how he or she will incorporate you into the process.
- If insurance is not available and money is tight, ask the counselor if you can pay on a sliding scale. Many therapists will slide their fees to correspond with your income.
- Ask your church about a counseling support fund. Sometimes a church will pay half of the counseling fee while you pay the other half.

- If counseling is not feasible due to your financial situation, look for a support group in your community. Contact the National Mental Health Association information center for referrals to local support groups and/or community resources: 1-800-969-NMHA or visit *www.nmha.org.*
- Check with your local hospital regarding educational meetings about adolescent development and sexual issues.
- Contact the Abstinence Clearinghouse at *www.abstinence.net* to see if they can recommend a counselor in your area.
- To find a doctor who is willing to talk with you and your daughter about sexual issues and support your values, contact the National Physicians Center for Family Resources at *www.physicianscenter.org* and ask if they can recommend a doctor in your area.

RESOURCES

The following resources may not reflect all of your beliefs and values. I have listed them as sources of information, but they should be reviewed and evaluated before you decide to make them available to your daughter.

ABSTINENCE

Real Sex: The Naked Truth About Chastity. Lauren F. Winner. Grand Rapids: Brazos Press, 2005.

Sex and Character. Deborah Cole and Maureen Gallagher Duran. Mesquite, TX: Haughton, 1998.

Sex Has a Price Tag: Discussions About Sexuality, Spirituality, and Self-Respect. Pam Stenzel. Grand Rapids: Zondervan, 2003.

Time for a Pure Revolution. Doug Herman. Wheaton, IL: Tyndale, 2004.

Other Resources
Abstinence Clearinghouse
801 East 41st Street
Sioux Falls, SD 57105
605-335-3643
www.abstinence.net

BODY IMAGE

Everything You Need to Know About Body Dysmorphic Disorder: Dealing with a Distorted Body Image. Pamela Walker. New York: Rosen, 1999.

"Mom, I feel fat!" Becoming your daughter's ally in developing a healthy body image. Sharon Hersh. Colorado Springs: Shaw Books, 2001.

The Pursuit of Beauty: Finding True Beauty That Will Last Forever. Katie Luce. Green Forest, AR: New Leaf Press, 1998.

Transforming Body Image: Learning to Love the Body You Have. Marcia Germaine Hutchinson. Berkeley, CA: Crossing Press, 1985.

What's Real, What's Ideal: Overcoming a Negative Body Image. Brangien Davis. Center City, MN: Hazelden Publishing and Educational Services, 1999.

Other Resources

Body Talk Series. The first twenty-eight-minute video in the series focuses on
   body-esteem issues for teens ages twelve and older. The second twenty-minute
   video deals with age-specific body-image issues for teens ages nine through
   twelve. Also available on DVD. Order from The Body Positive, 2550 9th
   Street, Suite 204B, Berkeley, CA 94710; 510-548-0101; fax: 510-548-4224;
   www.thebodypositive.org.

"Building Blocks for Children's Body Image." Article by Marius Griffin, January
   10, 2000. Produced by the Body Image Task Force, PO Box 360196,
   Melbourne, FL 32936; www.sizenet.com/showdoc.asp?id=201.

DATING AND ABUSIVE RELATIONSHIPS

Boundaries in Dating. Henry Cloud and John Townsend. Grand Rapids: Zondervan, 2000.

*But I Love Him: Protecting Your Teen Daughter from Controlling, Abusive Dating
   Relationships.* Jill Murray. New York: HarperCollins, 2000.

*Preparing Your Daughter for Every Woman's Battle: Creative Conversations About
   Sexual and Emotional Integrity.* Shannon Ethridge. Colorado Springs:
   WaterBrook, 2005.

Other Resources

Break the Cycle. Web site that provide links to other sites that offer information
   on abusive relationships, including information regarding legal rights. Contact
   888-988-TEEN or visit www.breakthecycle.com.

DEPRESSION

Depression Is the Pits, but I'm Getting Better: A Guide for Adolescents. E. Jane
   Garland. Woodbridge, VA: American Psychological Association, 1997.

Depression: What It Is, How to Beat It. Linda Wasmer Smith. Berkeley Heights,
   NJ: Enslow, 2000.

*"Help Me, I'm Sad": Recognizing, Treating, and Preventing Childhood and Adolescent
   Depression.* David G. Fassler and Lynne S. Dumas. New York: Penguin, 1998.

Lonely, Sad, and Angry: A Parent's Guide to Depression in Children and Adolescents.
   Barbara D. Ingersoll and Sam Goldstein. New York: Broadway Books, 1996.

"Mom, I hate my life!" Becoming your daughter's ally through the emotional ups and downs of adolescence. Sharon Hersh. Colorado Springs: Shaw Books, 2004.

More Than Moody: Recognizing and Treating Adolescent Depression. Harold S. Koplewicz. New York: Penguin Group, 2002.

Overcoming Teen Depression: A Guide for Parents. Miriam Kaufman. Canada: Firefly Books, 2000.

Teen Torment: Overcoming Verbal Abuse at Home and at School. Patricia Evans. Avon, MA: Adams Media, 2003.

When Nothing Matters Anymore: A Survival Guide for Depressed Teens. Bev Cobain. Minneapolis: Free Spirit, 1998.

Other Resources

Child and Adolescent Bipolar Foundation
1000 Skokie Boulevard
Suite 425
Wilmette, IL 60091
847-256-8525
Fax: 847-920-9498
www.cabf.org

Depression and Bipolar Support Alliance
730 North Franklin Street
Suite 501
Chicago, IL 60610-7224
800-826-3632
Fax: 312-642-7243
www.dbsalliance.org

DIFFICULT RELATIONSHIPS

Controlling People: How to Recognize, Understand, and Deal with People Who Try to Control You. Patricia Evans. Avon, MA: Adams Media, 2001.

Every Heart Restored: A Wife's Guide to Healing in the Wake of a Husband's Sexual Sin. Stephen Arterburn, Fred Stoeker, and Brenda Stoeker. Colorado Springs: WaterBrook, 2004.

The Verbally Abusive Relationship: How to Recognize It and How to Respond. Patricia
    Evans. Avon, MA: Adams Media, 1996
When Bad Things Happen to Good Marriages. Leslie Parrott. Grand Rapids:
    Zondervan, 2001.

Other Resources
Restoring the Soul
(Provides counseling and information regarding sexual sin and marriage struggles.)
7220 W. Jefferson Avenue
Suite 210
Lakewood, CO 80235
303-932-9777
Fax: 303-932-7555
www.restoringthesoul.com

FEMALE DEVELOPMENT
The Girls' Life Guide to Growing Up. Karen Bokram and Alexis Sinex, eds.
    Hillsboro, OR: Beyond Words, 2000.
Girltalk: All the Stuff Your Sister Never Told You. Carol Weston. New York: Harper-
    Trade, 1997.
It's Perfectly Normal: Changing Bodies, Growing Up, Sex, and Sexual Health. Robie
    H. Harris. Cambridge, MA: Candlewick Press, 1996.
Odd Girl Out: The Hidden Culture of Aggression in Girls. Rachel Simmons. New
    York: Harcourt, 2003.
*Queen Bees and Wannabees: Helping Your Daughter Survive Cliques, Gossip,
    Boyfriends, and Other Realities of Adolescence.* Rosalind Wiseman. New York:
    Crown, 2002.
*"Trust Me, Mom—Everyone Else Is Going!" The New Rules for Mothering Adolescent
    Girls.* Roni Cohen-Sandler. New York: Penguin, 2003.

Other Resources
Brio Magazine
Focus on the Family
(No street address required)
Colorado Springs, CO 80995

800-A-FAMILY

www.family.org

MOTHERING

Different Children, Different Needs: Understanding the Unique Personality of Your Child. Charles F. Boyd. Sisters, OR: Multnomah, 2004.

Growing Up with a Single Parent: What Hurts, What Helps. Sara McLanahan and Gary Sandefur. Cambridge, MA: Harvard University Press, 1996.

"I'm Not Mad, I Just Hate You!" A New Understanding of Mother-Daughter Conflict. Roni Cohen-Sandler and Michelle Silver. New York: Penguin, 2000.

Keep Talking: A Mother-Daughter Guide to the Pre-Teen Years. Lynda Madison. Kansas City, MO: Andrews McMeel, 1999.

Reviving Ophelia: Saving the Selves of Adolescent Girls. Mary Pipher. New York: Ballantine, 2002.

SEX EDUCATION

Beyond the Big Talk: Every Parent's Guide to Raising Sexually Healthy Teens. Debra W. Haffner. New York: New Market Press, 2002.

A Celebration of Sex: A Guide to Enjoying God's Gift of Sexual Intimacy. Douglas E. Rosenau. Nashville: Thomas Nelson, 2002.

Everything You Never Wanted Your Kids to Know About Sex (But Were Afraid They'd Ask): The Secrets to Surviving Your Child's Sexual Development from Birth to the Teens. Justin Richardson and Mark A. Schuster. New York: Three Rivers Press, 2003.

The Hidden Epidemic: Confronting Sexually Transmitted Disease. Thomas R. Eng and William T. Butler. Boulder, CO: NetLibrary, 1997.

Other Resources

Centers for Disease Control and Prevention

(Provides statistics and other information on teenage sexual behaviors as well as sexually transmitted diseases.)

1600 Clifton Road

Atlanta, GA 30333

800-311-3435

www.cdc.gov

Sex: Q & A. Booklet providing parents with information about teenage sexual issues. To order, contact National Physicians Center for Family Resources, PO Box 59692, Birmingham, AL 35259; 205-870-0234; www.physicianscenter.org.

STDs: The Facts. Brochure providing an overview of the epidemic of sexually transmitted diseases. To order, contact The Medical Institute, 1101 S. Capital of Texas Highway, Building B–Suite 100, Austin, TX 78746; 512-328-6268; www.medinstitute.org.

SEXUAL ABUSE AND HEALING

Restoring the Teenage Soul: Nurturing Sound Hearts and Minds in a Confused Culture. Margaret J. Meeker. Traverse City, MI: McKinley and Mann, 1999.

The Wounded Heart: Hope for Adult Victims of Childhood Sexual Abuse. Dan B. Allender. Colorado Springs: NavPress, 1992.

SEXUAL ADDICTION AND PORNOGRAPHY

An Affair of the Mind: One Woman's Courageous Battle to Salvage Her Family from the Devastation of Pornography. Laurie Hall. Colorado Springs: Focus on the Family, 1998.

Cybersex Exposed: Simple Fantasy or Obsession. Jennifer Schneider and Robert Weiss. Center City, MN: Hazelden Publishing and Educational Services, 2001.

Don't Call It Love: Recovery from Sexual Addiction. Patrick Carnes. New York: Bantam Books, 1992.

Other Resources

Sex Addicts Anonymous
PO Box 70949
Houston, TX 77270
800-477-8191
www.sexaa.org

YOUTH CULTURE

Living in the Image Culture: An Introductory Primer for Media Literacy Education. J. Francis Davis. Los Angeles: Center for Media and Values, 1992.

Understanding Today's Youth Culture. Walt Mueller. Wheaton, IL: Tyndale, 1999.

Other Resources

Living in the Image Culture by Francis Davis may also be ordered through the
Center for Media Literacy, PO Box 80669, Lincoln, NE 68501-0669;
800-228-4630; fax: 800-306-2330; www.medialit.org.

YouthCulture@Today Newsletter
Center for Parent/Youth Understanding
PO Box 414
Elizabethtown, PA 17022
717-361-8429
Fax: 717-361-8964
www.cpyu.org

Notes

Introduction

1. For up-to-date research and statistics on teens and sex, visit the following Web sites: (1) The Centers for Disease Control and Prevention—*www.cdc.gov*—provide a wide variety of reports, including Youth Risk Behavior Surveillance Surveys, "Sexual Behavior and Selected Health Measures: Men and Women 15–44 Years of Age," and "Teenagers in the United States: Sexual Activity, Contraceptive Use, and Childbearing." These reports access data from the National Survey of Family Growth. (2) The U.S. Department of Justice, Bureau of Justice Statistics—*www.ojp.usdoj.gov*—provides updated statistics on violent crimes against teens by intimate partners. (3) The National Longitudinal Study of Adolescent Health—*www.cpc.unc.edu/projects/addhealth*—provides statistics on the sexual behavior of teens as well as other health-related behaviors. (4) The Alan Guttmacher Institute—*www.guttmacher.org*—provides resources and information about sexual health. They publish several journals and reports on sexual health, including the *International Family Planning Perspectives* journal. (5) The Kaiser Family Foundation—*www.kff.org*—conducts teen surveys, such as the SexSmarts survey, and provides resources and information on major U.S. health-care issues. Many of their statistics come from government studies, such as the National Survey of Family Growth. The foundation also publishes the "Sex on TV" report, a biennial study measuring sexual content in the entertainment media. (6) The National Center for Missing and Exploited Children—*www.missingkids.com*—provides resources and information on protecting children from such threats as pornography and Internet victimization. They also offer a wide variety of publications on child-safety issues, including "Online Victimization: A Report on the Nation's Youth," a national survey on child victimization on the Internet.

2. 2002 National Survey of Family Growth, cited in U.S. Department of Health and Human Services, Centers for Disease Control and Prevention,

William D. Mosher, Anjani Chandra, and Jo Jones, "Sexual Behavior and Selected Health Measures: Men and Women 15–44 Years of Age, United States, 2002," *Advance Data from Vital and Health Statistics,* no. 362 (September 15, 2005): 11, www.cdc.gov/nchs/data/ad/ad362.pdf.

3. 2002 National Survey of Family Growth, cited in U.S. Department of Health and Human Services, Centers for Disease Control and Prevention, "Teenagers in the United States: Sexual Activity, Contraceptive Use, and Childbearing, 2002," *Vital and Health Statistics* 23, no. 24 (December 2004), table 3, www.cdc.gov/nchs/data/series/sr_23/sr23_024.pdf.

4. Centers for Disease Control, "Teenagers in the United States," table 3.

5. Centers for Disease Control, "Teenagers in the United States," table 3.

6. Hannah Brückner and Peter Bearman, "After the Promise: The STD Consequences of Adolescent Virginity Pledges," *Journal of Adolescent Health* 36 (2005): 275.

7. Centers for Disease Control, "Teenagers in the United States," table 29.

8. Henry J. Kaiser Family Foundation, "Sex on TV, 2005: A Kaiser Family Foundation Report," tables 20 and 21, www.kff.org/entmedia/upload/Sex-on-TV-4-Full-Report.pdf.

9. National Institute on Media and the Family, D. Gentile, "Teen-Oriented Radio and CD Content Analysis," 1999, cited in Campaign for a Commercial-Free Childhood Fact Sheet, "Marketing Sex to Children," www.commercialexploitation.com/factsheets/ccfc-facts%20marketingsex.pdf#search=?marketing%20sex%20to%20children'.

10. Center for Media and Popular Policy, S. R. Lichter, "Sexual Imagery in Popular Culture," 2000, cited in Campaign for a Commercial-Free Childhood Fact Sheet, "Marketing Sex to Children."

11. Planned Parenthood Federation of America, L. Harris, "Sexual Material on American Network Television During the 1987–88 Season," cited in American Academy of Pediatrics, "Sexuality, Contraception, and the Media," *Pediatrics* 107, no. 1 (January 2001).

12. 1997 Henry J. Kaiser Family Foundation and Children Now national surveys: "Talking with Kids About Tough Issues," cited in Kaiser Family Foundation Fact Sheet, "Teens and Sex: The Role of Popular TV," July 2001, www.kff.org/entmedia/loader.cfm?url=/commonspot/security/getfile.cfm&PageID=13556.

13. 2004 NBC News/*People* magazine poll, "National Survey of Young Teens' Sexual Attitudes and Behaviors," conducted in conjunction with the Katie Couric special "The 411: Teens and Sex," cited in Brian Alexander, "Sex Ed on the Web," MSNBC, January 27, 2005, www.msnbc.msn.com/id/6860487/4; Princeton Survey Research Associates International, "NBC/*People:* National Survey of Young Teens' Sexual Attitudes and Behaviors," http://msnbcmedia.msn.com/i/msnbc/Sections/TVNews/Dateline%20NBC/NBCTeenTopline.pdf.

14. U.S. Department of Health and Human Services, Centers for Disease Control and Prevention, 2003 National Youth Risk Behavior Survey, cited in "National Youth Risk Behavior Survey, 1991–2003: Trends in the Prevalence of Sexual Behaviors," www.cdc.gov/HealthyYouth/yrbs/pdfs/trends-sex.pdf.

15. See 1 Peter 5:8.

16. 1 Corinthians 6:16, 18.

CHAPTER 1

1. 2004 readership survey, "You Tell Us," *Young and Modern,* August 2004, 78.

2. 2003 readership survey, "Heart to Heart," *Seventeen,* September 2003, 128.

3. Hillard Weinstock, Stuart Berman, and Willard Cates Jr., "Sexually Transmitted Diseases Among American Youth: Incidence and Prevalence Estimates, 2000," *Perspectives on Sexual and Reproductive Health* 36, no. 1 (January/February 2004), www.agi-usa.org/pubs/journals/3600604.html.

4. Alan Guttmacher Institute, "U.S. Teenage Pregnancy Statistics: Overall Trends, Trends by Race and Ethnicity, and State-by-State Information," 2000, updated February 19, 2004, www.guttmacher.org/pubs/state_pregnancy_trends.pdf.

5. Alan Guttmacher Institute, "U.S. Teenage Pregnancy Statistics," 2.

6. 2003 readership survey, Melissa Daly, "Let's Talk About Sex," *Seventeen,* July 2003, 92.

7. Barbara Strauch, *The Primal Teen: What the New Discoveries About the Teenage Brain Tell Us About Our Kids* (New York: Anchor Books, 2003), 156.

8. Joan J. Brumberg, *The Body Project: An Intimate History of American Girls* (New York: Random House, 1997), cited in the National Institute on

Media and the Family Fact Sheet, "Media's Effect on Girls: Body Image and Gender Identity," September 6, 2002.

9. 2002 National Survey of Family Growth, cited in U.S. Department of Health and Human Services, Centers for Disease Control and Prevention, William D. Mosher, Anjani Chandra, and Jo Jones, "Sexual Behavior and Selected Health Measures: Men and Women 15–44 Years of Age, United States, 2002," *Advance Data from Vital and Health Statistics,* no. 362 (September 15, 2005): 25, www.cdc.gov/nchs/data/ad/ad362.pdf.

10. National Campaign to Prevent Teen Pregnancy, 2003 survey conducted by International Communications Research, cited in Joyce Howard Price, "Teens Want to Wait for Sex," *Washington Times,* December 2003.

11. 2002 National Survey of Family Growth, cited in Mosher, Chandra, and Jones, "Sexual Behavior and Selected Health Measures," 21–22, www.cdc .gov/nchs/data/ad/ad362.pdf.

12. William Miller et al., "Prevalence of Chlamydial and Gonococcal Infections Among Young Adults in the United States," *JAMA* 291, no. 18 (2004), cited in Rita Rubin, "Chlamydia Infection Prevalent Among Unsuspecting Young Americans," *USA Today,* May 12, 2004.

13. Mosher, Chandra, and Jones, "Sexual Behavior and Selected Health Measures," 37.

14. 2002 National Survey of Family Growth, cited in U.S. Department of Health and Human Services, Centers for Disease Control and Prevention, "Teenagers in the United States: Sexual Activity, Contraceptive Use, and Childbearing, 2002," *Vital and Health Statistics* 23, no. 24 (December 2004), table 15, www.cdc.gov/nchs/data/series/sr_23/sr23_024.pdf.

15. Mark Kastleman, "Teenagers as Victims," www.contentwatch.com/ learn_center/article.php?id=149.

16. Henry J. Kaiser Family Foundation and *Seventeen* magazine national survey, "Virginity and the First Time," October 2003, www.kff.org/entpartnerships/ upload/Virginity-and-the-First-Time-Summary-of-Findings.pdf.

17. Kaiser Family Foundation and *Seventeen* magazine survey, "Virginity and the First Time."

18. Hannah Brückner and Peter Bearman, "After the Promise: The STD Consequences of Adolescent Virginity Pledges," *Journal of Adolescent Health* 36 (2005): 274.

CHAPTER 2

1. Martha Manning, *Chasing Grace: Reflections of a Catholic Girl, Grown Up* (San Francisco: HarperSanFrancisco, 1996), 161.
2. 2002 National Longitudinal Study of Adolescent Health, cited in Robert W. Blum et al., "Mothers' Influence on Adolescents' Sexual Debut," *Journal of Adolescent Health* 31, no. 3 (2002); "Mothers' Influence on Teen Sex: Connections That Promote Postponing Sexual Intercourse," Center for Adolescent Health and Development, University of Minnesota, 2002, 18–19, http://allaboutkids.umn.edu/presskit/MonographMS.pdf.
3. Blum, "Mothers' Influence on Teen Sex," 18.
4. Blum, "Mothers' Influence on Teen Sex," 20.
5. Robert Blum, quoted in Gina Greene, "Teen Sex: Moms May Have Big Impact on Girls," CNN.Com/Health, http://archives.cnn.com/2002/HEALTH/parenting/09/04/teen.sex/index.html.
6. Galatians 3:12.
7. See Greene, "Teen Sex."
8. Dan Allender, "Sexual Disorders" (lecture, Colorado Christian University, Spring 1995).
9. Frederick Buechner, *Telling the Truth: The Gospel As Tragedy, Comedy, and Fairy Tale* (San Francisco: HarperSanFrancisco, 1977), 58.
10. See Hebrews 11:34, NIV.
11. Julian of Norwich, quoted in Sheila Upjohn, *All Shall Be Well: Daily Readings from Julian of Norwich* (Harrisburg, PA: Morehouse, 1992), 185.
12. See John 3:27–30.
13. These are truths my pastor Peter Hiett repeats over and over because he knows the healing path for men and women who have been sexually abused.
14. Hebrews 11:1.

CHAPTER 3

1. See Matthew 7:3, NIV.
2. Christiane Northrup, *Mother-Daughter Wisdom: Creating a Legacy of Physical and Emotional Health* (New York: Bantam Books, 2005), 469.
3. Psalm 103:3, 4.

4. Psalm 103:4, NIV.

5. Frederick Buechner, *Telling Secrets* (San Francisco: HarperSanFrancisco, 1991), 75.

6. Genesis 50:19, 20–21.

CHAPTER 4

1. Peter Bearman and Hannah Brückner, "Promising the Future: Abstinence Pledges and the Transition to First Intercourse," *American Journal of Sociology* 106 (2001), cited in Hannah Brückner and Peter Bearman, "After the Promise: The STD Consequences of Adolescent Virginity Pledges," *Journal of Adolescent Health* 36 (2005): 272, 276.

2. Adrienne Rich, *Of Woman Born: Motherhood As Experience and Institution* (New York: Norton, 1986), 114.

3. Henry J. Kaiser Family Foundation, "Sex on TV, 2005: A Kaiser Family Foundation Report," table 10, www.kff.org/entmedia/upload/Sex-on-TV-4-Full-Report.pdf.

4. Kaiser Family Foundation, "Sex on TV," table 21.

5. Crimes Against Children Research Center, national survey, "Online Victimization: A Report on the Nation's Youth," June 2000, ix, www.ncmec.org/en_US/publications/NC62.pdf.

6. Tom Piotrowski, "Read Your TV," Center for Parent/Youth Understanding, www.cpyu.org/Page.aspx?id=76985.

7. Tom Wolfe, *Hooking Up* (New York: Farrar Straus & Giroux, 2000), 1.

8. Dan Allender and Tremper Longman, *Intimate Allies: Rediscovering God's Design for Marriage and Becoming Soul Mates for Life* (Wheaton, IL; Tyndale, 1995), 212–13.

9. 2 Corinthians 4:13–15, emphasis added.

10. Isaiah 4:6, NIV.

CHAPTER 5

1. Statistics for sexual activity among teenage girls were nonexistent until 1971 when Johns Hopkins conducted its first National Survey of Young Women, which was repeated in 1976 and 1979. The statistics for sexual activity among this demographic were tabulated by the Alan Guttmacher

Institute based upon data from the 1982 and 1988 National Survey of Family Growth. See the Alan Guttmacher Institute, "Sex and America's Teenagers," 1994.

2. See Proverbs 19:26.

3. *Middle School Confessions,* directed by Ellen Goosenberg Kent, HBO Family, 2002.

4. U.S. Department of Health and Human Services, Centers for Disease Control and Prevention, "Youth Risk Behavior Surveillance, United States, 2003," *Morbidity and Mortality Weekly Report* 53, no. SS-2 (May 21, 2004): table 42, www.cdc.gov/mmwr/preview/mmwrhtml/ss5302a1.htm.

5. 2002 National Survey of Family Growth, cited in U.S. Department of Health and Human Services, Centers for Disease Control and Prevention, William D. Mosher, Anjani Chandra, and Jo Jones, "Sexual Behavior and Selected Health Measures: Men and Women 15–44 Years of Age, United States, 2002," *Advance Data from Vital and Health Statistics,* no. 362 (September 15, 2005): table 7, www.cdc.gov/nchs/data/ad/ad362.pdf.

6. Mosher, Chandra, and Jones, "Sexual Behavior and Selected Health Measures," table 7.

7. Mosher, Chandra, and Jones, "Sexual Behavior and Selected Health Measures," table 7.

8. Sharon Lamb, *The Secret Lives of Girls: What Good Girls Really Do— Sex Play, Aggression, and Their Guilt* (New York: Simon & Schuster, 2002), 7–9.

9. Naomi Wolf, "The Porn Myth," *New York Magazine,* NYMag.com, October 20, 2003, http://nymetro.com/nymetro/news/trends/n_9437.

10. Henry J. Kaiser Family Foundation, "Sex on TV, 2005: A Kaiser Family Foundation Report," table 16, www.kff.org/entmedia/upload/Sex-on-TV-4-Full-Report.pdf.

11. Kaiser Family Foundation, "Sex on TV," table 14.

12. Henry J. Kaiser Family Foundation and *YM Magazine,* "National Survey of Teens: Teens Talk About Dating, Intimacy, and Their Sexual Experiences," (1998), 11, www.kff.org/youthhivstds/upload/Kaiser-Family-Foundation-YM-Magazine-National-Survey-of-Teens-Teens-Talk-about-Dating-Intimacy-and-Their-Sexual-Experiences-Report.pdf.

13. 2004 NBC News/*People* magazine poll, "National Survey of Young Teens' Sexual Attitudes and Behaviors," conducted in conjunction with the Katie Couric special "The 411: Teens and Sex," cited in Brian Alexander, "Sex Ed on the Web," MSNBC, January 27, 2005, www.msnbc.msn.com/ id/6860487/4; Princeton Survey Research Associates International, "NBC/People: National Survey of Young Teens' Sexual Attitudes and Behaviors," http://msnbcmedia.msn.com/i/msnbc/Sections/TVNews/ Dateline%20NBC/NBCTeenTopline.pdf.

14. Joint United Nations Programme on HIV/AIDS (UNAIDS) and World Health Organization (WHO), "AIDS Epidemic Update," December 2004, www.unaids.org/wad2004/EPIupdate2004_html_en/epi04_02_en .htm#TopOfPage.

15. Hillard Weinstock, Stuart Berman, and Willard Cates Jr., "Sexually Transmitted Diseases Among American Youth: Incidence and Prevalence Estimates, 2000," *Perspectives on Sexual and Reproductive Health* 36, no. 1 (January/February 2004), www.agi-usa.org/pubs/journals/3600604.html.

16. U.S. Department of Health and Human Services, Centers for Disease Control and Prevention, "STD Surveillance 2004: National Profile," www.cdc.gov/std/stats/chlamydia.htm.

17. 2002 National Survey of Family Growth, cited in U.S. Department of Health and Human Services, Centers for Disease Control and Prevention, "Teenagers in the United States: Sexual Activity, Contraceptive Use, and Childbearing, 2002," *Vital and Health Statistics* 23, no. 24 (December 2004), table 7, www.cdc.gov/nchs/data/series/sr_23/sr23_024.pdf.

18. The Crimes Against Children Research Center, national survey, "Online Victimization: A Report on the Nation's Youth," June 2000, ix, www.ncmec.org/en_US/publications/NC62.pdf.

19. Centers for Disease Control, "Teenagers in the United States," tables 25 and 32.

20. The 1996 National Longitudinal Survey of Adolescent Health, wave II statistics, cited in Heritage Foundation, Robert E. Rector, Kirk A. Johnson, and Lauren R. Noyes, "Sexually Active Teenagers Are More Likely to Be Depressed and to Attempt Suicide," June 3, 2003.

21. See Susan M. Blake et al., "Effects of a Parent-Child Communications Intervention on Young Adolescents' Risk for Early Onset of Sexual Inter-

course," *Family Planning Perspectives* 33, no. 2 (2001); see also the 2002 National Longitudinal Study of Adolescent Health (Add Health), cited in Robert W. Blum, "Mothers' Influence on Teen Sex: Connections That Promote Postponing Sexual Intercourse," Center for Adolescent Health and Development, University of Minnesota, 2002, 18–19, http://allaboutkids.umn.edu/presskit/MonographMS.pdf.

22. 1 John 4:18.

23. I am indebted to my pastor, Peter Hiett, for telling a similar story and providing an entirely new perspective on my own game of "Sardines."

CHAPTER 6

1. Lauren F. Winner, *Real Sex: The Naked Truth About Chastity* (Grand Rapids: Brazos, 2005), 11–12.

2. See Genesis 1:31.

3. See Genesis 2:24 and Matthew 19:6.

4. Douglas E. Rosenau, *A Celebration of Sex for Newlyweds* (Nashville: Thomas Nelson, 2002), 123.

5. 2004 NBC News/*People* magazine poll, "National Survey of Young Teens' Sexual Attitudes and Behaviors," conducted in conjunction with the Katie Couric special "The 411: Teens and Sex," cited in Brian Alexander, "Sex Ed on the Web," MSNBC, January 27, 2005, www.msnbc.msn.com/id/National Survey of Young Teens' Sexual Attitudes and Behaviors," http://msnbcmedia.msn.com/i/msnbc/Sections/TVNews/Dateline%20NBC/NBCTeenTopline.pdf.

6. 2004 NBC News/*People* poll, cited in Alexander, "Sex Ed on the Web."

7. 1 Corinthians 6:16, 18.

8. Lewis Smedes, *Sex for Christians* (Grand Rapids: Eerdmans, 1994), 6.

9. *Vanilla Sky,* directed by Cameron Crowe, Paramount Pictures, 2001.

10. Genesis 2:24–25.

11. Helen Fisher, quoted in Barbara Strauch, *The Primal Teen: What the New Discoveries About the Teenage Brain Tell Us About Our Kids* (New York: Anchor Books, 2003), 150.

12. 1992 *Christianity Today* survey, cited in Haddon Robinson, "Sex, Remarriage, and Divorce," *Christianity Today,* December 14, 1992, www.christianitytoday.com/ct12000/135/45.0.html.

13. See Pam Stenzel, *Sex Has a Price Tag: Discussions About Sexuality, Spirituality, and Self-Respect* (Grand Rapids: Zondervan, 2003), 34.

14. Winner, *Real Sex,* 82–83.

15. See the National Marriage Project, "The State of Our Unions, 2001: The Social Health of Marriage in America," June 2001, cited in Glenn T. Stanton, "Do Half of All American Marriages Really End in Divorce?" *CitizenLink,* June 30, 2005, www.family.org/cforum/fosi/marriage/divorce/a0037056.cfm; see also Centers for Disease Control and Prevention, "Births, Marriages, Divorces, and Deaths: Provisional Data for April 2005," *National Vital Statistics Reports* 54, no. 6 (October 26, 2005), www.cdc.gov/nchs/data/nvsr/ nvsr54/nvsr54_06.pdf.

16. J. A. Davis and T. W. Smith, "General Social Surveys: 1972–1994," cited in Michael W. Wiederman, "Extramarital Sex: Prevalence and Correlates in a National Survey," 1997.

17. Matthew 19:5–6.

18. Dan Allender, *Intimate Allies: Rediscovering God's Design for Marriage and Becoming Soul Mates for Life* (Wheaton, IL: Tyndale, 1995), 308.

19. Peter Hiett, "God's Sneaky Way to Get a Person Crucified" (sermon, Lookout Mountain Community Church, Golden, Colorado, October 31, 2004).

20. Ephesians 2:15–16, NIV.

21. Hiett, "God's Sneaky Way."

CHAPTER 7

1. Sue Monk Kidd, *When the Heart Waits: Spiritual Direction for Life's Sacred Questions* (New York: HarperCollins, 1990), 22.

2. Ron Dahl, University of Pittsburgh Medical Center, quoted in Barbara Strauch, *The Primal Teen: What the New Discoveries About the Teenage Brain Tell Us About Our Kids* (New York: Anchor Books, 2003), 92.

3. See Psalm 90:4.

4. Curtis Sittenfeld, *Prep* (New York: Random House, 2005), 15.

5. Sittenfeld, *Prep,* 309.

6. Jill Murray, *But I Love Him: Protecting Your Teen Daughter from Controlling, Abusive Dating Relationships* (New York: Regan Books, 2000), 86.

7. Sittenfeld, *Prep,* 309.

8. Dallas Willard, *The Spirit of the Disciplines: Understanding How God Changes Lives* (San Francisco: HarperSanFrancisco, 1999), 92.

9. Romans 12:1.

10. 2 Corinthians 6:11–13.

11. Lauren Winner, *Real Sex: The Naked Truth About Chastity* (Grand Rapids: Brazos, 2005), 124.

12. See Winner, *Real Sex,* 18.

13. Sittenfeld, *Prep,* 320–21.

14. Winner, *Real Sex,* 127.

15. See Revelation 19:9, KJV.

16. *Newsweek* poll of thirteen- to nineteen-year-olds conducted in 2000, cited in Sharon Begley, "A World of Their Own," *Newsweek,* May 8, 2000.

17. The Barna Group, 1999 national survey, cited in "Barna by Topic: Teenagers," www.barna.org.

18. Peter Hiett, "The Last Idol" (sermon, Lookout Mountain Community Church, Golden, Colorado, April 3, 2005).

19. Jeremy Camp, "Beautiful One," copyright 2004, Chordant Music/EMI.

20. Psalm 103:3–5, author's paraphrase.

CHAPTER 8

1. See Robert J. Havighurst, *Developmental Tasks and Education* (New York: Longman, 1951), 30–55.

2. Jean Kilbourne, *Can't Buy My Love: How Advertising Changes the Way We Think and Feel* (New York: Touchstone Books, 1999), 148.

3. Kilbourne, *Can't Buy My Love,* 148–49.

4. Debra W. Haffner, *Beyond the Big Talk: Every Parent's Guide to Raising Sexually Healthy Teens* (New York: Newmarket, 2002), 52.

5. See Erik H. Erikson, *Childhood and Society* (New York: W. W. Norton, 1993).

6. *Bruce Almighty,* directed by Tom Shadyac, Universal Pictures, 2003.

7. Dan Allender, *How Children Raise Parents: The Art of Listening to Your Family* (Colorado Springs: WaterBrook, 2003), viii.

CHAPTER 9

1. Statistics cited in Jill Murray, *But I Love Him: Protecting Your Daughter from Controlling, Abusive Dating Relationships* (New York: Regan Books, 2000), 7.

2. National Crime Victimization Survey, in U.S. Department of Justice, Bureau of Justice Statistics Special Report, Callie Marie Rennison, "Intimate Partner Violence and Age of Victim, 1993–99," NCJ 187635, October 2001, Table 2, www.ojp.usdoj.gov/bjs.

3. National Institute of Justice and the Centers for Disease Control and Prevention, National Violence Against Women Survey, 1999, cited in U.S. Department of Justice, Patricia Tjaden and Nancy Thoennes, "Extent, Nature, and Consequences of Intimate Partner Violence," NCJ 181867, July 2000, www.ncjrs.org/pdffiles1/nij/181867.pdf.

4. University of Michigan Sexual Assault Prevention and Awareness Center, quoted in Murray, *But I Love Him*, 8.

5. U.S. Department of Health and Human Services, Centers for Disease Control and Prevention, "Youth Risk Behavior Surveillance, United States, 2003," *Morbidity and Mortality Weekly Report* 53, no. SS-2 (May 21, 2004): table 10, www.cdc.gov/mmwr/preview/mmwrhtml/ss5302a1.htm.

6. Murray, *But I Love Him*, 42.

7. Henry J. Kaiser Family Foundation, "National Survey of Youth Knowledge and Attitudes on Sexual Health Issues," February 2002, prepared for the National Center on Addiction and Substance Abuse (CASA) conference "Dangerous Liaisons: Substance Abuse and Sexual Behavior," www.kff.org/youthhivstds/loader.cfm?url=/commonspot/security/getfile.cfm&PageID=14906.

8. Lauren Winner, *Real Sex: The Naked Truth About Chastity* (Grand Rapids: Brazos, 2005), 77.

9. Research from a 1998 University of Maryland study, cited in Patricia Evans, *Teen Torment: Overcoming Verbal Abuse at Home and at School* (Avon, MA: Adams Media, 2003), 7.

10. Taken in part from Murray, *But I Love Him*, 117–18.

CHAPTER 10

1. Paraphrased from Dr. Jeffrey Satinover, "The Feathers of the Skylark." Used by permission.

2. Renee N. Altson, *Stumbling Toward Faith: My Longing to Heal from the Evil That God Allowed* (El Cajon, CA: Youth Specialties Books, 2004), 133.

3. Sharon Hersh, *Bravehearts: Unlocking the Courage to Love with Abandon* (Colorado Springs: WaterBrook, 2000), 10–11.

4. Ephesians 5:3, 8, 12–14.

5. Frederick Buechner, *Telling Secrets* (New York: HarperCollins, 1992), 3.

6. 2 Corinthians 12:8–9, NIV.

7. Steve Siler and John Mandeville, "Into the Light." Words and music by Steve Siler and John Mandeville, 2005 Silerland Music. Administered by the Copyright Company. ASCAP/Lifestyle of Worship BMI, www.musicforthesoul.org. Used by permission.

CHAPTER 11

1. Colossians 1:19–20.

2. 1 John 4:10, NIV.

3. Lewis Smedes, *Sex for Christians* (Grand Rapids: Eerdmans, 1976), 59.

4. Quoted and paraphrased from Fyodor Dostoevsky, *The Brothers Karamazov* (New York: Bantam Dell, 2003), 350.

5. I am indebted to my teacher Dr. Dan Allender of Mars Hill Graduate School and my pastor Peter Hiett for their influence on my thinking about the complexities of questions regarding sexual identity and responding to those who struggle.

CONCLUSION

1. Matthew 13:10–13.

2. Paraphrased and quoted from the story of the Samaritan woman in John 4.

3. See Genesis 2:23, NIV.

4. See Hebrews 13:5.

5. See Matthew 19:6.

6. I am indebted to Peter Hiett for his sermon "A Temptation from Paradise" (March 27, 2005), which inspired my writing of the story about the Samaritan woman. The following truths, which are echoed in the story, have been repeated by Peter many times over the years: "[Jesus] is the deepest ocean, undiminished by me"; "I know that [Jesus] is good and

that he is light and life and that I love him"; "Jesus is God in the flesh—the Lord—and I was made for him"; "[Jesus] cries, 'Bone of my bones and flesh of my flesh' when he sees me"; "[Jesus] longs to enter me and fill me and give me his life, himself, the Word, the Seed that bears fruit"; "[Jesus] completes me and in some way I complete him"; "When I hid and ran away and murdered and did things that cannot be talked about in the light of day, [Jesus] did not leave me or forsake me; for what God has joined together, no man can tear asunder."

7. John 12:32, NIV.

ABOUT THE AUTHOR

SHARON HERSH is a licensed professional counselor and the director of Women's Recovery and Renewal, a ministry of counseling, retreat, and support services for struggling women. She is an adjunct professor in counseling at Reformed Theological Seminary, Mars Hills Graduate School, and Colorado Christian University. She is the author of several books, including *Bravehearts, "Mom, I feel fat!" "Mom, I hate my life!"* and *"Mom, everyone else does!"* She is a sought-after speaker for conferences and retreats. Sharon lives with her family in Lone Tree, Colorado.

Be your daughter's greatest ally

Navigating an adolescent daughter's emotional life is one of a mom's toughest challenges. A teenage girl's volatile emotions can seemingly toss her—and you—like a hurricane. When a scary external world and a turbulent internal world collide, the result is sometimes overwhelming and confusing. Allow the Hand-in-Hand books to help you guide your daughter through this chaotic time, and assure her you are truly on her side.

SHAW BOOKS
www.shawbooks.com

WATERBROOK PRESS
www.waterbrookpress.com